Austral
Bush Survival
Skills

Kimberley Publications

Kimberley Publications

Australian
Bush Survival Skills

*A complete guide to
surviving in the wild*

Kevin Casey

Australian Bush Survival Skills
A complete guide to surviving in the wild

Published by:
Kimberley Publications PO Box 6095
Upper Mt. Gravatt QLD 4122 Australia

Every effort has been made to ensure this book is free from error or omissions. However, the Author, the Publisher or their respective employees or agents shall not accept responsibility for injury, loss or damage occasional to any person acting or refraining from action as a result of material in this book whether or not such injury, loss or damage is in any way due to any negligent act or omission, breach of duty or default on the part of the Publisher, the Author or their respective employees or agents.

COPYRIGHT © 2000

All rights reserved. This publication is copyright and may not be resold or reproduced in any manner (except excerpts thereof for bona fide study purposes in accordance with the Copyright Act) without prior consent of the publisher.

NATIONAL LIBRARY OF AUSTRALIA
CATALOGUING IN PUBLICATION DATA:

Casey, Kevin, 1955-
Australian bush survival skills:
a complete guide to surviving in the wild.

Bibliography.
ISBN 0 9587628 1 3

1. Survival skills - Australia - Handbooks, manuals, etc.
2. Wilderness survival - Australia - Handbooks, manuals, etc.
I. Title. II. Title: Complete guide to surviving in the wild.

613.690994

Contents

Photo: Rob Staszewski

Acknowledgements

This book would not have been possible without the assistance, advice and encouragement of numerous people. The author gratefully acknowledges the many individuals and organisations whose expertise and enthusiasm contributed to the completeness, accuracy and quality of this work.

Nick Vroomans, former Chief Survival Instructor for the Australian Defence Force & current director of Staying Alive Survival Services.
Robyn Keen and Michael Fruend, Mountain Designs Australia.
Brad Maryan, W.A. Society of Amateur Herpetologists.
Vince Allen, West Marine Products, California U.S.A.
Andrew Kemp.
Ron Chester & Michael Peers, Opal Shell Yacht Charters.
Joan Fowler.
Ross Buchanan, Bushpeople Publications / Silva compasses
Bill Edwards, Toyota Landcruiser 4WD Club (QLD).
Colin and Georgina Wright.
Bill & Barbara Brooker.
Damiano Visocnik.
Michael & Raylene Tiffin.
Rob Staszewski.
Luke Reynolds.
Stuart Coleman.
Belinda Dyer.
Gary Tischer.

Cover photo acknowledgements:

Front Cover: Top left - Belinda Dyer
Middle left - Andrew Kemp
Top right - Brad Maryan, WASAH
Middle right - Stuart Coleman

Back Cover: Bottom - Colin & Georgina Wright

Front Inside Cover: Top - Ron Chester,
Opal Shell Yacht Charters
Bottom left - Raylene Tiffin
Bottom right - Colin & Georgina Wright

Printed in Brisbane, Australia by Clark & Mackay,
1 Railway Parade, Rocklea QLD

ABOUT THE AUTHOR

Kevin Casey's extensive survival knowledge has been gleaned from first-hand experience in some of the world's most remote wild places, which he normally explores alone and with minimal equipment. When not wandering Central American jungles, kayaking Alaskan rivers or trekking in northern Australia, he lives in Brisbane.

IMPORTANT

Many of the survival techniques described in this book are for use in genuine emergencies only, where serious threat
to human life exists. In practising these skills
always comply with laws relating to wildlife protection, firearms and land use. Respect the sanc-
tity of National Parks and other protected areas and
look after the bush. The author and/or publishers cannot be held responsible or liable for any loss, damage,
injuries or prosecutions resulting from the use or mis-
use of information in this book.

Numerous certified courses are available in wilderness first
aid, mountaincraft, 4WD maintenance, boat handling,
climbing and survival. AUSTRALIAN BUSH SURVIVAL
SKILLS is meant to support organised and professional
outdoor training, not be a substitute for it. Information
in this guide will not make you a survival expert by itself; *you must practise* essential skills to achieve the
desired level of proficiency and confidence.

You alone are responsible for decisions you make
in a genuine survival situation. The more knowledge and practical experience you can ac-
quire, the better your chances. Survival
methods may need to be adjusted depending upon location and individual circumstances.

Photo: Damiano Visocnik

Introduction

The survival methods outlined in this book have saved thousands of lives, and they can save yours. Every year in Australia hikers become lost, vehicles get stranded in the desert, boats capsize offshore and exhausted climbers spend nights on cold mountains. No one is exempt from finding themselves in a survival situation, whether through pursuit of leisure activities or in the course of work. Farmers, surveyors, forestry workers and mining personnel spend much of their time in the bush, but a salesman driving between towns can just as easily run off the road and be confronted with unexpected survival challenges. An outdoor adventure gone wrong, a forced light aircraft landing, a flood or a bushfire can quickly put us in positions where we must rely solely upon our existing survival knowledge.

In today's world we depend on electronic wizardry and the infrastructure of society for daily existence. This increasing dependence means we no longer develop skills for coping with the harsh realities of the bush. In distancing ourselves from nature we lose touch with instincts and abilities that would otherwise save our lives in a natural setting. Advances in high-tech gear lull us into a false sense of security. We may own expensively fitted out 4WDs but have no practical experience in using their safety gear. We might carry the finest life raft on our boat but lack practice or training in detaching it quickly. We can bushwalk into an arid region toting the best water bag available, but what if it breaks? Can we repair it or improvise a substitute? More importantly, have we taken the time to learn and practise methods for getting water from the land?

Like all survival manuals this book describes how to obtain the essentials of water, food, shelter and fire in the wild. It outlines effective ways to deal with climate, geographic obstacles and medical emergencies. It describes methods for safe bush navigation and signalling of rescuers. Solutions to a whole range of survival problems are clearly provided, with an emphasis on self-reliance and regular honing of crucial skills. Where this book differs from other guides is in its commitment to relevance. The reader will find no elaborate diagrams showing the construction of large multi-person shelters from natural resources, as are common in other survival books. Smaller shelters are less environmentally destructive and far more practical for typical situations. The obligatory 'how to make 38 types of animal traps and snares' chapter is also absent. Most of these creations catch only the most cooperative creature stepping in just the right spot. Others (staked pits, spear deadfalls and trip-wire catapults) are potentially more deadly to their maker (or others) than intended prey. Controlled tests on snare catch rates have confirmed that the effort is rarely worth the gain.

Older survival manuals are rife with ideas that look good on paper but have limited practical use for persons stranded in the wild. This reference focuses on techniques that have been *proven to work* in the field. The author has personally tested and used a great many of the methods described. Where needed, additional specialised advice was obtained from the most competent practitioners in their respective fields. Traditional survival concepts have been picked apart to extract what matters, with an emphasis on practicality and safety.

AUSTRALIAN BUSH SURVIVAL SKILLS contains techniques and ideas not found in any other publication. It is a portable reference that should be carried by everyone who ventures into the outdoors - 4WD enthusiasts, bushwalkers, kayakers, boat owners and those who work or travel away from towns and cities.

No one will become a survival expert just by reading this (or any other) book. This guide is an excellent start but its role is meant to be supportive. Survival knowledge is only part of the equation - you must also be able to convert this knowledge into practical experience. This can be achieved only through your own commitment to practice and training.

Talk to anyone about survival and sooner or later two words will crop up - 'bush tucker'. Interest in bush foods, especially plants, has blossomed tremendously in the past decade. While this is a positive trend it is worrying that interest in more essential survival knowledge has not kept pace. This book strives to correct this imbalance. Bush tucker awareness must be viewed within the greater context of overall survival needs, where its significance is usually very minor indeed.

Survival cannot be learned by rote because each experience is different. Learning a sequence of steps for a particular task is fine but if weather, injury or broken equipment demands a different approach you must be ready to adjust. It's helpful to know that water can be obtained by pulling up certain surface tree roots, but is the effort worthwhile if you sweat litres in the process? To survive you must balance acquired knowledge with flexibility, hard-won experience with common sense.

As well as being aware of basic principles you must appreciate the exceptions to the rule.

Tenacity is the foundation upon which human survival is based. Survivors have an upbeat stubbornness, concrete personal values and self control. Loss of mental resolve rather than physical exhaustion causes many people to give up in the face of daunting odds. Without the will to live the information in this book is of little use. A positive mental outlook is the most valuable survival tool we carry into wild places. This attitude is easier to achieve when backed up by realistic confidence in our outdoor skills.

Acquiring survival know-how is only the beginning - the next step is training. Make a list of individual techniques you would like to practise and set aside a day, a weekend or longer to try them out. Ongoing training is a must, especially with more difficult activities. It's one thing to read about starting a fire without matches and another to get it to work when your life depends on it.

Make a special effort to perfect the described techniques for obtaining fresh water. This book advances the concept of Water Transpiration Bags as the most effective water procurement method for arid regions. Until very recently the solar still was globally touted as the ultimate water gathering device, but Australian research has shown that properly used transpiration bags are simpler, less labour-intensive and far more productive.

Outdoor equipment is increasingly sophisticated. Modern clothing fibres are lighter and stronger, and many are both waterproof and breathable. New harness systems make shouldering a rucksack more comfortable, and 4WD vehicles can be equipped with a wealth of safety features for outback travel. We have hand-held satellite phones that let us ring to or from virtually anywhere on earth, GPS units to keep us from getting lost and personal radio beacons to let others know we're in trouble. Hydration systems allow us to drink on the move without removing the rucksack, and hand-held desalinators pump sea water in one end and expel fresh water from the other. Gear can make a difference between life and death so its selection must be carefully considered.

This book shows you how to create your own pocket-size survival kit, to be carried whenever you go bush. Appropriate kits for boat or vehicle are also described. When all other gear is lost these kits will help keep you alive in a range of environments.

Ecological considerations are no less important in a survival situation, where excessive exploitation of natural resources can harm your chances. Minimum impact bush travel is no longer just a vague goal; it is a planetary necessity and a responsibility we can't ignore. In genuine emergencies the need to stay alive outweighs environmental concerns, but there is a clear distinction between taking what nature offers you for survival and wastefully degrading the bush. A skilled survivor is a pre-server of the wild, not a plunderer.

Make this book a starting point for expanding your survival aware-ness but don't stop here. Expertise and advice are available from many sources. Complete a training course in 4WD maintenance or enrol in an accredited first aid program. Find yourself an expert in rock climbing, boat handling, snow safety or whatever area you need to work on, and learn from them. Supplement personal survival practice with a formal-ised course in mountaincraft, sea survival or search and rescue. In Aus-tralia we have access to some of the best survival training in the world, but too few of us utilise it.

An excellent way to obtain localised knowledge of bush survival skills is from Aboriginal people in remote communities. A bush tucker trip or fishing expedition with experts can be very rewarding in regions where the old ways are still practised. Permission to visit Aboriginal land must always be obtained beforehand. As an invited visitor, respect sacred sites and the wishes of the community. Indigenous Australians are happy to share their unique bush knowledge with everyone.

Perfecting survival skills is enjoyable and satisfying. The sense of achievement is tangible, and builds with each success. By learning to apply the methods in this book you will improve your understanding of the natural world and strengthen your relationship with it. You will be better prepared to deal with the unexpected, and more capable of emerging from a bush or coastal mishap alive and well.

Kevin Casey

The Human Survivor

Physically we don't compare well with other animals when it comes to survival. Our naked bodies offer a feeble barrier to cold or heat. We cannot out-run cranky feral bulls or out-swim crocodiles. Our sense of smell is inferior to that of many other mammals and our bodies don't store water well. Fortunately, from an evolutionary standpoint these physical drawbacks have actually helped us. They have forced us to create and adapt, to use our superior brains to compensate for physical shortcomings. Our intelligence has made us the most successful survivors on earth.

The human body can endure a range of hardships when forced to do so. The will to live is a powerful weapon in its own right. Self-discipline and a pugnacious attitude will get you through many outdoor challenges, even with little or no training. A knowledge of survival techniques removes much of our fear but even skilled survivors must maintain mental self-control and stay focused in putting their abilities to use. History abounds with situations where people have been forced to go from relative luxury to the hardships of a hand to mouth existence, often with little warning. In Australia more and more of us are buying four-wheel drives, venturing offshore in small boats, scaling up difficult mountains and exploring remote regions. Modern equipment continues to make outdoor pursuits safer, but gear is no substitute for knowledge, skill and self confidence.

Fear can be the biggest killer in a survival incident. It can lead to irrational decision-making or expand into full-blown panic. Fear is useful when it goads us into needed activity but when it turns to panic our skills are virtually nullified. Fear prevents us from adapting to an unfamiliar environment and new circumstances.

If mental adjustments aren't made in the bush, death can result from stubborn inflexibility. People stuck in deserts have been found dead next to waterholes because they refused to drink water deemed too dirty. Others have died of dehydration with a canteen full of water beside them, having taken the idea of rationing too far. There is one case of a plane crash where two men and a woman awaited rescue on a snow-covered mountain. Unable to light a fire, one of the men suggested they huddle together to conserve body warmth. The woman declined, explaining she 'didn't know them well enough'. Days later rescuers found the men barely alive, still huddled together. The woman was metres away, dead from exposure. In the bush *we must change our priorities* and adjust personal values to fit the needs of the moment.

Reluctance to eat unfamiliar foods is natural but shouldn't inhibit the survival process. Over the past twenty years in various countries the author has sampled foods ranging from donkey stew, earthworms, ants, grasshoppers and termites to feral goat, raw fish, mangrove snails, wild plants and assorted reptiles, all with no ill effects. Squeamishness about eating such items is a reflection of prejudice rather than safety or palatability issues. Many wild bush grains and fruits have been scientifically tested for nutrients and found more sustaining than their cultivated counterparts, and the quality of protein found in earthworms, termites and other 'undesirable' animal foods is very high.

For urban survivors the unexpected means little more than a flat tyre, a sudden downpour or a sports injury. In the city there is always help at hand. Because of this we are rarely placed in situations demanding sustained improvisation, prolonged discomfort or a true test of physical limitations. Civilisation removes our need to hunt for food, build a fire, find water or construct urgent shelter. In the technological age we have become divorced from the earth, our ancestral instincts replaced by dependence on machinery. To master survival skills we must relearn the basics.

SURVIVAL OF THE FITTEST

Physical toughness was more evident in our ancestors than in today's urban dweller. Hands were not as soft, bones were stronger and physical activity was the rule rather than the exception. In countless group survival disasters, cardiovascular and muscular fitness has proven a significant factor in determining who lives and who perishes. Today, tribal people around the globe are more in tune with their physical relationship to the environment. A need to adapt to harsh landscapes evolves into physical toughness. Nepali Sherpas tread barefoot through the Himalayas and Kalahari Bushmen survive in desolate African desert. In Australia, early settlers often remarked on the fine musculature and amazing endurance of Aborigines they met and the speed with which they recovered from serious injuries. Today's more sedentary human has relinquished much of this physical stamina.

Preparation for outdoor adventure should include some fitness training. This is one of the most ignored components of survival planning. Outback drivers must be fit enough to handle strenuous jobs such as manual winching, digging vehicles from mud bogs and lifting tyres onto wheels. If your plans involve carrying a heavy rucksack over tough terrain for two weeks, go on some day hikes beforehand to get used to the load. Novice bushwalkers tend to underestimate the demands on feet during lengthy treks. Heavy boots need more leg strength to lift than normal footwear. Boots should be worn frequently in the weeks leading up to a strenuous hike.

Swimming, walking, bike riding and aerobic work-outs all contribute to muscle tone and cardiovascular health. A walking regimen can be gradually built up. Start with short, leisurely strolls and gradually advance to sustained striding. Walking up and down hills on rugged bush tracks is excellent training. When riding a bicycle uphill, lift up off the seat to use pure leg power rather than the gears. This is an especially good exercise for rock climbers.

You don't need to be an athlete to survive in the bush. Your goal should be a reasonable degree of general fitness in keeping with your age, body shape and anticipated activities. Take it slowly in the outdoors and listen to your body when it tells you to rest.

In addition to physical toughness a survivor needs determination, initiative and ingenuity. Life may depend upon finding unique solutions to seemingly insurmountable problems. A cave explorer in the U.S., swept into a narrow underground cavern by surging water, landed in a section which offered no way to climb out. He alerted rescuers by tying wool from his jumper to the legs of bats he captured. The bats were spotted by residents of a nearby town who reorganised a search party (the initial search was abandoned when he was not found after four days). The man was eventually located and rescued.

In rare cases people have survived for months on snow-shrouded mountains and in the most inhospitable jungles. In the Pacific during World War II a man was rescued after drifting alone in a life raft for an astonishing 133 days. He collected rainwater in the raft and caught fish with a hook made from a single nail.

Personal character plays a fundamental role in survival. When life is at stake the ability to maintain emotional control is a deciding factor. People who make it through emergency situations are often amazed at the resolve they were able to summon at crucial moments. The ability to create positive, rational action from a position of uncertainty is the essence of survival strategy. To stay alive we must put our character and strengths to work for us.

SURVIVAL STRESSES

Know your enemies. Being in a survival situation means coping with new physical and mental stresses.

Physical Stresses:

1. PAIN   *Pain from injury or illness decreases morale and impedes movement.*

2. HEAT OR COLD   *High temperatures can lead to dehydration or heat stroke. Cold costs the body precious energy, slows down mental responses and can lead to hypothermia.*

3. THIRST/HUNGER   *Thirst is a sign of dehydration, which must be attended to immediately. Hunger is less urgent but cannot be ignored in long-term scenarios.*

4. FATIGUE/SLEEP DEPRIVATION   *In an outdoor emergency the physical demands of staying alive mean less rest and less sleep. Energy conservation is paramount.*

Psychological Stresses:

1. ANXIETY AND FEAR   *These impair decision making, cause extra output of calories through tension and waste water through additional perspiration.*

2. BOREDOM   *Many situations require patience. Resting and waiting may be more helpful than activity. Mental discipline is needed to fight boredom. Establishing a routine will help.*

3. LONELINESS   *People vary in their need for company, but loneliness can be a real threat to morale.*

4. GROUP STRESSES   *Personality/leadership conflicts.*

Few stories better illustrate the human capacity for survival than the saga of Brisbane medical student James Scott, who withstood 43 days trapped in the mountains of Nepal from 22 December 1991. Caught in heavy and unexpected snowfall while hiking across a mountain pass, Scott decided to turn back toward his starting point. Blizzard conditions quickly reduced visibility to under ten metres and within minutes the trail vanished under a blanket of snow. Cold and wet, Scott decided to descend to a creek, intending to use it as a navigation landmark. The landscape became increasingly treacherous but he eventually found a large rock overhang offering shelter from snow and wind. He subsequently tried to climb out of the area but the combination of atrocious weather, steep terrain and increasing weakness from hunger forced him to stay put. With no food he clung to life in the cliff-side shelter until rescued on 3 February 1992. His sister was a major force in the organisation of air searches during Scott's time in the mountains. Their account of the ordeal (*Lost in the Himalayas, James Scott / Joanne Robertson, Lothian 1993*) is an accurate and level-headed description of an unprecedented experience.

In a Himalayan midwinter at 3500 metres a person with basic clothing and no food would be expected to survive no more than ten days. How then did Scott hang on for a month and a half? Though he termed himself 'an ordinary person who fell into an extraordinary situation', he survived for reasons that are both tangible and instructive. The history of human survival shows that some common factors contribute to an individual's ability to pull through against the odds. In James Scott's case these advantages can be broken down as follows:

1. **Physical condition:** Scott was young, fit and aware of his body's capabilities. He was athletic and solidly built. This was a major advantage. During such a long period without food a scrawnier physique would have succumbed to cold and hunger more quickly.

2. **Medical knowledge:** Scott was a medical student with a good understanding of human physiology. While trapped in the mountains he effectively dealt with hypothermia, attended to wounds and scrapes and carried an adequate first aid kit. Fastidious attention to the health of his feet almost certainly staved off serious frostbite.

3. **Equipment:** Maximum use was made of gear available. Scott's sleeping bag, anorak and extra clothing saved his life. Spare socks were placed over his hands to preserve warmth. He made sure he was always able to change into dry clothing. Extra shirts and shorts were wrapped

around his head to slow down heat loss. A sleeping bag cover served as a receptacle for melting snow.

4. Setting priorities: Scott knew that keeping as warm and dry as possible was his only chance. He recognised the potential of that rock overhang as suitable shelter and made himself as comfortable as circumstances allowed. Had he not been able to get out of the wind and snow he would have perished very quickly.

5. Character: Several sensible and life-saving decisions were made during this ordeal. Mentally, Scott retained an impressive degree of control, showing common sense and emotional discipline where others might have succumbed to despair. In the first crucial days he avoided the traditional killer in such situations - panic. By rereading his few books, thinking of home and maintaining a daily routine he was able to focus his mind on more than the immediate predicament. He showed initiative in attempts to light a fire without matches, test nearby plants for food and improve methods of extracting water from snow.

6. Rescue: Scott's sister Joanne played a vital role in helping coordinate searches, and this substantially increased Scott's chances of rescue. Despite being almost too weak to move, he effectively signalled to an approaching helicopter from a clearing near the shelter. This clearing was one of the most prominent in the entire valley, the rest of which was heavily forested. Maximum visibility from the air is crucial in rescues from densely wooded mountains. Scott recognised the importance of this clearing when he first selected the overhang as a refuge. Without this open area and with no way to light a signal fire he would have been invisible to air searchers in almost any other part of the valley.

Taken separately, no single one of these advantages would have been enough to produce a positive outcome. When combined they were just enough to keep a determined man alive. Such is the nature of survival. It is tempting to oversimplify the reasons why a person survives (media obsession with Scott's chocolate bars is a case in point - these were consumed in the first two days and were irrelevant in the context of a 43-day ordeal).

Every survival situation presents its own challenges. Confidence, knowledge, physical fitness and a clear set of personal values contribute to improved chances, and each day that passes makes these qualities progressively more important. Survivors must make a personal commitment to explore all avenues of self-assistance.

THE RULE OF THREES

In a survival situation you must carefully consider which actions to take first. The *RULE OF THREES* is an easy way to remember what needs to be done and in what order. It applies to all environments on land and sea, anywhere in the world.

PROTECT YOURSELF

1. FIRST AID - *Protect the body from injury or illness. Without oxygen you can be brain dead within THREE MINUTES.*

2. CLOTHING, SHELTER AND FIRE - *Protect the body from the elements. Cold, heat or immersion can kill within THREE HOURS.*

PREPARE FOR RESCUE

3. RESCUE - *Make yourself visible. If you have told someone where you're going and given a firm overdue time, search and rescue operations should get under way within THREE DAYS.*

KEEP THE BODY FUNCTIONING

4. WATER - *Water procurement is a major concern. In unfavourable conditions death by dehydration may occur within THREE DAYS.*

5. FOOD - *Lack of food progressively weakens the body and can be life-threatening within THIRTY DAYS.*

Survival prospects are increased by proceeding through each step of *The Rule of Threes* in order. Individual circumstances and common sense dictate any changes to the sequence. It is worth noting that many people consider finding water to be the first survival priority. This is sometimes the case, but protecting yourself from intense heat with appropriate clothing, shelter and by resting in shade decreases your *need* for water. Similarly your food requirements are lessened in cold climates if you can protect yourself from wind, rain and cold temperatures at the outset.

A thorough preparation for rescue builds morale, occupies your time and can save your life. Too many people have perished by failing to maximise their visibility to searchers. Organise a signalling plan.

PREPARATION

There is a common misconception that survival is solely for those who end up in an unexpected situation. Nothing could be further from the truth. Most people survive not because of their reactions to emergencies but because they prevent them from happening in the first place. We frequently hear of individuals being plucked from the sea, airlifted from a mountain or lost in the bush for days. Often these incidents result from bad preparation or inexperience which escalates into a disaster. What doesn't make the news are the thousands of others who carry decent maps, wear their life jackets, tell people where they're going, pack proper clothing and look after their vehicles. Survival is not what happens to you when things go bad, it is an ongoing process that begins even before you enter the bush.

Survival means anticipating your most urgent needs before they arise and putting in the time to prepare yourself, your vehicle and your equipment. It is a state of mind in which you must constantly ask yourself 'what if?'. What if I break down here? What if that waterhole is dry when I reach it? What if I can't get a fire going? Your optimism must be tempered with the understanding that life doesn't always go according to plan. Survival is about creating alternatives for yourself in challenging situations - in other words, always having a 'Plan B'.

Too many bush tragedies stem directly from inadequate preparation. It is useful to know how to find water in the desert but better to carry enough in the first place. It is satisfying to be able to identify fifty species of edible plants but more productive to pack sufficient food before you go. It is wise to read in this book about making snow caves but even wiser to go out and practise making one.

Before any wilderness excursion, whether a two hour bushwalk or a two month 4WD expedition, make checklists of what you think you'll need. If driving, give your vehicle a thorough checkup. Talk to those who regularly make similar trips. Check that your safety gear, first aid kit, food, water, fuel and other requirements are appropriate for what you're planning. Ensure you are mentally and physically ready for the journey. Carry a survival kit and know how to use what's in it. Tell at least two responsible people exactly where you're heading and when they can expect to hear from you again. Practise your bush skills regularly and participate in any courses or training that will add to your safety in the wild. In the bush, what you don't know can certainly hurt you.

AUSTRALIA – Beautiful one minute, deadly the next...

Do you plan to travel in a remotely populated area for your holidays?
Do you employ people who are required to travel through or work in remotely populated areas?
Have you or your staff been trained and prepared for survival and self-help situations?
Staying Alive Survival Services will dramatically improve your chances of returning home safely.
Training is the key and Staying Alive Survival Services can design a course which suits your individual or group needs.
Many hundreds of remote area workers, casual travellers and military people have placed their faith in the expert hands of Australia's leading survival training company.
We provide more than just the best training and advice. Staying Alive Survival Services offers you a complete consultative and backup service anywhere in Australia.

Don't risk it - get the facts.

Call -   (07) 3374 4554
Mobile -   0419 796 382
Fax -   (07) 3374 4664
e-mail -   stayalivesurvival@bigpond.com.au

**PO Box 5116
Kenmore East
QLD 4069**

Training for life

The author's basic survival kit - Butterfly wound closures, sticking plaster, fishing gear, safety pins, needles and thread, glow sticks, blister pads, magnifying glass, compass, scalpel blades, disposable lighter wrapped in fishing line, candle, condom, pencil, water purification tablets, signal mirror, wire leader. It all fits into the tin shown at right. Matches, fire-lighting aids and a roller bandage (for sprains/snakebite etc.) are carried in another pocket. Photos: Andrew Kemp

A belt bag with twin water bottles is ideal for storing personal survival gear.

Survival Kits

Two types of kits should be carried as standard gear on bush journeys. The first is a very basic personal kit which never leaves your pocket. The second is a more elaborate kit for boat or vehicle. In an outdoor emergency your survival could rest upon the carefully chosen items in these kits.

PERSONAL KIT

When on foot in the wild you should carry a personal survival kit. This collection of small but essential items fits into an old tobacco tin, spice tin or metal sticking plaster container. Fist-sized boiled lolly tins are ideal. The theory is that if it is small and flat it will not get left behind because it's 'too much of a bother'. The best place to carry it is in a secure shirt or trouser pocket. The kit container should be metal. Lesser materials don't stand up to rough bush treatment and may not keep contents clean and dry. You should be able to completely seal the lid with tape to make the whole thing waterproof.

Larger, more comprehensive kits should be standard gear in motor vehicles and water craft, but don't dismiss the need for a personal kit that *always* stays with you. Situations where people are stranded and separated from boats, vehicles, kayaks or rucksacks are common. A personal kit stored safely in a pocket or clipped to your belt may be all the gear you have left.

A personal survival kit should include the following:

1. MATCHES

Marine matches are ideal. The ignitable material is generous and goes halfway up the match. Normal waterproof matches are also suitable for the kit.

Matches are a precious survival item. Your life might depend on a single match. Store carefully and use sparingly. When lighting a match protect it from the wind as much as possible.

2. LIGHTER/FLINT

Pack either a disposable lighter or a flint. Striking a flint against steel creates a friction spark. Direct this toward a small pile of fine tinder to set it alight. Even a wet flint will do its job if tinder is dry. Flints are available from camping stores. A disposable lighter is more convenient to use but won't work if it gets wet (most do dry out eventually).

3. CANDLE

It is a frustrating experience that happens to us all - the match blows out or your finger is scorched before you can get the fire started. A candle is the answer because you can hold it in place much longer than a match. Normal sized candles must be pared down to fit into the tin. An alternative is to use birthday candles.

4. COMPASS

You can buy quality miniature compasses not much wider than a ten-cent piece. Carry one in the kit as a backup in case your main compass is lost or broken. Spend the money on a good one that's easy to read. The pointer needles in cheaper varieties tend to stick as they swing around. When buying a compass always check that there are no bubbles in the fluid.

5. FISHING GEAR

Some line, 4-6 hooks, two swivels and two lead sinkers are sufficient. Additional sinkers can be improvised with suitably shaped pebbles. Use a light line and carry mostly smaller hooks. If your travels take you to tropical coasts you might want to add a 20 cm length of wire leader. Wire leader is incredibly strong and great for gear repairs. Longer leader lengths may also be useful in making small game snares.

Fishing line is an indispensable all-purpose survival item. It can help you catch yabbies, crabs or birds in an emergency. You can use it to tie a groundsheet to branches for shelter, fasten prongs to a spear tip or create a new shoelace.

In crocodile country it is risky to climb down steep, muddy river banks to collect water. Fishing line provides a safe method. Stand a discreet distance up the bank and tie the end of the line to your billy. Lower it into the water and then pull it hand over hand toward you. Water containers can be lowered into cliff fissures or tree hollows the same way.

6. MAGNIFYING GLASS

In strong sunshine you can start a fire quickly by directing a pinpoint of magnified sunlight toward a ball of tinder. In a survival situation use your magnifier first, your flint second and your precious matches last.

7. BASIC MEDICAL NEEDS

It makes sense to carry a few medical items in the survival tin, separate from your first aid kit. Contents depend upon anticipated needs and any medical conditions you may have. Some suggestions:

1. *Pain relieving tablets*
2. *Antibiotics for general infection*
3. *Antihistamine (for allergic reactions to bee stings, bites, etc.).*
4. *Butterfly bandages*
(a suture substitute to keep the edges of small wounds together)
5. *Sterile scalpel blade*
6. *Sticking plasters*
7. *Water purification tablets*

WARNING: In the bush there is some danger in taking pain relieving tablets for headache. Headache is one of the first signs of dehydration, so you may actually need water rather than pain relief. Pain relieving medication can mask symptoms of dehydration, possibly allowing it to accelerate to dangerous levels.

8. CONDOM

Non-lubricated condoms make ideal emergency water containers. They hold up to a litre of water and are compact, lightweight and easy to carry. A medium-sized plastic freezer bag is an alternative water carrier, but not as strong or flexible.

9. SEWING GEAR

Pack two or three needles with large eyes and some strong thread to take care of sewing repairs to clothes, packs and tents. In desperate times they can be used to suture wounds. Wind the thread around the needles for storage. Sewing needles are handy for splinter removal and draining foot blisters. Include three or four strong safety pins in the kit as well.

10. PENCIL

Include a pencil (around 7 cm long) for note taking and map drawing. Write vital things down - don't try to rely on memory.

11. SALT

Salt is constantly lost through urination and sweating and must be replaced to maintain health. Store two or three heaped tablespoons of table salt in a small plastic bag or carry a rehydration powder instead.

12. SIGNAL REFLECTOR

A signal mirror should be carried. The heliograph type is best (this is a square reflector with a round sighting hole through the middle). Alternatively, polish the inside of your tin lid until shiny. This then becomes your reflector.

13. GLOW LIGHT

These 4 cm long plastic tubes contain chemicals which create a glowing green light when mixed together. The light produced lasts over 12 hours and is sufficient to light up a snow cave or read a map. For attracting attention in the dark, wave one in the air to help searchers pinpoint your location. Secured to the shank of a fish hook they also make great nocturnal fishing lures.

This simple kit can save your life if you are stranded in the bush. Confine its use to real emergencies and keep it with you at all times when on foot. You could be injured away from camp during a pack-less excursion or get lost heading back to the campsite. This happens more often than you might imagine and can be very serious in exposed conditions.

Remote-area kayakers and canoeists should keep the kit on their person rather than in the craft. If you hit a rock or log and are thrown clear, the kayak can vanish downstream with all the gear. Recovery of kayak and equipment may be days away if it happens at all.

Check the kit's contents regularly for deterioration and replenish as needed. Wrap duct tape or other heavy duty tape around the edge of the lid to keep moisture out. Use a tape you can remove and reapply several times without it losing its stickiness. Carry spare tape.

A **sharp knife** is your most important survival tool. A durable folding knife that locks open is a practical choice and should *always* be carried when travelling on foot. Keep it separate from the kit in a belt sheath or zippered pocket. In the bush a knife is used often, whereas the survival kit is usually left undisturbed the whole trip. Expend the effort to keep knives sharp. A dull knife will more likely cut you than a sharp one because extra force is needed to use it. Dull blades have a tendency to slip and glance off surfaces instead of cutting into them.

VEHICLE KIT

Four wheel drive and boating enthusiasts need a more comprehensive survival kit. This must be securely stored but easily accessible. You should be able to grab it and go without fumbling around. In a worst-case scenario (vehicle on fire, sinking boat, etc.) there will not be time to dig under gear or untie a confusion of knots to get to it.

The vehicle survival kit should be stored in something easily carried on foot if necessary. It has to be durable enough to withstand the daily jostling of car or boat travel. A large, stiff camera bag with shoulder strap is ideal. This container should be waterproof and large enough to hold the following items:

1. KNIFE

This is a spare in addition to your personal belt knife. Store in a leather sheath with a secure fastening. Keep it sharp and minimise contact with sea water. Store your sharpening gear with the knife. If you do a lot of fishing you may want to pack a separate filleting knife for saltwater use. This should also be sheathed for safe storage.

2. EMERGENCY FOOD

The aim is maximum energy for minimum weight. Beef jerky, energy bars, dried fruit and nuts are suitable. Bushwalkers often remove food from its initial packaging and re-store in plastic bags to save space, but food for the vehicle kit will keep longer if left in the original sealed wrapping. Many items will keep long enough to last more than one trip, but monitor use-by dates. To maintain salt levels in hot weather, electro-lyte powder is preferable to salt tablets. It replaces minerals and vitamins lost through sweating as well as the salt.

Protein, fat and salt are the immediate priorities to keep the body going in a survival scenario. Along northern coasts you will generally find enough of these once you know how to look. Inland regions are less bountiful.

Ensure your emergency food supply contains plenty of these three essentials as well as recognised high-energy foods (honey, sultanas, etc.). Remember that protein, fat and salt need a lot of water to be properly digested. Eat them freely only when water is plentiful.

3. SIGNAL FLARES

Red and green flares are indispensable for attracting attention in the bush or at sea. Pack two or three mini-flares in the survival kit. Keep them away from children and follow the directions carefully. Treat them with the same caution you would apply to a firearm.

4. DISPOSABLE LIGHTERS / MATCHES

Carry two or three disposable lighters for fire-making as well as a supply of waterproof matches. Store the lighters in a plastic bag to keep dry. If travelling through cold, soggy country a couple of fuel tablets are also worth including. These are available from camping outlets and are a real help in getting a fire going when conditions are uncooperative.

5. TORCH

Take a durable torch with long-life batteries (and spares). Torches are a frequently lost item in the bush. Pack a brightly coloured one that you can't miss when breaking camp.

6. OVERSIZED PLASTIC BAGS

A clear plastic bag about two metres long, one metre wide and 150 microns thick provides several survival functions. It keeps gear dry during river crossings and in cold, windy weather serves as an emergency sleeping bag. You can use it as a rain poncho by cutting out holes for arms and head. One of its most important uses is in producing valuable drinking water through plant transpiration (see Water chapter). When driving in arid regions take several bags, with at least three in the survival kit.

7. BILLY

A two or three litre aluminium billy gives more cooking options than a fire alone because you can boil water. It's also a handy place to store most of the items listed. Inside the billy these are better protected for packing inside the vehicle kit bag.

A cup of tea is always a morale booster in the bush, and another good reason to include a billy with lid in your kit.

8. TARP

Many survivors stranded in isolated areas have watched in dismay as search planes passed overhead without seeing them. To increase rescue prospects it is vital to increase your visibility on the ground. There may not be time to light a signal fire but it only takes seconds to spread out a bright orange or blue tarp. Place this flat on the ground well clear of trees and other visual obstructions.

9. WATER

Take enough for each person and plenty for the radiator. Separate containers are best in case one breaks. Keep containers upright and secure them against the jostling of the vehicle. As a rule of thumb an absolute minimum of 9 litres per person and 18 litres for the vehicle is advisable. Carry more if you are heading into isolated areas.

Take water with you whenever you venture even a short distance from the vehicle, even if this is no more than a plastic litre bottle or a small water bag hanging from your belt.

A comprehensive survival kit should be standard gear for remote area 4WD trips. In an emergency you can find all you need in one container.

Photo: Colin & Georgina Wright

Whatever other gear you take into the wild, always carry a pocket-sized personal survival kit. You never know when you might need it.

Survival Priorities
First Aid

1. Take a course in basic first aid or wilderness first aid. Learn how to perform heart/lung resuscitation and other essential emergency procedures.

2. Prevention equals safety. Most accidents stem from bad judgement, poor preparation or carelessness.

3. Carry a suitable first aid kit in the bush.

4. Priorities in a medical emergency: prevent further injury, check consciousness, maintain respiration and heartbeat, stop any bleeding and treat for shock.

5. By definition, first aid aims to keep a person alive until proper medical help is obtained. In remote areas this help might be days or weeks away, or not available at all. Improvisation and long-term solutions may be needed.

6. If driving in isolated regions, seriously consider an HF radio or other way to communicate with the Royal Flying Doctor Service. The investment could save your life.

7. Think carefully about moving an injured person. It may be safer and quicker to bring help to the patient.

8. Some knowledge of bush medicine can be helpful. Many Australian plants have proven medicinal uses.

9. You may have to treat yourself. First aid courses tend to teach techniques as they are used on another person but it's important to understand the need for 'self-aid'. Can you wrap your own snake-bitten arm, splint your own broken bones or treat your own heat exhaustion? Your life may depend on knowing how.

First Aid

Protecting yourself is the first priority in any survival incident. Self-protection encompasses first aid, clothing, shelter, fire-making and other factors, but of all these first aid is the most urgent. In a medical emergency death can occur within minutes.

Even if you have completed a first aid course in the past it's a good idea to take a refresher course before going bush. If your training was some time ago it may now be out of date. Many first aid techniques have been improved over the years. By keeping up to date and practising skills you will be more able to respond swiftly and calmly in a crisis. Courses are offered by a number of organisations including the Australian Red Cross Society and the St. John Ambulance Association.

Safety and prevention come first. Accidents are no accident - they mostly result from poor planning, overestimation of physical abilities, carelessness or plain stupidity. Once an incident has occurred the safety of the injured and all other persons is the priority. Dangerous rescues and hasty decisions can lead to further injuries and worsen the situation. *Nothing causes death more quickly in a survival situation than serious physical injury or illness.*

In administering first aid, take the victim's medical history into account and make an assessment based on what *you know* has occurred. Check vital signs and record times as applicable:

Breathing: Count breaths per minute, listen for noisy breathing (suggesting a blocked airway) and check if breaths are shallow or deep.

Pulse: Check the heart beat rate per minute.

Consciousness: Is there any response when you touch, pinch or speak to the patient?

Skin: Is the skin hot or cold, dry or perspiring? Is the colour normal or is it flushed or pale?

This survey of vital signs is the initial basis upon which first aid is administered. Perform it quickly but calmly in the order shown.

When recording times and the changing status of vital signs, don't rely on memory. Write everything down. Those who go for help should take the information with them. The more facts rescue and medical personnel have about a patient's condition the better they can assist. This information should include the name, age and sex of the casualty, the type of incident and the first aider's diagnosis determined from vital signs and other observations. Record the date, time and nature of the mishap and how it has been managed so far. Give the patient's location as precisely as possible - provide map grid coordinates, page references from your bushwalking book, prominent nearby landmarks or anything that will aid rescuers. Tell them what time you left the casualty to summon help and where you are calling from if reporting by phone. The name and phone number of the patient's next of kin should also be supplied.

In urgent cases it may be better to bring help to the patient rather than try an evacuation. The incapacitated should only be moved if evacuation is a quicker and safer option than waiting for help. If there is danger that the condition will worsen from the stresses of transport, *do not move the patient*. The police or Royal Flying Doctor Service should be contacted by two-way radio or satellite telephone.

FIRST AID KIT

A first aid kit is something you hope you'll rarely have to use. In trackless country a quality kit is vital. Paranoia about carrying a few extra grams of weight leads many backpackers to skimp on first aid gear. This is a mistake. Compared to food, tent and other essentials, medical supplies are light in weight and take up little space in the pack. The items on the following list can all be obtained from your local chemist and are provided as a suggestion for longer treks. Use the list as a guide, to be pared down or modified for your own trip. The compiling of first aid kits is a personal matter, ultimately dependant upon medical history, climate, terrain, conditions anticipated and individual whim. The use of brand names is unavoidable, but in most cases other brands may be available which do a similar job to those listed.

Total weight of the following kit is around half a kilo. Pack it in a sturdy plastic bag and store in a padded part of the pack. A kit for the glove box or boat could be expanded to include additional items, since weight is less of a concern. First aid supplies and medications must be readily accessible - don't bury them under piles of other gear. With serious injury, seconds make all the difference.

ITEM	QUANTITY
Stingose gel	25 grams
Elastoplast Fingertip dressing	1
Gastrolyte tablets (for dehydration)	15
Sterile oval eye patch	1
Water purification tablets	24
Combine pads (pressure dressings) 9x10 cm	2
Cotton crepe roller bandage 7.5x2.3 cm	1
Cotton crepe roller bandage 10x2.3 cm	1
Butterfly closure strips	6
Sterile surgical gloves	1 pair
Melolite absorbent dressings 7.5x5 cm	2
Panadol tablets	8
Panadeine tablets	8
Betadine antiseptic	25 grams
Cotton balls	12
Cotton tip buds	8
Alcohol swabs	10
Emergency suture and needle set	2
Sterile surgical blades	2
Antifungal cream	10 grams
Conforming gauze bandage	1
Triangular bandage	1
Opsite wound dressings 6.5x5 cm	2
Opsite wound dressings 9x8.5 cm	2
Small scissors	1
Small sharp-pointed tweezers	1
Splinter probe	1
Safety pins	10
Transpore adhesive tape	1 roll
Zinc Oxide cream	1 tube
Maximum protection sunscreen	1 tube
Adhesive blister pads	several
Salt tablets or table salt	4 tblspns
Medicated soap	1 bar
Haemostat (mosquito clamp)	1

Electrolyte replacement drink powder (to keep up salt and mineral levels) can be carried separately from the first aid kit.

Some prescription-only medications can be useful, including antibiotics in their various forms and perhaps a stronger painkiller for serious injuries. Consult your doctor about what you feel you might need.

It isn't possible to prepare for every conceivable medical dilemma but the kit above will see you through the most common problems. If your trip is a brief jaunt rather than a full-fledged expedition you may be able to do without some items and reduce quantities. Size of the expedition party also makes a difference to what is carried. You wouldn't normally pack Airsplints, a space blanket or a thermometer on solo journeys but in a party of three or four they should be included.

WILDERNESS AND REMOTE AREA FIRST AID COURSES

A ustralia-wide quality first-aid training courses for Professional Outdoor Leaders, travellers and remote area workers. Call for information on Australia's best Outdoor First Aid Kits and our Newsletter. Visit our new web page: www.outdoorsafety.com

The Safety Network
P.O. Box 320
Katoomba NSW 2780
ph/fax: 02 4782 4419
wfac@wfac.aust.com

The most prevalent outdoor ailments are minor ones - foot blisters, insect bites, cuts, abrasions and the occasional muscle strain. Sunburn is a self-inflicted condition that is wholly preventable. With protective clothing, sunscreen and a decent hat it shouldn't happen.

"What if I break a leg while I'm out in the middle of nowhere?" This is a common worry. As far as broken limbs are concerned an ounce of prevention is worth everything. Serious injuries occur most often when unnecessary chances are taken when fatigued. Descending a steep rocky gully near the end of an exhausting day's trek is asking for trouble. Experienced walkers plan ahead to avoid such high risk situations.

Carry a comprehensive first aid guidebook with your kit. This brief chapter is no substitute for a proper first aid reference. Unless you have medical training or practise first aid regularly it's difficult to keep up with all the symptoms and treatments you need to remember. In isolated areas medical help or evacuation can be delayed and there may be some extended care. Improvisation will probably be necessary in making splints, stretchers and other necessities. These can be fashioned from bark, branches or materials found in your vehicle.

LOSS OF CONSCIOUSNESS

A bad mistake with unconscious patients is to leave them lying on their backs. This shouldn't be done because suffocation may result from the tongue or vomit blocking the airway. Turn the patient over into the recovery position. Then remove any vomit from the mouth. Vomiting is a common occurrence in unconscious persons. Check that the tongue has fallen away from the back of the throat, and reposition the neck and jaw if needed to achieve a clear airway. Loss of consciousness must always be viewed as very serious.

HEART/LUNG RESUSCITATION

Turn the patient face up if there is no sign of breathing and begin mouth to mouth (or mouth to nose) resuscitation. Lift the jaw to open the airway and give five full breaths in ten seconds. Check for circulation in the carotid artery. If circulation is evident continue with air resuscitation at the rate of fifteen full ventilations per minute. Check the circulation after one minute, and every two minutes thereafter. If breathing resumes, place the patient in the recovery position and keep the airway clear.

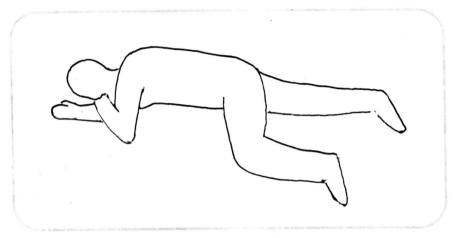

The recovery position.

If circulation is not present upon checking the carotid artery, begin cardiac compressions. Put the heel of one hand over the sternum and lock the other hand on top, either by intertwining the fingers or grabbing your wrist. If you're by yourself, give two breaths and fifteen chest compressions (four cycles per minute). With two resuscitators the first gives one breath, then the other gives 5 compressions. This cycle is repeated 12 times per minute. If these actions are successful some colour should return to the patient's face and a carotid pulse will be detected with each compression.

A common error with inexperienced resuscitators is to blow into the mouth too hard. All you need is enough breath to make the chest rise gently. Blowing too forcibly may inflate the stomach, possibly sending gastric contents up to clog the airway. This may make further resuscitation impossible. Be steady, calm and gentle when resuscitating, especially with children.

BLEEDING AND SHOCK

Treatment for external bleeding is to apply firm direct pressure over the wound. Keep pressure on the area with a firm bandage. Apply a second dressing even more firmly over the top if the first one leaks. Do not just slow the bleeding - stop it totally. Once bandaged, elevate the affected part and keep the patient still.

Arterial bleeding is very serious. It is characterised by rapid, pulsing spurts of bright red blood. Direct pressure will normally work if applied properly. Compressing the artery at a higher pressure point (groin, underside of the upper arm, etc.) may also be necessary.

Internal bleeding may be caused by trauma or disease, and is harder to detect. Coughing up or vomiting blood are symptoms, as is blood being passed in faeces. However, it is possible to have internal bleeding without these signs. A serious fall, car smash or sharp blow can cause damage to organs such as the liver or spleen or trauma to large blood vessels. Symptoms of this sort of injury include a painful, tender or rigid abdomen. You won't be able to stop internal bleeding, so the priority is to check the patient for signs of advancing shock and treat that.

Both external and internal bleeding can be accompanied by shock. With serious bleeding the onset of shock is virtually a certainty. *Shock can kill.* Learn to read the signs. Pulse rate per minute will increase but its strength will decrease. Skin will feel cold, look pale and show increased sweating. Loss of consciousness may follow.

To treat shock your first objective is to stop any bleeding. Then recline the patient and elevate the legs. Loosen restrictive clothing and keep the person warm but not hot. Give plenty of fluids. Diluted soup or juice is good, or you can just add 1/4 teaspoon salt and four teaspoons sugar to a litre of water. If rescue is under four hours away the giving of drinks is not necessary. A patient in advanced shock from loss of blood requires quick evacuation. Intravenous fluids and other care beyond the scope of first aid will be desperately needed.

BLOCKED AIRWAY

This occurs when objects (usually food) become lodged in the back of the throat. Symptoms include choking, clutching at the throat and an inability to talk. Noisy breathing suggests a partial blockage. As the situation worsens the face may turn blue from lack of oxygen and the victim soon collapses into unconsciousness. If the obstruction is not cleared within minutes, death will occur from respiratory arrest.

Try to get the patient to cough. Look into the mouth to see if the object is visible. Some probing with fingers may get it out, but ensure you don't inadvertently push it further along instead. Next try a few hard slaps between the shoulder blades; this works best with the patient upside down. If there is still no success get behind the victim, encircle with your arms and execute the Heimlich Manoeuvre. Clasp one fist inside the other hand and place just under the rib cage. Give a quick, hard inward tug. This forcibly expels air from the lungs and often dislodges the object. Performed properly, the Heimlich Manoeuvre has an excellent success rate.

CARDIAC ARREST

The stopping of the heart is quickly evident. The patient is deeply unconscious with no reaction to pain and no pulse. Any breathing will be slow and fading away. There may be a blue tinge to the face. Immediate cardiopulmonary resuscitation should be started and continued until you are relieved by medical personnel or until the patient is deceased. Contrary to the miraculous recoveries seen on television doctor shows, heart/lung resuscitation is used primarily to keep the brain going until more advanced medical treatment can be given. For it to restore full heart and lung function after both have stopped is a very rare occurrence.

Cardiac arrest shouldn't be confused with heart attack, even though it may be one of the complications arising from it. Heart attack occurs when an artery leading to the heart muscle is blocked. The signs are well known - pain in the chest, arms, back or jaw. Unlike indigestion, the level of pain and feeling of tightness does not alter noticeably as the patient breathes in and out. Heart attacks are often accompanied by shortness of breath, nausea and vomiting. Aside from complete rest and small sips of water there is not much that can be done in a remote bush setting for a heart attack victim. If cardiac arrest occurs, start CPR.

FRACTURES

Bone fractures can range from slight cracks to multiple breaks of major bones. Bleeding is usually present in adjacent damaged tissue. Symptoms of a fracture include pain, tenderness and swelling at the site. The patient will be unable to move the affected part, which may be visibly irregular in shape. With major fractures blood loss and shock are potentially fatal. Control bleeding with a sterile dressing, bandage firmly and then splint the limb. Splints should be padded and long enough to completely immobilise the joints on either side of the break. Splints support the affected area and control pain caused by movement. Inflatable Airsplints are ideal, but you can improvise. Pad some straight tree branches with jumpers, poncho or folded tarp. Tie a partially inflated sleeping mat around the limb or use the lumbar pad from your rucksack. Padded tent poles may also be used as splints.

It's not often easy to tell if an ankle is broken or merely sprained. With both there is pain and swelling but with breaks there is usually also a visible misalignment and a 'crunchy' feeling as the foot is moved. If the ankle is believed to be broken, apply a splint from the knee to the bottom of the foot.

Wrist and forearm fractures are splinted, then supported with a sling made from a triangular bandage. Tie the supported arm against the chest with a bandage wrapped around the upper torso. Handle a fractured rib by bandaging right around the chest. With a break on the right-hand rib cage the right arm can be strapped against the chest in a sling; this may give some relief. Minor rib fractures cause sharp pain that increases at inhalation. They generally heal themselves over time.

Spinal fractures are normally the result of severe neck movement caused by trauma. Being dumped on your head by a large wave, coming off a bike head first or diving into shallow water are common causes. The patient may be unconscious with a slow pulse (less than fifty beats per minute). *Do not* move the patient unless absolutely necessary. Place padded clothing on either side of the head to keep it still. Summoning assistance is preferable to moving the patient. If movement is unavoidable, someone should hold the victim's head so it doesn't flop around.

First aid courses provide instruction in making arm slings and limb splints but you should also practise such skills on your own. You must be able apply a range of first aid techniques not only to others but to yourself. In a survival situation you may have to practise 'self-aid'.

HEAD INJURY

A blow to the head can cause a concussion, skull fracture, cerebral compression or fractured neck vertebrae. Signs of concussion include loss of consciousness, confusion, memory loss, headache and decreased coordination. In some cases the patient may only be unconscious for seconds. Brief convulsions may occur. Rest the patient and watch very closely for 24 hours. A relapse into unconsciousness can indicate continued bleeding inside the skull. Unconscious periods of over half a minute are cause for evacuation, even if consciousness is restored.

Cerebral compression is basically a build up of fluid or blood inside the skull, putting excessive pressure on the brain. This is a very serious injury indicated by increasingly severe headache, nausea, vomiting, disorientation and drowsiness. Consciousness will be regained either temporarily or not at all, so evacuation must be immediate. Keep the head in the same position relative to the rest of the body.

APPENDICITIS

An inflamed appendix is most likely to occur in people between 15 and 24 years of age, but can affect other age groups as well. Appendicitis strikes 1 in 500 people every year. If medical help is reached in time, treatment consists of surgical removal of the swollen appendix. However, a ruptured appendix left totally untreated is fatal. Urgent evacuation is essential if appendicitis is suspected.

Appendicitis can be difficult to diagnose, especially in the early stages. Usually it starts with pain near the navel. The pain migrates toward the right side of the lower abdomen, usually within twelve hours. Pain then becomes steadier and more localised. Touching the affected area, sneezing, breathing deeply, coughing and movement worsen the pain. There may be nausea, vomiting and constipation. A low fever may develop. In later stages there may be some abdominal swelling. If the appendix ruptures the pain may suddenly vanish, only to return within hours and become more intense. At this point the pain may be felt over the whole abdomen, which will feel hard to the touch. Pale skin, vomiting, listlessness and fever are normally present.

Appendicitis patients must not be given any food or pain medication. If vomiting has stopped, small sips of water may be given if hospitalization is unlikely within four hours.

EYE INJURIES

Specks of dust, sand and other foreign bodies can easily get into your eyes in the bush. Prevention goes a long way. Wear sunglasses that protect as much of the eye area as possible. Roll up car windows on dusty roads and wear a mossie net when small insects are a problem. Objects on the white of the eye can be carefully brushed toward the tear duct with a clean moistened tissue or cloth. If the material is in the clear part of the eye try flushing it out with water or eyewash solution.

Slivers of glass, wood or metal that penetrate the eye and remain firmly embedded are dealt with differently. Place a ring-shaped pad over the affected eye and then cover both eyes. Covering material *must not* touch the protruding object. Evacuate the patient on a stretcher.

A blow to the eye can cause blood under the cornea (the clear part of the eye). This is more noticeable with the patient sitting down. The eye will be painful and the patient may have some nausea and vomiting. Rest the patient with the head upright, keeping head movement to a minimum. Blood under the cornea can result in loss of sight in that eye, so waste no time in evacuating the patient by stretcher.

INFECTED WOUNDS

In the bush it is doubly important to take good care of cuts and abrasions to avoid infection. A localised infection becomes red, painful and swollen. Clear fluid or pus may escape from the wound. The first step is to remove any foreign material with heat-sterilised tweezers. Clean the surrounding skin with a suitable antiseptic such as Betadine. Apply a sterile dressing and bandage. Check and clean the wound daily and apply a fresh dressing.

In a healthy person, minor cuts tend to heal themselves with minimal care and the infection remains small and localised. Uncontrolled infection is a more serious matter that can lead to debilitating illness, loss of limb or death.

Infection which has spread to the bloodstream is detected by pain and a sense of heat and pressure at the wound site. A fever (over 37.5 degrees) is accompanied by telltale red streaks leading away from the wound. Pus is normally present and the affected limb will be difficult to move. Infections stemming from leg wounds are characterised by swollen lymph nodes in the groin. Head or neck injuries affect lymph nodes in the armpit.

Treat this level of infection promptly. Swab away any pus with sterile gauze held by heat-sterilised tweezers and wash the wound with clean warm water. Apply a sterile dressing, but not too tightly. Clean and redress the wound twice daily and avoid pulling the edges closed. If you're a regular visitor to remote areas you may have suitable prescription antibiotics in your first aid kit and know how to use them. Administer these if you understand the dosage and procedure. With or without antibiotics the patient must be evacuated urgently to a medical facility.

An innovative First Aid Kit System

Survival Pack

EQUIP +

HANDS ON FIRST AID

Telephone 0011 618 9319 8818   e-mail admin@equip.com.au   www.equip.com.au

Equip products are endorsed by WMI Australasia

The Wilderness Medicine Institute Provides Quality, Hands-On Education For The Recognition, Treatment & Prevention Of Wilderness Emergencies.

For Course Information

Telephone 0011 618 9321 1263
e-mail   perth@tmvc.com.au
www.wildernessmed.com

BURNS

Minor superficial burns should be cooled as quickly as possible with cold water. If a cool stream or waterhole is available, immerse the burned area for 5 - 10 minutes, long enough to relieve some of the pain but not so long that the patient becomes chilled. Burns with broken skin should be covered with a sterile dressing. Give plenty of fluids. Medicated creams are available for use with burns *on unbroken skin only* - ask your chemist.

A patient with superficial burns over more than 9% of the body should be evacuated at once, as should a person with burns to critical areas (feet, hands, groin, face, etc.). Nine percent of the body surface is roughly the amount of skin covering one arm or the entire head.

Sunburn and minor campfire burns are painful but not normally life-threatening. Deeper burns are another matter. The skin may be charred, and because nerve endings have been destroyed the victim will only feel pain in the superficial surrounding burns. A real danger with deep burns is shock brought on by the intense pain and sudden loss of body fluids.

Cool deep burns with liberal amounts of cold running water. Keep this up for up to 15 minutes or until the patient begins to feel chilled. Take off burnt clothing but cut around any fabric that is sticking to the burn. Cover with a sterile dressing and keep air away from the burn as much as you can - this is vital. Moistening the dressing may bring some relief from the intense pain. Fluid loss is very high with deep burns so give small drinks often. With deep burns the current wisdom is to urgently evacuate if the burnt surface area exceeds 3%. With all burns the pain level, location and effect on mobility and normal function determine the best course of action.

BLISTERS

Foot blisters range from mildly annoying to painfully debilitating. If ignored they will slow down a trip or ruin it completely.

Prevention starts with the correct boots. These must fit properly, offer support in the right places and be fully broken in. Blisters form from friction and heat caused by the rubbing that goes on inside the boot. Attend to blisters the moment you become aware of them. *Do not wait.* Cover the tender spot with an adhesive blister pad. These come in assorted shapes and thicknesses and offer a protective barrier against further friction.

The trick is to get to the pressure spot early when it's still just a slight tenderness or a faint reddening of the skin. If covered before it becomes a full-blown blister it will usually cause no further trouble. Take off the blister pad at night to let air get to the spot and cover again in the morning if needed.

Don't be heroic with blisters. If you ignore them they'll become painful enough to impair your ability to continue on schedule. Serious blisters may need to be punctured and drained. To do this, prick the edge with a sterilised needle, gently press out the fluid with a sterile pad and cover with a sterile dressing.

There seem to be two divergent opinions regarding the subject of looking after feet while trekking. The 'tough it out' theory suggests you put your boots on in the morning and leave them on until the end of the day, barring any major problems. The 'pampering' method subscribes to the concept that the better you treat your feet the better they will treat you. It includes some or all of the following procedures: taking boots off to air the feet at hourly rest stops, anointing them periodically with rubbing alcohol and/or foot powder and changing socks at every stop (the old pair are suspended from the outside of the pack to dry as you walk).

SNAKEBITE

Suburban gardeners trying to kill snakes are more susceptible to snakebite than careful trekkers in remote country. More people are bitten harassing these reptiles than are bitten from accidentally treading on them. Leave them alone. Most snakes are reluctant to bite in defence and will happily move along if you let them.

Each year in Australia about 2000 people are bitten by snakes, usually on the hand, lower leg or forearm. Only around 10% of these need treatment with antivenene. At the moment snakebite fatalities in Australia average only two or three deaths per year. This extremely low rate is attributed to improved first aid techniques and the increased availability and effectiveness of modern antivenenes. Often when snakes bite they don't inject much (or any) venom.

The old 'cut, suck and tourniquet' treatment is a thing of the past. The modern method is to apply a firm pressure bandage to the bite site and along as much of the limb as possible. A 7.5 cm or 10 cm wide cotton crepe roller bandage from the first aid kit is excellent for the job. Once the bite itself is covered, continue wrapping the bandage up the length of the limb in a spiral motion with firm even pressure, and back down the limb again if the bandage is long enough. Use roughly the same pressure as you would on a sprained ankle. The bandage must *not* be so firm that you are cutting off circulation to the limb.

The next step is to immobilise the limb with a splint. Any limb movement hastens the spread of venom through the body. Splint legs into a straight position. Splint forearms up to the elbow and support with a sling. For bites to the torso or face apply firm pressure only, using the palm of the hand. Victims should stay as still and as calm as possible to slow the spread of the venom. Don't bother trying to wash venom away from the bite area. If you are wearing long trousers when bitten just leave them on. The movement needed to take them off will cause more venom to enter the bloodstream. Minimising movement is vital both before and after the pressure bandage has been applied.

The Death Adder has a triangular head, a thick body and a distinctive tail, and flattens its body when threatened. **Photo: Brad Maryan, WASAH**

Staying composed when bitten by a snake is easier said than done, but the pressure and immobilisation treatment is very effective when administered without delay. If applied promptly and correctly the prospect of serious illness or death from snakebite is very minimal. If far from help and on your own when seriously bitten you should avoid the temptation to rush off on foot - the exertion just causes more venom to enter your system. Instead, remain calm, bandage and immobilise the limb to restrict venom flow and rest in the shade.

Snakes may vary in colour from region to region. The Mulga Snake is often referred to as the 'King Brown', but it might be coppery, pale brown, olive or (like this specimen) almost black. These snakes strike very rapidly and may grow to over two metres in length. Photo: Brad Maryan, WASAH

HEAT EXHAUSTION

High temperatures can lead to heat exhaustion quickly, especially with exertion. Symptoms include profuse sweating, flushed hot skin and a feeling of weakness. There may be headache, some dizziness and confusion. Because the blood is rushing to the surface of the skin to keep things cool, the supply to the brain suffers.

Mild heat exhaustion can accelerate into severe heat stroke very rapidly. Take *immediate action* when it is obvious the body is overheating. First, get the victim to rest in the shade with the feet up. Remove excess clothing and fan the body to cool it down. Provide plenty of cool drinks (water or a rehydration beverage, never alcohol). These should be given as frequent sips at intervals rather than all at once. The victim should continue to rest in the shade until urine has returned to its normal light colour. Give the body plenty of time to recuperate at its own pace.

Along with water loss, sweating reduces the level of salts (electrolytes) in our bodies. When these are depleted we risk developing muscle cramps.

Table salt or salt tablets should always be carried in hot weather. Packet soup powders are very salty and are a convenient pack food. They make a good choice for evening meals when you've been walking in the heat all day. A number of rehydration drink powders are available (Gastrolyte, Gatorade, Staminade etc.). These are specifically designed to replace the salts and minerals lost through sweating. Carry a quantity in an outside pocket of your pack to mix with water at rest stops.

Prickly heat is a less serious but still irritating problem for outdoor travellers. A combination of blocked sweat glands, chafing clothing and profuse sweating leads to redness and itching. Humid, windless conditions make it worse. Several preparations are available to treat it. Tea tree oil (store-bought or applied from crushed leaves) works well for many sufferers.

HEAT STROKE

Heat stroke occurs when the body's cooling mechanism breaks down completely. This is a life-threatening development indicative of severe dehydration. Sweating stops completely and the skin becomes dry, hot and pale. Dizziness, nausea, blurred vision, vomiting and delirium may soon follow, then loss of consciousness and death. Treatment for heat stroke must be rapid and aggressive. In addition to shade, rest, clothing removal and vigorous fanning you may need to use other cooling methods. Cover the body with wet cloths and if possible immerse in cool (but not icy cold) water. Massage limbs by stroking towards the torso. This helps move the cooled blood near the skin surface back toward the heart.

SNOW BLINDNESS

Snow blindness is caused by exposure to too much glare. The eyes become red, watery and acutely sensitive to light. There is often a 'gritty' sensation under the eyelids. Headache is common.

Snow blindness can occur in cloudy conditions as well as bright sunshine. Sometimes there is a delayed reaction with symptoms. After climbing a snowy mountain you might not feel the full effects until back in camp.

Dark goggles or sunglasses should always be worn in snow regions. Snow blindness usually heals itself, though this may take a few days. It is a painful condition and little can be done for relief except to apply cold compresses and stay in the dark. Anaesthetic eye drops and anti-inflammatory ointment can also help.

Glare on the water can also be damaging to the eyes. Polarising sunglasses are essential for kayaking, fishing or boating trips. Aside from the water itself, white sand is also a strong sunlight reflector.

HYPOTHERMIA

Inadequate clothing and exposure to wind, cold, rain or snow can bring on hypothermia. Floating in water also robs the body of warmth. The water need not be freezing cold; what seems merely refreshing during a ten minute swim may be cold enough to kill after prolonged immersion. Learn to recognise signs of hypothermia so it can be treated at the earliest possible stage.

The first evidence of hypothermia is shivering which becomes increasingly intense. The patient feels cold and fatigued and the skin may be pale. Muscle coordination decreases, speech becomes slurred and there may be uncharacteristic mood changes. The simplest tasks (unzipping a tent flap, putting on a glove) become difficult. *Advanced hypothermia* is characterised by lethargy, confusion or delirious behaviour. At this late stage shivering ceases and the patient loses consciousness. Death may follow rapidly after loss of consciousness.

The aim in treating hypothermia is to prevent further loss of body heat. Get the patient out of the rain, snow or wind. If there are dry clothes or a sleeping bag to change into, remove the wet clothes. You may need to exhale your breath into the sleeping bag to warm it up first. Treat *mild hypothermia* by increasing warmth through exercise or gentle application of external warmth. A fit and well-nourished person might run on the spot to get warm. Give the patient high energy foods (chocolate, honey, muesli bars, etc.) and warm beverages but no alcohol. Sharing body heat with a warm person in a sleeping bag is effective.

Advanced hypothermia is potentially fatal and is treated differently to mild hypothermia. It occurs when the body core temperature dips to 32 degrees. An ominous sign that hypothermia has progressed to the advanced stage is when all shivering stops. Your main aims should be to stop all heat loss, ensure there is no physical exertion (keep the patient still) and most importantly *do not rapidly rewarm*. External rewarming of an *advanced hypothermia* patient in a first aid setting has its dangers because of stresses on the heart and the problem of drawing blood out and away from the body core where it's needed. Patients suffering advanced hypothermia are on a survival knife edge. Extreme care must be taken not to put added strains on the fragile circulatory system.

FROSTBITE

Frostbite isn't common in Australia, but it can occur. Basically it's the freezing of body tissue, usually on toes, fingers, ears and nose. When the body gets cold, circulation to the extremities decreases making them more vulnerable. At first the affected part is very painful, then becomes numb. Skin looks pale and waxy, and in severe cases may show purple blotches. Tight boots make matters worse in cold weather because they further restrict circulation through the feet.

Prevent frostbite by dressing warmly all over and keep up fluid intake. One of the effects of frostbite is to dehydrate the affected tissue. Put numb hands under armpits or blow warm breath on them. Mittens are better than gloves because the fingers can warm each other. If feet get numb, take boots off and warm your feet. One of the best ways is to place them on a companion's stomach. Massage also helps.

To treat serious frostbite, keep frozen tissue from thawing until you're totally sure there is no chance it could re-freeze. Once thawed the tissue is very fragile. Rapid rewarming in water at 40 - 42 degrees Centigrade is the accepted treatment. You have to maintain this steady temperature for 30-45 minutes until skin colour improves. If the water cools too much and slows down the rate of thaw the damage to tissue will be greater. Keep pressure off the affected part and *do not* apply direct heat to it. Give aspirin or a stronger pain killer if necessary - rewarming frostbitten areas can be excruciating. Apply a dressing.

In a remote setting with minimal gear (and no thermometer) this controlled rewarming process may be difficult or impossible, in which case it's better to leave the affected part frozen and concentrate efforts on an urgent evacuation.

BUSH MEDICINE

Aboriginal people have been using wild plants as medicinal remedies for centuries. Early colonists also utilised native and introduced plants for various ailments. Scientists have established the chemical basis for many of these remedies, some of which have potential uses in a survival scenario. *It is not recommended that plants be taken internally, however, as many are highly poisonous.* Problems with plant identification are compounded by the difficulty in knowing the correct quantities to use. The survivor is better off learning a few external plant applications that are easy to remember and known to be safe.

The benefits of aromatic eucalyptus oil in relieving cold symptoms is well documented. Aborigines in some parts of Australia still treat head colds, coughs and headaches with a range of natural inhalants. These include the crushed leaf tips of young paperbarks and weeping tea trees, which are sniffed deeply. Other aromatic plants used in this way include ragworts, lemon grasses and fuchsia bushes. Those who believe in fighting colds with Vitamin C can do no better than the fruit of the billygoat plum (*Terminalia ferdinandiana*), found in Top End woodlands. The small green fruits ripen at the start of the dry season, and contain sixty times more Vitamin C than oranges.

Native plants which have effective antiseptic properties are relevant to the survivor faced with injury in a remote setting. Bark from red river gums may be boiled to produce a red liquid for applying to minor cuts and skin irritations. For larger wounds the pounded inner bark of stringybark trees is packed into the wound. This is covered with a bandage made of paperbark tied on with natural fibres. The milky sap of the caustic bush (*Sarcostemma australe*) is dabbed on suppurating wounds and dries to form a protective natural 'bandaid'. Kinos (gums) from tannin-rich eucalypts such as bloodwood trees and ghost gums are astringent and promote rapid healing. Cunjevoi roots are pounded and applied to insect bites and stingray wounds, while the milky juice is rubbed on the skin as an antidote to the sting of giant nettle trees.

Some bush items serve as medical tools. Thorns from the mimosa bush (*Acacia farnesiana*) can be used to remove splinters. The sinews from larger animals such as kangaroos were turned into sutures by early colonial physicians.

An excellent reference on the subject of natural remedies is BUSH MEDICINE (*Tim Low, Harper Collins 1990*). It describes in detail the use of medicinal plants by Aborigines and early colonists.

Don't forget medical aids you might have in your travelling pantry. Garlic juice (diluted with water) is a powerful antiseptic suitable for cuts or swelling. A dab of Vegemite applied to an attached leech will cause it to let go, and vinegar is the accepted remedy for jellyfish stings.

Some natural remedies are unusual but effective. Urine is a sterile antiseptic sometimes used to wash out wounds when nothing else is at hand. Many people throughout the world still enlist leeches for treatment of bruises. Some jungle tribes use fire ants as a suture substitute, pressing the mandibles across the wound so they pinch the two sides closed. The ant's body is then broken off and the pincers left in place.

USING PLANT PREPARATIONS

To be safe, confine yourself to easily recognisable, nonpoisonous plants with proven medicinal benefits.

1. POULTICES - These are commonly used on sprains and suppurating sores. The leaves, root or whole plant is mashed and shaped into a flat pad. A leaf or section of paperbark is placed on top and held in place with cord or 'bush string'.

2. INFUSIONS - Crush or cut up a handful of the plant, place in a container and pour half a litre of boiling water over the top. Stir well and let it cool.

3. JUICE - Pound leaves and stems with a rock or branch to extract the juice, which is applied to wounds. The remaining pulp is smeared on the surrounding skin.

4. DECOCTIONS - These are normally made from plant roots which are cut up and mashed, soaked in water for an hour or more and then brought to a boil. The fluid is then simmered to reduce volume by 30%.

Plant potency depends on the age of the plant, time of year and other factors. Best results are obtained with fresh plants applied immediately after preparation, but you could also divide into two or three portions to be used at intervals.

Survival Priorities
Clothing

1. In the absence of a medical emergency, protection from the elements is normally your first survival priority.

2. Clothing should be loose-fitting to permit freedom of movement. Dress for the cold using the layering system.

3. Cotton and wool aren't the only choices for outdoor wear. New clothing fibres incorporate advanced technology to provide optimum efficiency and comfort in a range of conditions. Some fabrics are waterproof but breathable.

4. Protect yourself from the sun with a wide-brimmed hat, loose trousers and a long-sleeved shirt. Use maximum protection sunscreen liberally on exposed skin. Take advantage of shade and don't let the body overheat.

5. Wear suitable outdoor footwear that protects against spiky plants and provides arch and ankle support. Modern boots are tough but increasingly light in weight. Gaiters provide an additional barrier in spinifex country. Carry moccasins for camp wear or emergencies.

6. Wet, Windy and Weary is the recipe for hypothermia. Carry lightweight windproof and waterproof clothing. Have at least one spare set of dry clothing packed at all times. Don't underestimate the effects of wind chill.

7. Wear a head covering in cold weather to preserve body heat. Heat loss from a bare head is substantial. Outer jackets with deep lined pockets are best for warming hands.

8. Clothing has additional survival purposes. Use it as a flotation aid, a bait net or to pad first aid splints. Brightly coloured clothing is useful for signalling rescuers.

Clothing

Protection from the elements is often the first step in controlling a survival situation. Being able to maintain the body at a comfortable, safe temperature will help keep you alive. Preparation for a bush trip starts with selection of appropriate clothing and equipment for the conditions. If separated from your gear you may have to rely solely upon what you're wearing for a long period. Bush materials can be used to create makeshift clothing but this is not as effective as the real thing.

Listen to your body. It will tell you when you are overheated or getting chilled. Heed its signals and act promptly. A naked healthy human maintains a comfortable temperature only as long as the environment stays between 28 and 34 degrees centigrade. Above 34 we sweat more and need to increase water intake. Below 28 we must put on clothing and start moving around to keep warm. High humidity, unsuitable attire and lack of shade worsen the effects of heat, while wind chill and wet clothing add to the dangers of cold.

FOOTWEAR

Feet receive constant punishment in the bush and must be protected. Exposed feet don't cope well against spiny plants, surprised snakes, hot ground, rough terrain or cold temperatures. With outdoor boots, comfort and fit are everything. If they don't feel right when you try them on in the store, keep looking until you find a pair that does. The idea that slightly uncomfortable boots can somehow be 'broken in' is a myth. There may be some softening and shaping of the leather to the contours of your foot with increased use but the support, fit and comfort must be there from the beginning. Before undertaking a long trek take some day trips with a weighted pack to see how new boots perform. If nothing else, wear them around the back yard for a month or so to get used to them.

A boot's sole should offer protection underfoot as well as a degree of grip on slippery surfaces. Hard rubber soles don't grip as well as softer rubber but they last longer. Vibram soles are commonly used in the making of quality boots.

Leather boots should not be dried out by a fire. This shrinks and cracks the leather and shortens the life of the boot. When returning from a hike, clean dirt and mud off with water, using a nylon brush if needed. Dirt particles that are left behind work their way into seams and weaken the boot. Nikwax is a good waterproofing agent for boots, and also works on Gore-Tex. It can be applied to wet or dry boots.

The author's Trezeta Sherwoods (shown with gaiters) are a typical example of modern boot technology. Leather and Gore-Tex lining are combined to create a breathable boot that is incredibly durable but without the cumbersome weight found in older-style leather boots. Gaiters are a useful addition in snake country and regions where spiky undergrowth is prevalent. **Photo: Andrew Kemp**

On the trail, reasonably thick socks of at least 50% wool are best. A thinner pair of socks may be worn underneath to reduce the chafing and friction that leads to blisters. Carry spare pairs and change often. Hanging socks from the top of the pack is the easiest way to dry them on the move.

Gaiters earn their keep in snow, deep mud or thorny undergrowth. The bottom strap attaches around the sole of the boot and the gaiter fabric extends upward to just below the knee. Gaiters protect the lower legs and keep snow, mud, stones and other debris from entering boots.

Ultra-lightweight moccasins or slippers are good for wearing around camp or for brief excursions away from the tent. Moccasins also provide short-term emergency footwear if your boots come to grief.

DRESSING TO STAY ALIVE

Being suitably dressed for the outdoors is a survival necessity. Aim for lightweight, versatile clothing that dries quickly and packs into a small space. In the past, clothing selection meant choosing cotton for the heat and wool for the cold. Today, outdoor clothing incorporates state-of-the-art fabric technology so it's easy to select attire that handles a range of conditions and activities.

THE LAYERING SYSTEM

In cool conditions wear several thinner layers of clothing rather than one thick layer. Add or subtract layers as temperature and activity levels change.

1. The inner underwear layer should wick moisture away from the body, breathe freely and still insulate when wet.

2. The second layer should do all of the above but also be windproof and allow maximum freedom of movement.

3. The third layer should be completely windproof and waterproof, but made from a breathable fabric that allows body vapour to escape. Gore-Tex or similar fabrics are commonly used in this layer. In extreme conditions more than three layers may be needed.

Shirts, shorts and trousers must be loose-fitting enough to allow freedom of movement. Long-sleeve shirts are best so you can roll down the sleeves for sun protection. Jeans offer a good barrier against snagging undergrowth but are heavier than cotton drill trousers and take longer to dry when soaked. Durable cotton work wear is practical for the bush, but many of the new-age fabrics will be lighter and have advantages over cotton in certain environments. In changeable weather, ensure you have clothing suited to layering - lightweight, breathable and warm. Snug-fitting garments *do not* give better protection from the cold. What keeps you warm is the heated air trapped between clothing and skin. Tight, restrictive clothing reduces this trapped air.

One of the more useful features on outdoor jackets is the armpit-zip, which provides extra ventilation during periods of strenuous activity. Another handy idea is the double-ended zip, which lets you unzip the jacket from either end. Being able to unzip from the bottom means more freedom of movement for legs during climbing. Elastic at the bottom of jackets and at sleeve ends helps keep warmed air from escaping. An attached hood with drawstring is essential for cold, windy conditions. A cold weather jacket should extend well below the waist to protect the vulnerable lower torso from chill.

Protection from the elements is crucial to survival, and starts with the right clothing for the environment.   Photo: Michael Tiffin

With natural fibres the basic rule is to wear cotton in the heat and wool in the cold. Wool takes considerably longer than cotton to dry out but retains some of its warmth when soaked.

Don't pack more clothing than you need. Take a good look at what you want to bring and pare it down to a functional but safe minimum. The compactness and low weight of today's innovative outdoor gear means you can pack a lot into a smaller space and be ready for any weather.

Fly nets should fit over the outside of your hat brim and hang down away from your face. Those that have see-through netting in the front and lightweight sunshade material in back (to shield the neck) are ideal.

Protect your hands. Urban life does nothing to toughen up hands, and just one day of serious outdoor activity can result in small cuts and abrasions. Roadside 4WD maintenance, shelter building, digging, fishing and other tasks leave unprotected hands prone to injury and infection. Carry gloves and use them.

Always carry clothing for the outdoors inside your vehicle. This sounds obvious, but business people often drive between remote country towns carrying no extra clothing other than what is on their backs. Polyester shirts, business suits and dress shoes are not ideal attire for a vehicle breakdown or outdoor emergency. Have a spare set of protective clothing in the vehicle which includes gloves, hat, decent boots and suitable clothing for the environment.

BEATING THE HEAT

In choosing bush clothing it helps to understand how the body reacts to temperature extremes. Overheating affects the body in several ways. Sweating increases and blood vessels near the surface of the skin dilate. We need to drink more but are less inclined to eat. Our bodies both generate and dissipate heat, and in normal circumstances do a first-rate job. Trouble starts when we don't drink enough, push too hard in high temperatures or wear too many clothes during exercise. Exposure to serious sunburn or the intense heat of a bush fire puts huge strains on the body's cooling system. When *body core temperature* reaches 38 we are dangerously overheated, and above 40 degrees we suffer heat stroke. Above 45 degrees some nasty things start happening to the proteins in our cells, and death is not far off.

The body's metabolism constantly generates its own heat, measured in calories (4.19 kilojoules equals one calorie). In one day we might generate between 2000 and 5000 calories, the exact amount determined by how hard the body works. The fuel for this process is the food we eat. When we use muscles the blood within them warms up and blood vessels dilate, sending more blood toward the skin where the extra heat can be lost.

The main way we dissipate heat is through evaporation of sweat. The evaporation of a litre of perspiration absorbs 500 - 600 heat calories. It is possible to sweat out up to 1.5 litres each hour, so if the evaporation process starts to break down the heat has nowhere to go and our body temperature rises alarmingly. It is not the sweat itself that cools us but its evaporation upon contact with the air. This is why loose clothing is so important in the heat. Tight clothing that doesn't breathe inhibits the evaporation process.

BATTLING THE SUN

Sunshine is strongest at high altitudes, in the tropics and in places where snow or water reflects it back at you. Sun protection is crucial to survival. In the long term skin cancers can kill. More immediate hazards are sunburn, snow blindness and increased fluid loss.

Sunburn affects survival chances in many ways. Unprotected skin absorbs maximum heat and maintains that heat long after you're out of the sun. More water must be consumed to counter this. Weeping blisters that form as a result of sunburn shed additional body fluid. The pain of sunburn makes movement unpleasant and may be so bad that sleep is impossible.

Prevention is fundamental. Wear long loose fitting trousers, a long-sleeve cotton shirt with collar, wide-brimmed hat and appropriate footwear to combat the sun. Attach a chin strap to your hat if it doesn't already have one. Legionnaire's hats cover the neck and also offer good protection. All exposed skin needs a liberal dose of sunscreen (at least 15 SPF). Skin experts recommend using over a tablespoon on each leg, a dessert-spoonful on each arm and at least a teaspoonful over your face and neck. Don't forget the tops of ears. Sunscreen is best applied 20 minutes before any sun exposure. Zinc cream is good for problem areas such as nose, lips and backs of hands (an area often overlooked by hikers and canoeists). Reduce your exposure to sunlight between 10am and 3pm when UV rays are strongest.

The UPF Classification System

Many new fabrics are now UPF (Ultraviolet Protection Factor) rated and carry a tag showing the rating.
The Australian Radiation Laboratory's UPF Classification System gives the following guidelines:

UPF ratings of 15 or 20 block 93.3% to 95.8% of UV and offer *Good Protection.*
UPF ratings of 25, 30 or 35 block 95.9% to 97.4% of UV and offer *Very Good Protection.*
UPF ratings of 40, 45, 50 or 50+ block over 97.5% of UV and offer *Excellent Protection.*

Wear sunglasses to shield eyes from glare and to provide a barrier against sharp branches as you walk. The polarised type are best for fishing. They cut down on surface reflections and give better visibility down through the water. Secure sunglasses with a neck strap.

Dressing for sun protection.

Photo: Andrew Kemp

Versatility is the key to hot weather wear. If wearing only a T-shirt, shorts and thongs you can't increase your protection level while on the move. On the other hand, if you had a hat on you could angle the brim to shade your face. With a loose, long-sleeve shirt you could roll down sleeves to protect your arms and turn up the collar to shade your neck. Lightweight, loose fitting trousers can be left long out in the sun but rolled up above the knees in the shade. Dress so you can always adjust clothing to suit the weather.

COLD COMFORT

Take the cold seriously. Avoid the combination of 'Wet, Windy and Weary' at all costs. Loss of body heat can rapidly lead to hypothermia, when the body's ability to maintain temperature breaks down.

Sustained cold is a deadly foe because the survivor is affected mentally as well as physically. Responses slow down, rational decisions become harder to make and a lethargic attitude sets in. Slight tiredness soon degenerates to full exhaustion, taking away the will and initiative to battle on.

WIND CHILL FACTOR

Wind helps in the heat by increasing sweat evaporation but in the cold it removes existing surface warmth much faster than cold alone. Even in temperatures around 20 degrees, high winds can rob the body of enough heat to bring on hypothermia, especially if wet clothing is added to the equation. The effects of wind chill are multiplied as wind speed increases. It seems reasonable to assume a 10 km/h wind would rob you of twice the heat of a 5 km/h wind, but in reality it strips away *four times* the heat. When dressing in layers for the cold, ensure the outer layer or the one just beneath it is windproof.

Preparation prevents most cold-related problems. Wear clothing that protects you from cold temperatures, rain and wind, and pay special attention to hands, feet and head. Huge amounts of body heat are lost from an uncovered head. Carry *at least* one set of spare clothing in plastic bags so you can change out of wet attire. Select a sleeping bag and tent that are up to the task if the weather should turn bad. Keep up food and water intake in the cold - when well fed and fully hydrated you can fight its effects more effectively. It is easy to become complacent about drinking water in cold weather but a steady fluid intake is vital for proper circulation. Being fully hydrated will help delay the onset of hypothermia and frostbite.

Normal human body temperature is between 36 and 37.5 degrees centigrade. Between 32 and 35 degrees, mild hypothermia sets in. Around the 32 degree mark the mental processes are noticeably affected and advanced hypothermia starts to take hold.

As activity level increases, remove clothing layers to keep a comfortable temperature. Overheating during exercise in cool weather leaves you clammy and chilled after you stop. Wearing too many clothes is as bad as wearing too little - stay within the comfort zone. Photo: Damiano Visocnik

To negotiate slippery rocks your footwear must grip well. Always have a spare set of dry clothing in the pack in case you receive a dunking on the way across.
Photo: Damiano Visocnik

67

Survival Priorities
Shelter

1. In extreme conditions, being without shelter can lead to death within three hours. Whether on foot or in a vehicle always carry shelter materials (tent, bivvy bag, tarp etc.).

2. Fatigue and sleep deprivation are common in survival episodes. If you can shield yourself from weather and get some sleep your chances are much improved.

3. Avoid direct contact with the ground. Use a tarp, ground-sheet, layer of grass, sleeping mat or plastic bags. Snow, damp earth and dew will chill you and prevent rest.

4. If you must build an emergency shelter keep it small to minimise impact on the bush. Practise shelter-building tech-niques on private property (with prior permission), not in state forests or other protected areas.

5. Keep alert for natural shelters as you pass through ter-rain. You may have to backtrack to the nearest one in an emergency. Small shelters are easiest to warm. Note avail-ability of nearby water and firewood supplies.

6. Choose shelter locations to avoid hazards such as flood risk, falling tree branches or rocks, wind exposure, damp, cold and lightning danger. Check for ants' nests and avoid camping too close to rushing water - the noise may drown out sounds of rescuers or approaching danger.

7. Position shelter so wind is not blowing into the entrance.

7. Ensure proper ventilation in all shelters, and especially in alpine regions where falling snow can cut off air supply. Never cook inside a vehicle.

Shelter

With the versatility and sturdiness of modern tents we can shelter effectively in virtually any Australian environment - snowcapped mountains, windblown desert or dripping rainforest. A lighter alternative to the tent is the bivvy bag, a waterproof breathable cocoon used with or without a sleeping bag. Other functional shelters can be created with nothing more than a tarp, poncho or groundsheet. A large plastic bag can be used during the day to procure water through condensation, then turned into a sleeping bag after dusk.

Being nourished, hydrated and well clothed is your first line of defence against the elements, but this isn't always enough. Shelter is a crucial element in survival strategy. Any gear or methods that might increase a shelter's efficiency are worth a try. Resist the urge to cut corners in organising shelter. Note wind direction, ground slope and potential hazards and take the time to create a shelter you can count on.

Shelters can be built from branches, foliage, bark, large stones and other natural materials. A thatched lean-to, rough tepee or simple A-frame structure may save your life where no tent is available. However, it is wasteful to deface vegetation for shelter when less destructive options are available. Practise your construction skills on a friend's property (with previous permission), not in protected bush areas. When using large stones in the construction, return these to their original positions when leaving the area.

TENTS

Provided you avoid the 'bargain pup tents' sold in some department and surplus stores, choosing a tent is easy. Find one that's light and as small as is bearable for the number of persons meant to occupy it. A separate fly sheet to go over the top is an advantage; so is a double floor. It pays to spend the extra money on a quality tent. Ensure there is reinforced stitching at weak points such as corners and seams.

Tents are not only for overnight use. In a blizzard or sandstorm they provide immediate protection at short notice. Give all the stitched seams a good going over with seam sealant. This will make a big difference in keeping the inside dry in driving rain.

Embed the pegs securely in the soil to give the tent stability in the wind. For camping with a vehicle, metal spikes with hooks at one end are handy to remove. Bushwalkers normally carry plastic pegs. When the ground is unsuitable for pegging, weigh down guy ropes with logs, stones or your pack. Put a groundsheet under the tent to protect the floor from sharp branches and rocks.

Tent design continues to improve. Many modern tents are now double-skinned, with innumerable variations on the basic A-frame, tunnel and dome shapes. Your own selection depends upon intended use, but whatever the shape or size it must be taut when erected. Uniform tension across the entire fabric ensures less flapping in the wind. Snow and rain rolls off better when loose spots are eliminated. Taut doesn't mean overstretched - zippers on tent flaps don't function well when stretched too tightly in any direction.

Dome tents are a bit heavier than tunnel-shaped tents but have more room inside.
Photo: Luke Reynolds

Many one-person tents feature a large screened area along the top for maximum visibility and ventilation. An attachable waterproof fly sheet can be rolled over the top and secured around the edges when it rains.

Look after your tent poles. If a section of pole doesn't work it affects the soundness of the whole tent. Smooth saplings can be used as emergency pole substitutes, but may need to be wrapped or padded.

Don't put off getting the tent up - it should be your first task at a new campsite.

BIVOUAC BAGS

A one-person bivouac (bivvy) bag with mosquito netting is practical and much lighter than a tent with poles, and is adequate for many environments. Basically it's a waterproof sleeping bag cover. Because its area is smaller than a tent it is easier to keep warm. On the down side, condensation may be slightly more of a problem, especially in the cheaper models which are cotton lined rather than 100% Gore-Tex (or similar breathable fabric). Always air out your sleeping bag after a night in the bivvy to dry out accumulated moisture. Intermittent unzipping during the night also allows excess water vapour to escape.

A bivvy with an external loop at the head end is good for keeping the fabric up off your face, when the loop is tied to an overhead branch. There is normally room inside for the sleeping bag, sleeping mat and a few other bits and pieces. The pack stays outside, which isn't a problem if you have safely secured all food inside the pack. Suspending the pack from a branch should keep all but the most determined scavengers away from your supplies.

This 100% Gore-Tex bivvy bag features tabs for pegging it out in windy conditions. Tabs at the zippered opening lift the fine insect mesh away from the face when tied with cord to an overhanging branch. The sleeping mat fits inside. In tropical areas a sleeping bag may not be needed. In the morning the bivvy is turned inside out to dry any condensation. Total weight is less than a kilo.

DEBRIS HUT

One of the least damaging natural shelters is the debris hut. This makes use of sticks, leaves and dead wood lying on the ground. No living material is needed. Branches are formed into a rough framework dense enough to support the smaller twigs, leaf litter and compacted soil heaped on top to form roof and walls. Given enough of the right material a debris hut makes a very effective barrier against wind and snow. You can use fishing line, cord or plant fibres to lash together the frame of sticks. If pliant and long enough the sticks themselves can be roughly woven together. Total rain-proofing is hard to achieve in a debris hut but with good material and plenty of time you can come close. Dig a trench around the shelter to direct rainwater away from your floor. Don't position the shelter in a gully or other low point in the landscape.

Just like tents, debris huts can be dome shaped, tunnel shaped or styled as a rough A-frame. What you end up with depends on available wood (and its pliability), nature of the terrain and how much time you're willing to spend putting it together.

COVERED HOLLOW

Wind and nightly chill are primary considerations when seeking shelter. One easy option is to use natural depressions in the ground (or dig one where the ground is soft). A few dead branches are then placed across the top, and shrubbery spread across these to form a sort of roof. In sandy areas, position some clothing around the edges to keep sand from blowing into the shelter.

Covered hollows perform well as emergency wind shelters, but aren't the place to be when it rains - they quickly turn into giant puddles. Selecting a hollow with a slight slope for drainage can help. If necessary dig a trench to guide water away downhill.

Take Shelter Early

Don't delay in organising shelter in a survival scenario. The quicker you can protect yourself from the elements and obtain quality rest the better you will be able to cope with the stresses of the situation.

A-FRAME SHELTER

Making camp in tea-tree swamps, flood plains or other wet country is a challenge. The best bet is to head for dry patches safe from further flooding. Be alert for snakes which also gravitate toward shrinking islands of high ground. You'll want to be a half-metre or so above the soggy ground, and for this a basic A-frame shelter is the answer. Staying off the ground is also desirable in desert country where ground temperatures can exceed 50 degrees. In rainforests an A-frame allows nocturnal ground animals to scurry safely underneath, and puts some distance between you and the leeches. An A-frame keeps you up above a light snow cover in conditions where snow cave building is impractical. As an all-purpose natural shelter it is hard to beat, and its open nature lets the breezes pass through.

The best A-frame roof is a lightweight tarp or groundsheet. Thatching with interlocking layers of shrubbery will keep most of the sun and much of the wind from reaching you, but rain-proofing is difficult with foliage alone. If you have time on your hands and access to large-leaved plants such as cunjevoi, rain-proofing is not out of the question.

For the A-frame you need seven sturdy branches. Each should be a metre longer than your height and about as thick as your forearm. Err on the side of strength, for it must be able to support your weight.

Step 1: After cutting or breaking off the poles, select two and lash them into an A-shape.

Step 2: Tie the top of the A-shape to a nearby tree trunk. This supports and stabilises the entire shelter.

Step 3: Put up the second A-frame parallel to the first. The distance between the two should equal your height plus about 70 cm. Holding the second A-shape upright, place your fifth pole over the tops of both frames and lash securely. This ridge pole needn't be as heavy as the others; it only has to support the roof tarp.

Step 4: The next step is a sleeping platform. Make a stretcher using the two remaining poles and a groundsheet. Tie the groundsheet to create a tube shape, then push the poles through. The ends of the stretcher poles are then pulled apart and set on the outside of the A-frame poles. If you have no groundsheet, two or three large, heavy-duty plastic bags of suitable width work very well. The narrower your sleeping platform the higher above the ground it will be.

Step 5: Stretch a tarp over the ridge pole to form a waterproof roof. Lash the corners to nearby branches. In insect-plagued regions hang some mosquito netting from the ridge pole.

The beginnings of an A-frame shelter - lash the tops of the first two poles to a tree for stability, then position another two poles parallel to the first. A ridge pole connects the two. Ensure that all rope work is firm and secure, and that the poles are thick and strong enough to support your weight.

Use the two remaining poles to make a stretcher bed. Form a tube around the poles with a groundsheet, tarp or a couple of large heavy-duty plastic bags.

Place the poles of the stretcher bed on the outside of the A-frame. Test the bed with your weight, then lash securely at each corner.

The completed A-frame with tarp roof. To increase comfort, spare clothing is placed on top of the stretcher bed as padding. This is a simple but very effective shelter, suitable for overnight use or as a daytime refuge.

OTHER SHELTERS

In rocky gorges look for natural shelter such as caves. Even a slight rock overhang is better than nothing. Beware of caves in areas where a lot of loose rock has collected at the base of cliffs - this indicates instability in the rocks above. Camping in sandstone escarpment country is a pleasure, but put ample distance between your sleeping bag and the cliff face. It isn't uncommon in parts of Kakadu and the Kimberley to be regularly awoken by the crash of boulders falling from nearby cliff tops.

Use a hollow log for shelter if it's large enough. Check that it's not already housing an ant colony, venomous snake or other undesirables. In rainforests seek out large fig trees. Vertical root buttresses at the tree's base offer a good shield from wind, and the sheer size of overhead branches serves as a reasonable barrier to rain.

Toppled trees may provide a small space underneath which offers some protection. Tie your groundsheet to trees to form a windbreak or stretch it between overhead branches to keep off rain or sun. In snow country stretch some cord between two trees, drape the groundsheet over that and tie the four corners near ground level to create an A-frame.

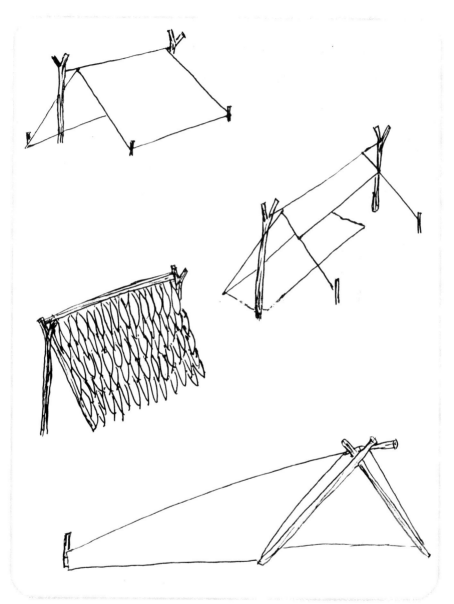

The difference that shelter makes to survival chances cannot be overemphasised. When building a shelter, spend at least as much time constructing a comfortable bed as you do on the shelter itself. Get your body up off the ground. The difference in comfort and temperature between sleeping on the ground and sleeping just a few centimetres above it is substantial. For cushioning use clothing, a rucksack, a layer of grass or some heavy duty plastic bags stuffed with greenery.

In rainforests the spaces between fig tree root buttresses are handy for waiting out a passing thunderstorm. Beware of ants' nests.　　Photo: Andrew Kemp

The author has met hikers who leave tents at home on long trips so they can cram more food into the pack instead. This is not sound strategy. Over the course of a two or three week hike the energy used up by tossing and turning against the chill, swatting mosquitoes and being generally uncomfortable exceeds that provided by the extra food. If you don't get a good night's sleep your daily progress suffers. Think hard about leaving your tent behind. At least pack a bivvy bag - they are even light and small enough to fit in a roomy belt bag.

Caves are an emergency shelter option in Top End escarpment country.

With a groundsheet and some cord you can have a shelter up in two minutes.

BUILDING A SNOW SHELTER

Every year tens of thousands of Australians head for the snow to ski, snowboard or bushwalk. Only a very small percentage have experience in creating shelter with snow. In a blizzard it is easy to become disorientated, lose sight of a trail and wander off in the wrong direction. The threat of hypothermia or panic-induced injury is great in these circumstances, so the best option may be to build a snow cave or similar shelter. A snow shovel makes the job much easier but isn't essential. The following shelters need no previous experience, training or special gear to construct. One of the best things about making a snow shelter is that the process itself keeps you warm. You may even need to take off extra clothing as you go so you don't overheat.

Caught in a snowstorm, the normal impulse is to flee quickly to a lower elevation. If distances are short and the terrain not too steep this is a viable plan, but at other times it will either be impractical or too dangerous. You might not have the time or energy to get down. Even if you do, suitable shelter may actually be harder to find at lower elevations. Another point is that you'll be more visible from the air in open snow than in dense forest. In the snow, leave brightly coloured objects outside the shelter entrance. Hang attention-getting objects from a stick to prevent them being buried under snowfall.

Instead of trying to leave the snow behind, make use of its benefits. Snow insulates well as long as you're not touching it. It makes an effective windbreak and is an easy building material to use. In really gusty conditions a snow cave may provide better wind protection than a tent. In the Himalayas, fierce winds have been known to pick tents off ledges and blow them down the face of cliffs with the occupants still tumbling around inside.

Keep hands and forearms dry while digging out the shelter. Put plastic bags over hands if you have no waterproof gloves. Lacking a snow shovel, dig with a cooking pot, toilet trowel, flat rock or your covered hands. Don't let yourself get too hot while digging.

SNOW CAVES

Select a deep drift or a slope of less than 30 degrees for the excavation. Well compacted snow is preferable. Dig a tunnel horizontally into the snow a metre deep, then angle upwards to create an enlarged sleeping area with a rounded roof. The doorway and entrance tunnel should be arch shaped. The main idea with snow caves is that the sleep-

If caught in a snowstorm erect your tent or prepare a snow shelter. Waiting a day or more for weather to clear is safer than trying to travel in high winds and blizzard conditions.   Photo: Stuart Coleman

ing platform must be higher than the entrance to trap heat. The roof should be at least 50 centimetres thick to prevent collapse. The less compacted the snow, the more roof thickness you will need for safety. A dome-shaped ceiling provides maximum support and reduces drips.

Two or three air vent holes are then poked through the roof and the doorway is sealed with a block of snow or rucksack. Make ventilation holes roughly the width of a tennis ball, and check periodically that they aren't getting clogged with falling snow. Insulate yourself against the snow floor as much as possible using clothing, groundsheet, self-inflating mat and sleeping bag. Even skis or an empty pack will help. If separated from gear, layer some foliage over the sleeping ledge to keep you off the snow.

Provided there is adequate overhead ventilation, candles can be used to light the snow cave. Take your gear inside the cave - if left outside it may get buried during the night and be hard to find.

Variations on the snow cave theme abound. On flat ground with only a light covering, collect snow into a large pile and hollow out the centre to accommodate your body. At the very least you can pile up a curved wall of snow for protection against prevailing winds as you lie behind it. Another option is to dig a trench and roof the top with branches, plastic groundsheet or your pack (supported by skis). Seek out natural holes formed at the base of boulders, trees and fallen logs which can be further enclosed with plastic sheeting or branches. With all snow shelters, *pay strict attention to the need for ventilation.* During heavy falls, vent holes will need to be reopened regularly with a stick, ski pole or your arm. Be vigilant against the possibility of oxygen being cut off to the shelter. Without outside air you can perish while you sleep. If there are several of you, one person should stay awake at all times to stand 'ventilation watch' while others sleep.

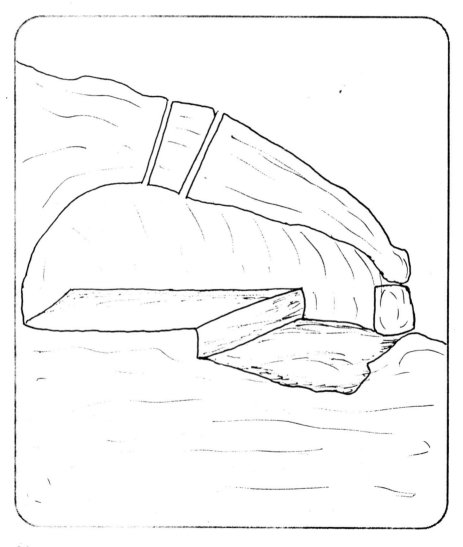

SETTING UP CAMP

Start scanning the landscape for a promising campsite while there is still plenty of light. Leave enough time to pitch the tent, prepare a meal, have a wash, etc. Camping early acquaints you with the surroundings and allows time to check out potential problems.

The ideal campsite is flat, close to water, well-drained, free from dense undergrowth and safe from falling rocks or branches. Where feral pig or cattle footprints are evident take care you don't plonk your tent directly in the path of their normal route to a drink. Large bulls can be noisy and aggressive when they find a tent blocking their favourite trail.

TIPS FOR MAKING CAMP:

1. Camp near water but not in its path. Never camp in a dry creek bed. Flash floods upstream can rush down the riverbed in a torrent, even when no rain has fallen in the immediate area.

The sand in the foreground seems the ideal spot to pitch a tent but it's a poor campsite choice. A site amongst the trees beyond the opposite bank would be shadier, out of flash flood danger and more environmentally responsible.

2. Stay clear of exposed ridges in high winds and during lightning storms.

3. Leave nothing behind. Pack out every last scrap of rubbish. *DO NOT burn it or bury it.* Take it out with you.

4. If a fire is necessary, camp close to available fuel. Confine the fire within a stone border, keep it small and make sure it's out when you leave the site.

5. Shade is essential for summer camping but don't site your shelter underneath overhanging branches that can fall on you overnight.

6. Insulate yourself from direct contact with the ground. Self-inflating sleeping mats are comfortable and shield the body from cold damp earth. A sleep mat is just as important in hot deserts. The sand beneath you can stay unbearably hot even after the sun has set.

7. Take note of wind direction. Angle the tent so wind isn't blowing straight in the entrance. When you have wet gear to dry out, determine the direction of sunrise and site your camp to make best use of its first rays.

8. Camping too close to rapids or waterfalls makes it hard to hear approaching danger. The roar of rushing water drowns out sounds of people or animals approaching and can make you oblivious to falling trees, rock slides and even thunder. You may not hear rescuers.

9. Practise responsible hygiene. Don't let soap, toothpaste or shampoo get into waterways. This promotes harmful algae growth which kills aquatic creatures. Wash dishes in a plastic tray rather than at the water's edge. To bathe, collect water in a bucket or billy and pour it over yourself, well away from the creek. Soap up then rinse again with the bucket; a billy bath uses little water. Carry a toilet trowel. Outdoor shops sell plastic ones that are tough but lightweight. Dig a hole for burying both faeces and toilet paper - the deeper the better. Burn the toilet paper in the hole before covering it up with a layer of soil.

The sign of an experienced overnight camper is no sign at all - aside from footprints, a person passing the site on the morning of departure should spot no evidence that anyone had spent the night there. For soldiers on reconnaissance missions in enemy territory the need to leave no evidence behind is crucial. For modern travellers the same goal is just as desirable for ecological reasons.

If a large group is staying in the bush awhile, dig a latrine up to a metre and a half deep to handle solid waste. After each use sprinkle some earth over the top to control flies and speed decomposition. Select a site well away from water sources and downwind from tents. Substitutes for toilet paper abound in the bush - moss, smooth rocks, leaves and clumps of grass. Snowballs are very effective.

Clean clothing insulates best. Socks and underwear should be washed daily if possible. In tropical areas try to wash (or at least rinse out) what you've worn that day, changing to fresh clothes for sleeping.

Baking soda is an excellent substitute for body soap and toothpaste, and a good scouring aid for the billy. Laundry and dishwashing detergents are unnecessary for short trips. A minimalist approach to cooking gear and regular rinsing of clothing is the way to go. It's easy enough to give everything a real wash when you get home.

Survival Priorities
FIRE

1. Always carry fire-lighting gear in the bush. Fire can warm you, cook food, boil water, signal rescuers and dry clothing.

2. Matches are a precious survival item. Store in a water-proof container and use as sparingly as possible.

3. Learn how to create matchless fires with flint, magnifying glass, car battery or by making a fire bow drill.

4. Tinder is an essential ingredient in fire-making. Learn to identify quality tinder and carry some with you.

5. Fire is dangerous - observe safety procedures. Put fires out completely when finished with them.

6. Gather all your tinder, kindling and larger fuel beforehand. Store inside the shelter if necessary.

7. Learn to make an efficient teepee-style fire.

8. Use deadwood and keep fires as small as you can. Keep gear a safe distance from wandering sparks.

9. Hardwoods burn longer but are slower to get going. Softwoods catch fire more easily but burn down quickly.

10. Use natural windbreaks or create one to protect your fire from gusty winds. Fires for warmth can be situated near a rock face to benefit from reflected heat.

11. When lighting your fire, let it 'breathe'. Too much fuel at the start will smother it.

12. Don't use wet rocks near a fire - they might explode.

Fire-making

Fire is one of the most versatile aids to human survival. Its smoke preserves food, signals rescuers and keeps insects away. Its warmth provides comfort in the cold and dries out gear in wet weather. Fire lets you cook food and purify dubious water by boiling. Aboriginal people use fire in additional ways, such as in spear-making and to flush out game while hunting.

The ability to light a fire without matches is viewed by many as the ultimate survival skill. There is satisfaction in creating fire without help from man-made items but this is an art demanding patience, energy, determination and plenty of practice, not to mention the right sort of wood. Few wilderness enthusiasts learn the techniques properly and fewer still practise them regularly, but this vital skill can save lives. In many outdoor situations the need for fire is urgent. Availability of matches, flints or a magnifying glass is never guaranteed.

Practise fire-lighting skills under a variety of conditions. Getting a fire going in the northern dry season is no problem but a drizzly, windswept ridge in alpine Tasmania is another matter. Murphy's Law seems to apply to fire lighting in the bush - the more desperately you need a fire the more likely conditions will frustrate your attempts to light one.

GETTING IT STARTED

Lighting a fire in the bush is easiest with quality matches or a cigarette lighter. With cheap plastic lighters you can hold your thumb down on the lever to keep the flame going until the tinder catches fire. Metal lighters are heavier and get hot quickly in the hand. Cut down match wastage by lighting a candle whenever you strike a match - then light your fire with the candle. Always store matches and lighters in waterproof containers.

Fire needs a steady supply of air, heat and fuel to keep going. Organise tinder, kindling and larger pieces beforehand. The key to a successful fire is vigilance - keep a close eye on its progress. Feed it what it needs and it will work for you. Fires for warmth, signalling or cooking are all built differently - learn how to make the right fire for the right job.

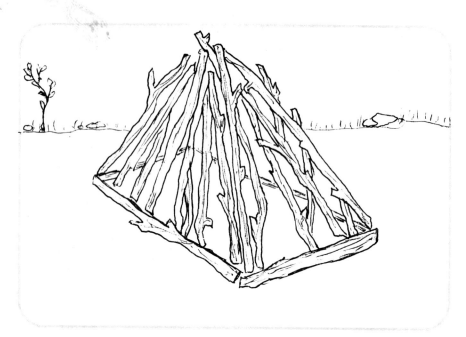

TEEPEE FIRE: As the wood burns it falls inward, leaving glowing coals at the base. Make an opening on one side of the 'teepee' so you can reach in and light the tinder in the centre. Space the sticks so air can get to the fire.

TINDER

Any fine fibrous material that catches fire quickly makes good tinder. The best tinder needs only a tiny spark to start it smoking. Tinder must be completely dry and packed loosely before lighting.

Fibrous bark, dried grass, pine needles and crumbled dead gum leaves make good tinder. Old abandoned bird nests and the sawdust produced by borer wasps and grubs are excellent. Cotton wool balls from the first aid kit are ideal in the absence of natural tinder. Carry a plastic camera film canister containing half a dozen paraffin-soaked cotton balls for occasions when natural tinder won't cooperate. In wet country always carry collected tinder with you, sealed in a plastic bag.

Tinder is the foundation upon which all outdoor fires are built. Try to keep some aside for the next fire. If the only tinder available is coarse tree bark, use a rock to pound it to a finer consistency. Cut, rub, twist or crush natural tinder fibres until they are almost powdery. Effort put into tinder preparation is rewarded when you must get a fire going quickly.

Fire-lighting short-cuts: Photo: Andrew Kemp

Top   -   *Fire starter blocks, flint with striker, crushed gum leaves for tinder.*
Middle   -   *Lighter, paraffin-soaked cotton balls, all-in-one magnesium flint.*
Bottom   -   *12-hour candle, old bird's nest (ideal tinder), marine matches.*

Some of these items go into the personal survival kit tin, but a second waterproof container for fire-lighting gear is also a good idea. This should be small enough to fit in your pocket.

KINDLING

Kindling is the next step up from tinder. Small, dry twigs no thicker than a pencil are best. Coupled with small pieces of soft wood, these create a quick-burning fire that in turn ignites the larger pieces of wood positioned above them. Think of kindling as the 'bridge' between tinder and your main fuel. In the absence of tinder, small blocks of paraffin or chemically treated fire sticks will ignite most small kindling. Aids such as these take up little room and can help in difficult conditions.

Snap the ends off dead branches for kindling. Roots pulled from the ground (even from sand) retain moisture and are of little use as kindling. When twigs are damp on the outside use your knife to pare into the dry centre. Sticks can be 'feathered' by making a series of long, shallow cuts along their length. This provides more surface area so they burn quickly. Always shave the wood away from you.

91

WOOD FUEL

Break dry pieces from dead standing trees to feed the fire. A hatchet or axe isn't needed to collect firewood if you stick to pieces of manageable size. Heavier hardwoods give a more intense, long-lasting heat than softwoods. Damp or green wood will burn once the fire is well alight but produces plenty of smoke. Add damp wood to the fire if your aim is to ward off biting insects or alert rescuers. A combination of green and dry wood makes a fire burn longer than dry wood alone.

Dry palm tree leaves burn well but the trunks do not. Soft woods from swamps are rarely good fuel but most pines are excellent. In rainforests many trees are dead beneath the vines that cover them. The vines are often the only thing holding them upright.

For cooking fires you shouldn't need sticks more than 20 centimetres long and a couple of centimetres thick. This size gives good control of heat with little fuel waste. Fires for warmth or signalling require bigger logs, but aim for control and steady fuelling rather than size.

Break larger branches in two by dropping them on a rock. A less violent method is to place them on the fire so they burn through the middle.

OTHER FUELS

In parts of Australia where wood is scarce you'll have to look for fuel alternatives. Dried animal droppings are one of the most useful. Kangaroos, feral cattle, donkeys and goats provide a ready source. The drier the dropping the less smoke it will produce. Don't underestimate the value of animal droppings. Very dry kangaroo dung crumbled onto a pile of tinder is one of the best fire-lighting aids known.

If stranded with a vehicle you can use oil or petrol to fuel a fire. Extreme caution is needed around combustible liquids. Never light them directly. Fashion a wick out of suitable material and light that instead, keeping a safe distance. Use small quantities. Petrol mixed with sand can be burned inside a tin; otherwise just place the mixture in a hole dug in the ground. Oil burns better when mixed with antifreeze or petrol.

Most animal fats burn fiercely. Put the fat in an old tin and use a cloth wick to light it. Punch some holes near the top of the tin so more air gets inside.

In desperate times use any fuel you can find. Moss, old seaweed and desiccated fungus works if dry enough. Rubber car tyres soaked in oil produce a thick, black smoke ideal for signalling.

FIRE WITHOUT MATCHES

Waterproof matches are an invaluable survival item but there are several ways to start a fire without them. Basic principles (dry tinder, plenty of air, collecting fuel beforehand, etc.) must be strictly followed, as there is less room for error than with match fires.

FLINT

Some flints come with a separate steel striker. Others consist of an all-in-one unit with a sparking insert on one side and a shaving edge on the other. Use your knife to scrape off the flaky substance to add to tinder, then strike along the sparking insert to direct sparks toward the pile. The trick with flint work is blowing the captured spark to life before it dies. Tinder must be bone dry.

MAGNIFYING LENS

Strong sunlight focused through a magnifying glass lights a fire very quickly if you hold the glass steady. Narrow the light down to a small hot pinpoint in the centre of the tinder. Once it starts smoking a few gentle puffs of breath bring it to life. In the absence of a magnifying glass you can use a camera lens, binocular lens or a curved piece of bottle instead.

CAR BATTERY

WARNING: *For safety, always remove the battery from the car before using it to start a fire.*

A vehicle battery can provide a spark to light your tinder. Using suitable hand protection, connect a length of electrical wire to each terminal and slowly bring the other ends together until a spark jumps. Direct this spark onto the tinder or a small petrol-soaked rag. If you carry steel wool pads in your vehicle the following method works like a charm: attach jumper leads to the battery and clamp the other ends onto a steel wool pad, which is placed in the middle of a pile of tinder and kindling. The steel wool ignites quickly and gives off plenty of heat.

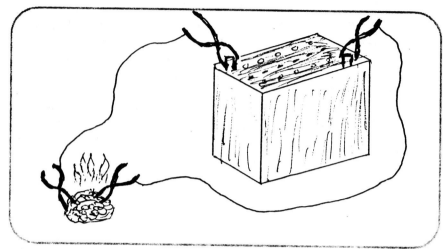

The car battery / steel wool fire-lighting method.

AMMUNITION / CHEMICALS

Ammunition can be used to start a fire. Pour half the powder from one cartridge onto your tinder pile to assist ignition.

When combined, some common chemicals easily ignite with a bit of friction. One combination you may already have in a bush setting is Condy's crystals (potassium permanganate) and sugar. Mix nine parts crystals to one part sugar. To ignite the mixture apply friction by grinding between two stones. Store crystals and sugar separately and keep both dry.

THE BOW DRILL

Creating fire solely from bush materials can be mastered with practice. One of the best ways is with a bow drill crafted from available wood. This can be made with a sharp rock as cutting tool and natural fibre for the bow, but a knife and some cord speed up the process.

A bow drill uses friction to produce enough heat to ignite a carefully placed piece of tinder. It consists of four parts - drill rod, pressure block, strung hardwood bow and hearth.

Fashion the drill rod from a hardwood stick about 40 cm long and 4 cm thick. Round both ends and carve one to a point. This is the 'business end' of the drill. For the pressure block you need a piece of hardwood roughly the size and shape of a chalk board eraser. This should be solid but small enough to fit comfortably in your hand. In the centre of one side carve a depression into the wood. This will hold the top end of the drill rod in place as you drill. A suitably shaped flat rock would also do as a pressure block.

The bow is simply a hardwood stick about 60 cm long and 2 cm thick. A length of string or cord is tied to both ends, but loosely enough so that you will be able to wind one loop around the drill rod. A shoelace works just as well.

Unlike an archery bow, no tension is needed in the branch. The simplest way to make your bow is to find a sapling branching into a Y-shape and cut it to size, as shown:

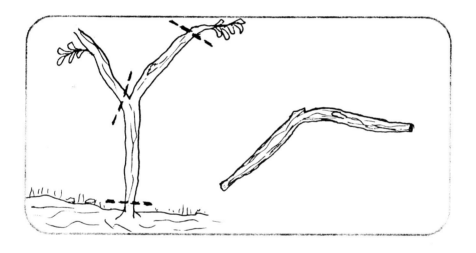

The final necessity is the hearth. This is a flat softwood base into which the pointed end of the drill rod is spun to create friction. At one edge of the hearth, cut a V-shaped notch into the wood. Turn the hearth over and then cut a small hole directly above the notch underneath.

To work the bow drill, place the hearth on flat ground, notch side down, hole side up. Put a small pile of tinder beneath the notch. Place the sharp end of the drill rod into the hole. Wrap one loop of the bow cord around the drill rod and slide the loop down to the middle of the rod. If you have previously cut a shallow notch around the drill rod's centre this will keep the cord from slipping as you drill.

With the bow in place the pressure block goes over the top of the drill rod, the end of which fits into the little depression you've made in the block. To use the bow drill, kneel close to the hearth. Put some tinder underneath the hearth's V-notch. With one hand, push and pull the bow to cause the drill rod to rotate back and forth quickly. Your other hand holds onto the pressure block, bearing down on the drill rod to increase friction. The combination of pressure from above and constant spinning soon creates enough heat at the bottom of the rod to create a very fine, hot wood powder which falls through the notch and lands on the tinder. Switch hands if you get tired but keep it rotating until the tinder starts to smoke. Maintain spin and pressure as the smoke increases, then gently blow on the tinder to turn the smoke to flame. Pick up the tinder pile in your hands to give it more air - don't try blowing it to life while it's still under the notch.

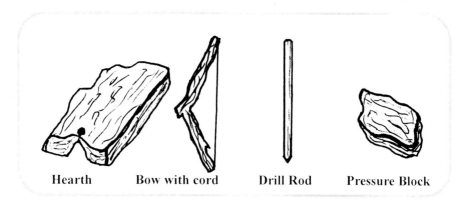

Hearth   Bow with cord   Drill Rod   Pressure Block

The fire bow drill in action - dry tinder and consistent spinning bring success.

Knowing how hard to press on the block, how fast to spin the drill and when to try blowing on the tinder is all a matter of practice. It's possible to succeed on your first go at making and using a bow drill but don't count on it. This is a survival skill that is best tried out before you are in a desperate situation. Use the driest wood you can find for all parts of the bow drill. The carving of notch, hole and drill tip normally removes enough wet surface wood so your friction areas are dry.

HAND DRILL

This 'poor cousin' of the bow drill operates on the same principle except there are only two pieces - a hearth and a pointed drill stick. The stick is rotated back and forth by a brisk rubbing of the hands while applying downward pressure. You work your way from the top to the bottom of the stick, repeating the process continuously to rotate the rod in brief, rapid bursts. Friction created this way is less consistent than with a bow drill, but with bone dry wood it is certainly worth a try. A pinch of dry sand in the friction hole will help speed up the task. For a hand drill the spinning rod need not be much thicker than 10-15 millimetres in diameter.

The hand drill.

FIRE PLOUGH

This friction method requires a flat softwood base and a hardwood stick. A straight groove is cut along the middle of the base and one end of the stick is rubbed back and forth along it. With the right wood and steady friction a small powdery tinder soon accumulates in the groove. This smokes and eventually ignites. A 9 to 1 mixture of Condy's crystals and sugar can be sprinkled into the groove for quicker ignition.

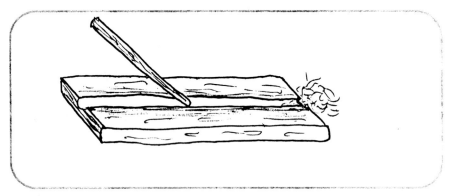

The Fire Plough.

FIRE FOR SURVIVAL

Fire plays a supportive role in bushcraft. It helps make all survival priorities easier to achieve. Knowing how to light the right kind of fire at the right time can save your life.

Conserve energy when handling fires. One of the easiest ways to keep an established fire going is by feeding logs into it by their ends. Five logs are placed on the ground around the fire, radiating out in a starfish shape. As the fire dies down one or more logs are pushed a bit further in to keep it going.

Fires for personal warmth must be sited carefully to take advantage of natural heat reflectors such as vertical rock. A small, carefully tended fire backed by a natural or man-made reflector offers better sustained heat than a large bonfire and consumes less wood.

Keep out of the wind. When fuel is scarce you may lose more body heat from wind chill than you gain from a small open fire. Fierce winds make fire-lighting difficult and burn fuel too quickly.

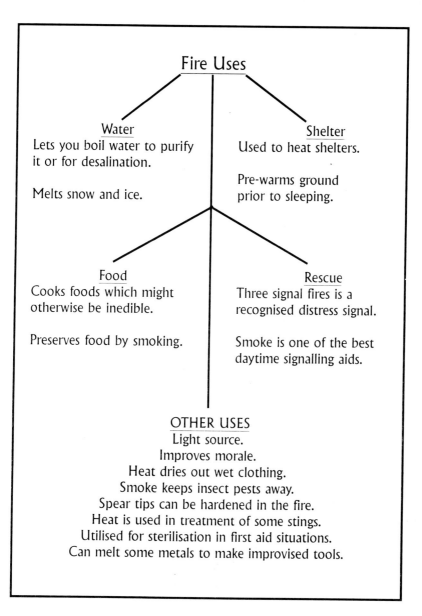

Fire Uses

Water
Lets you boil water to purify it or for desalination.

Melts snow and ice.

Shelter
Used to heat shelters.

Pre-warms ground prior to sleeping.

Food
Cooks foods which might otherwise be inedible.

Preserves food by smoking.

Rescue
Three signal fires is a recognised distress signal.

Smoke is one of the best daytime signalling aids.

OTHER USES
Light source.
Improves morale.
Heat dries out wet clothing.
Smoke keeps insect pests away.
Spear tips can be hardened in the fire.
Heat is used in treatment of some stings.
Utilised for sterilisation in first aid situations.
Can melt some metals to make improvised tools.

When fire is necessary on wet ground or snow the best option is a raised platform. Simplest is a layer of stones covered with soil or sand with the fire built on top. Various layered combinations of earth, green branches, sand and rocks are possible. Use whatever you have to keep the fire separate from the moist ground.

In flooded areas you will need to support the fire platform even higher.

Combat high winds by digging a trench about 30 cm deep, 90 cm long and 30 cm wide. Line the bottom with stones and build a normal teepee fire on top of that. This makes a handy cooking fire.

FIRE FOR COOKING

Cooking is one of the most important uses for fire. Cooking kills bacteria and parasites that may be present in food and makes proteins more digestible. Some plants must be cooked to neutralise their toxins. Psychologically there are few better morale boosters in a tough situation than a cooked meal.

Flame is almost never used in bush cooking (other than for boiling water). Slower cooking techniques are preferable - the food is less likely to get scorched and retains more nutrients. Food should be cooked only as long as needed. The aim is maximum energy and vitamins for minimum effort. Overcooking valuable food is self-defeating.

With practice you can get quite good at balancing a billy in the fire, but eventually you're going to lose the contents. Instead, support cooking vessels on flat rocks or suspend them above the fire. For vehicle travel a camp oven is useful, though some outback veterans use nothing more than an old metal refrigerator shelf placed over a trench fire. All cooking takes place on top of the grating.

Choose the cooking method that best preserves the food's nutritional value. In order, the best methods are as follows:

1. Steaming - This is the best method for survival purposes, and is especially effective with fish. Food items are wrapped in wet leaves, clay or mud and steamed underground in a shallow pit containing hot rocks or coals. Cover completely - no steam should escape during cooking. Another method uses a billy containing a few centimetres of simmering water, into which a tin containing the food is placed. Put the lid on the billy to trap the steam. For vegetables or wild plants the billy needn't remain on the fire. Take it off, put in the tin containing the food straight away, cover and leave for ten minutes.

2. Boiling - Two rules to remember with boiling are (a) use a lid to hold in the nutrients and (b) drink the resulting liquid after eating the boiled food - otherwise you're throwing away half the vitamins. The only time water from boiling should be discarded is when you are boiling the toxins or irritants out of wild plants. Boiling food kills any parasites.

Finding a natural boiling vessel when you have no pot or billy is a problem in Australia. In other parts of the world bamboo is commonly used. A suitably shaped bark container is one idea. Another is to fill a small rocky depression with water, build a fire nearby, heat stones in it

101

until red-hot and drop these in the water until it comes to a boil. However, fiddling with hot stones is tedious and risks burns.

3. Baking - Make your own camp oven from any suitable metal box or food tin that's large enough. Let a trench fire burn down to coals and place the 'oven' in the trench with them. Surround the oven with coals, pile some on top and seal the lot by covering with earth. Cooking time depends on size of the meal and amount of coals.

4. Roasting - Traditional roasting of meat on a spit is not much good from a survival standpoint because the meat must be constantly turned for even cooking and valuable fat is lost in the process.

THE ABORIGINAL WAY

Traditional Aboriginal cooking techniques are ideal for the survivor, as utensils, pots or a stove may not be available.

Vegetables, wild seed damper and tubers are cooked in the hot ashes. Deadwood from old wattle trees makes excellent ash for cooking. Place the items on the hot ground over the ash and cover thoroughly with another layer of ash. Any unburnt twigs or large embers are brushed out of the way first.

Fish, reptiles and small game may be placed directly on the hot coals. Shellfish are steamed open quickly on smaller coals away from the flame.

Roast kangaroos and other large game by making a ground oven. Dig a pit and balance firewood across the opening. Several stones are placed on top of the wood. As the firewood burns down, the hot rocks and coals fall into the bottom of the pit. Chunks of termite mound or old seashells may be substituted for rocks to heat the oven.

Brush most of the ash and coals out of the pit, leaving the layer of red-hot stones. Place food directly on top of the stones or wrap in paperbark first. Smaller foods are less likely to burn if enclosed in a bundle of flexible bark.

Large slabs of paperbark or other natural covering are placed over the food. Earth is piled on top of that to seal the oven from the air. Vigilance is then needed. Once the oven is covered no steam should escape.

The size of the pit, number of stones needed and cooking time vary depending upon the type of food. Larger game may take several hours. Four hours is a good minimum to work with for a large leg of lamb or an item of similar size. Reduce this time for fish.

There's no hurry unearthing the food. The beauty of a properly sealed ground oven is that overcooking is impossible. The heat in the oven is at its hottest the moment you seal the food in the hole. Once it's covered the heat dissipates very gradually over many hours. Unlike a fan-forced oven in the home, a ground oven isn't bombarded with continuous heat; it only uses what's there at the start. This results in tender, perfectly cooked food that retains its juices.

The ground oven is a simple but effective survival cooking method. Start by piling branches and stones across the top of the hole and lighting a fire underneath. The hot stones and coals will fall into the pit.

Survival Priorities
Search and Rescue

1. Most rescues occur within 72 hours of activation. Therefore, get rescue devices ready early. Prepare for rescue as soon as possible in a survival episode.

2. Searches often commence early in the morning, so survivors must be ready to signal before first light.

3. Rescue aids can be active (EPIRBs, flares, mirrors, torches, radios, fires etc.) or passive (tarps, ground signals etc.).

4. Safety equipment is beneficial only if you understand how to use it. On land or at sea, death can result from lack of training in using safety gear.

5. Three signal fires (30 metres apart) are a universal distress signal, as are three gunshots, three whistles etc.

6. An approaching rescue plane might be heard from 10 km away, but from there it can pass over your head in only three minutes. Have signalling materials ready to go within that time. You may only get one chance - make it count.

7. For signalling, use fire by night and smoke by day.

8. STAY WITH YOUR VEHICLE. It contains useful survival aids and is much easier to spot than a person on foot.

9. When awaiting rescue have one fire going at all times and two ready to light at a moment's notice. NEVER pour petrol directly on a fire to get it going quickly. The most efficient signal fire is log cabin style, one metre square, one metre high and filled with quick-burning material.

10. Always tell someone your itinerary and stick to it.

Search and Rescue

Whether you're a searcher or a person awaiting rescue you need to have an understanding of search patterns and procedures. The terrain and number of people available to search will determine the most sensible search plan.

On land the success or failure of searches hinges largely on how accurately travellers have stuck to their planned route. Chances of rescue are excellent if you have told at least two responsible persons where you're going and provided maps and an itinerary. They should also be given a definite date to raise the alarm if you don't emerge by the given time. Just as importantly, a person who has registered with National Parks or another authority and promised to notify them upon trip completion should keep that promise. Each year search and rescue organisations venture out to find bushwalkers, climbers, boaties and others in trouble. While some are genuine distress situations, a huge number are false alarms - people who forget to check in with authorities, accidentally turn on EPIRBs or decide to change plans without telling anyone. Search and rescue is an expensive and dangerous business, in many cases assisted by volunteers. We have all seen the stories in the news - inexperienced walkers trying to climb mountains beyond their abilities, fishermen drifting out to sea in tinnies with no life jackets or spare outboard, drivers who visit deserts without adequate water or repair kits.

SEARCH PATTERNS

When searchers know the route taken a number of search patterns are possible. Two of the most common are the fan search and the base line search. The fan method makes the last known position a central starting point. Base line searches cover a width of terrain along the presumed route of the lost party. If there are more than one searcher they should stay within visible and/or shouting range of each other at all times. Ribbons or other methods to regularly mark the search route are advisable. After the initial search is made the search area may be expanded.

When terrain permits this can be done on foot. Large-scale searches in open country are best performed by air.

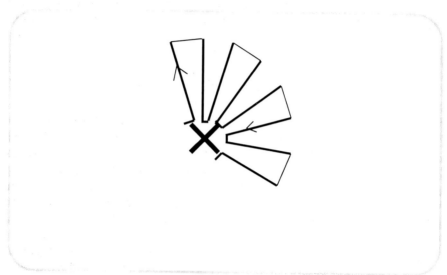

Fan search.

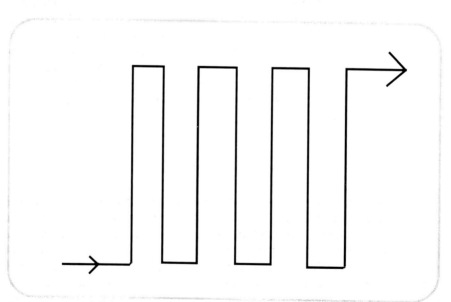

Base line search.

Aircraft cover a designated search area in a manner similar to the base line search - a series of parallel passes, heading towards and away from the sun for increased visibility of reflective wreckage or ground signals. In adverse weather air searches may be delayed. If the last position is known a sequence of gradually increasing squares is flown outwards from that spot.

HELICOPTER RESCUE

In rugged areas the actual rescue often involves a helicopter. Try to make the pilot's job easier by preparing a safe landing site. A large stretch of dry riverbank is ideal. You may have to do some work to create a safe site. Helicopters need level ground to land on, preferably with a gradient of less than 5 degrees. The landing spot should be free of tree stumps and large loose rocks, have a clear approach from the air and be about thirty metres in diameter. Mark the centre touchdown point with a large 'H', using whatever you have. Damping down a dry site reduces dust. Once the helicopter has safely landed, follow the pilot's instructions. Don't approach while rotors are turning unless directed by the pilot. In that case keep your head low and *never* approach from the rear - this is a blind spot for the pilot.

All this assumes you are not too weak or injured to prepare a landing site. If you're incapacitated it will be up to the pilot to decide whether to winch you up or send someone down to get you. Winching usually involves placing a loop harness underneath both armpits. After securing it and giving the thumbs up sign, keep your arms at your sides while being winched upwards. Keep in mind that static electricity can build up on a winch cable. Avoid possible shock by letting the cable touch the ground before grabbing it.

SIGNALLING

Signalling is one of the most important but least practised of all survival skills. After attending to first aid and protecting yourself from the elements, rescue preparation is the next priority in most survival situations. If you've told at least two people where you're going and when to raise the alarm if you don't show, it shouldn't be long before someone comes looking. Most rescues succeed within three days of initiation so make preparations as early as you can. Be ready early in the day as searches often get going before first light.

The basic aim in signalling is to *increase the size of your position on earth*. In other words, you want to create big, noticeable signals that are visible from any direction.

Make your position visible from the air by using any colourful, shiny or reflective objects. Car mirrors, polished hubcaps and brightly coloured tarps are ideal for attracting attention if you're with a stranded vehicle. A proper signalling mirror is even better. At sea, orange life jackets and sails contrast well against the colour of the ocean.

If there is a choice, select a signalling site on high open ground. On flat ground lay out the standard S.O.S. signal with branches, stones or other materials, aiming for maximum colour contrast with the earth.

Three fires in a triangular pattern is an internationally recognised distress signal. Position them 30 metres apart and have them ready to light when a passing aircraft is heard. If fuel is plentiful and you're physically able to look after a full-time fire the best strategy is to have one fire going at all times, with the other two ready to light at short notice. You might have no more than three minutes from the time you hear a plane in the distance until it passes near your position. Survival may hinge upon how well you use those minutes to make yourself visible.

'Log cabin' fires are ideal for signalling. Make them one metre square and one metre high. The height is important - it increases visibility at night, and by day the intense vertical heat sends your smoke column straight up in the air. This is vital in dense forest. The advice found in many survival manuals is to site signal fires on open riverbanks, sandbars or large clearings to maximise visibility. This is fine when there is no wind, but such locations are very prone to wind draughts. A healthy wind will blow all the smoke sideways, dissipating it through nearby trees until it is all but invisible above the canopy. In these situations the base of a tall tree is a better site - the tree guides the heated smoke up along its length almost like a chimney, and it emerges at the canopy intact and visible.

Once you have stacked enough branches to create the log cabin 'box', place a 10 cm layer of twigs on the ground inside. These twigs keep your kindling and tinder off the damp ground and leave some room for you to stick your hand underneath to light the base. Quick-igniting dead shrubbery is then piled loosely on top of the twigs to a height just above the top of the 'cabin'. Daytime signalling calls for maximum smoke, so have a supply of greenery at hand to keep piling on top. A ratio of 3 (foliage/green wood) to 1 (dead wood) gives the best smoke production. Don't pack it in too tightly - good air circulation is critical for quick ignition.

The Log Cabin Fire gives maximum visibility and height for signalling.

Collect plenty of dry tinder and bigger twigs as well as some green branches to create smoke. Experiment with different leaves, grasses and wood to determine which ignite quickest or produce smoke best. Cover firewood to keep it dry, and keep it off wet ground.

One of the most convenient signalling aids is a small isolated tree. Dry grass and twigs are strategically placed to ignite the foliage, setting the whole tree alight. A single tree burns for a long time and produces plenty of smoke. The only problem with this method is the risk that the fire could jump to other trees. Even if you are hundreds of metres from other trees or shrubs, a single spark held aloft by wind could travel a great distance and start a forest fire. Position is critical.

Fire safety is essential. Construct signal fires so there is minimal risk to surrounding terrain. Be careful if using petrol to help get a fire started. Never pour petrol directly onto a fire - this is asking for serious burns. Instead, soak a cloth in the petrol and place this on the pile of tinder, lighting it only after you have carried the petrol container a safe distance away.

Aside from showing rescuers your location, smoke gives an aircraft the wind direction. You'll need to decide whether dark or light smoke is more visible against the ground. In snow or light-coloured sand, dark smoke shows up well. Rubber and oil are the best ingredients to produce dark smoke. Tyres or rubber floor mats soaked in oil are ideal if you're with a vehicle. Against the background of a green forest or dark landscape a light-coloured smoke is best. Produce it with green leaves, grass or damp wood. Ensure all materials to get your smoke fire going are ready to be fired up in a matter of seconds.

Just as three fires signal distress, so do three flashing lights, three loud whistles or three gunshots. Fire is one of the best but not the only type of ground signal. An S.O.S. scraped in soil, snow or sand is very visible if placed in a clearing. Make it big enough. Always obliterate S.O.S. signals on the ground when rescued. These cause confusion if left in place.

Aside from its other survival uses a brightly coloured tarpaulin is an excellent signalling device. Spread it out in an open area and secure the corners to the ground. You might also write an S.O.S in the middle of it with a contrasting colour (i.e. white sand letters on top of a blue tarp). Bright blue is easy to spot in the desert, while orange works well against a forested background.

Memorising ground-to-air codes and body signals is something few of us bother with, but knowing a few of the more common signals can make your status much clearer to aerial rescuers.

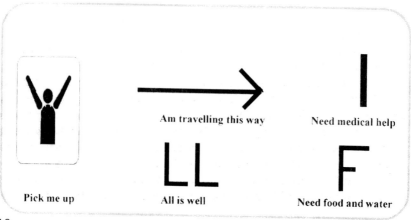

Pick me up   Am travelling this way   Need medical help

                    All is well   Need food and water

If an all-night fire is impossible, signal in the dark with a torch using three flashes at a time. Glow lights (that you bend to combine chemicals that produce greenish light) are also effective. Use flares if you have them. Some kinds are reversible, with a flare for night use at one end and smoke for day use at the other.

Don't leave your vehicle or walk away from plane wreckage except in special circumstances. These large objects are easier to see from the air than you are. If you must take off on foot, leave a message behind detailing when you left, where you're going and other pertinent details such as medical status. Mark your route as you walk. The simplest way is to create arrows showing your direction, using rocks on the ground or scrapings in the soil. Carved arrows in tree bark or bent branches also give an indication.

Morse code is now officially obsolete, superseded by more advanced communications. One of the more exciting of these is the satellite telephone which allows communication to and from anywhere in Australia. Other equipment that can speed up your rescue includes an HF Radio and a GPS (Global Positioning System). The radio tells police or the Royal Flying Doctor Service you're in trouble and the GPS tells them exactly where you are on the planet, give or take 30 metres or so.

EPIRBs and other transmitters that send out regular distress bleeps are great inventions, but some are less effective at long range. Generally, emergency rescue transmitters should be turned on immediately and used at regular intervals. However, with a finite battery life and limited range it may be better in rare instances to conserve battery power and wait until there is maximum chance of the signal being picked up. Some portable two-way radios work well only in line-of-sight situations. In mountainous country, head for high clear ground for signalling.

Personal EPIRBs (emergency rescue beacons) and hand-held GPS units are becoming popular with remote area walkers. Both can be lifesavers in a sticky situation. Technology is no substitute for common sense, however, and like all such devices they have limitations. Most GPS units are designed more for boaters or drivers than hikers. Get one that serves your purpose in the area where it will be used.

At sea the EPIRB is an essential survival item. Unfortunately, a huge problem in this country is the number which are improperly disposed of or accidentally set off. There is at least one case of a boat owner who threw out a beacon he thought was defective. It was activated when it landed in the bin, alerting Search and Rescue who had to track it down.

This is not an isolated incident. Looking at the statistics between October 1, 1989 and December 31, 1998, a total of 24,301 EPIRBs were activated in Australia, with the signals picked up by Australian Search and Rescue (AusSAR) in Canberra. Of these only 666 were genuine distress calls, resulting in the rescue of 1895 people. The other 23,635 were either accidental or the work of pranksters. That's a rate of only one bona fide distress call for every 36 EPIRB activations. It is Search and Rescue's job to respond to each and every one of these beacon calls, often at a cost of thousands of dollars.

Two massive sea search and rescue operations were conducted in Australia in the late 1990s. One was the highly publicized rescue of two racing yachtsmen in the southern Indian Ocean in January 1997. The boat of Frenchman Thierry Dubois rolled 180 degrees and stayed upside down, so he got his life raft ready and pulled the cord. It inflated only halfway, then huge seas tore it loose. Unable to get back inside the yacht because of a jammed hatch, Dubois held on to the rudders of the upturned craft with two activated rescue beacons hanging around his neck. When an RAAF Orion aircraft from Perth first dropped a life raft to him he swam fifty metres to grab it and climbed in, only to be flipped straight back into the water by the first big wave. Another life raft was dropped from a second Orion twenty-five minutes later and Dubois clambered in. Later the HMAS Adelaide arrived in the area and he was winched to safety by the ship's helicopter.

The second missing sailor was Tony Bullimore aboard the 18 metre Exide Challenger, also upturned in the same heavy seas. Immediately activating his emergency beacon, the British sailor unsuccessfully tried to unfasten his life raft, now underwater in freezing temperatures. Donning a survival suit, he grabbed what little food and water he could access and took refuge on a narrow shelf in the bow. Soon running out of both food and water, he used a hand-held filter desalinator to stay hydrated. Four days later an inflatable dinghy from the Australian warship HMAS Adelaide came alongside the stricken craft. A crewman rapped on the hull with a hammer. Bullimore heard the sounds, swam out of the upside-down yacht and was plucked from the sea. During the ordeal he lost a fingertip (crushed by a slamming hatch door) and showed symptoms of mild frostbite on his face and extremities. He was in the early stages of hypothermia and moderately dehydrated. His core body temperature had fallen to 36.1 (normal is 38 degrees) and he'd lost weight. The intense penetrating cold was his worst enemy, though it did help to numb the pain in his crushed finger.

Survival inside an overturned boat in some of the roughest and coldest seas on earth is a formidable achievement and testimony to Bullimore's extensive ocean experience and practical approach to his problems. Knowing his boat was unsinkable he turned on his emergency beacons, climbed into a survival suit and waited things out as best he could. At times he entertained thoughts of venturing under the freezing water to get stored food or to have another go at untying the raft. Sensibly he chose to remain in the driest part of the boat, warding off hypothermia as long as possible. He is alive today thanks to an exceptional rescue effort and because he kept a level head.

Planning and coordination of the rescue was impressive. Both missing yachts were closer to Antarctica than any other land mass, and until this rescue no Australian warship had ever been in latitudes so far south.

An even larger scale rescue occurred the following year during the 1998 Sydney to Hobart Yacht Race. 115 yachts participated but only 44 made it to Hobart. Five yachts sank, six sailors perished and over 50 people were winched to safety. Nine helicopters, 42 aeroplanes, a navy ship and well over 300 individuals took part in rescue efforts. During the race, wind gusts were recorded at over 90 knots and yachts were confronted with foaming waves as high as 5-storey buildings. Rescue conditions were extremely hazardous, especially for the helicopters which had to fly low enough to winch but high enough to avoid being flung into the sea by unpredictable waves.

Survival Priorities
WATER

1. More than 75% of Australia's landscape is classified as arid. Your body starts to break down after only a few days without water. Finding a supply is a primary concern.

2. Reduce the body's water loss by resting in shade, prefer-ably up off the hot ground. Don't talk, smoke, drink alcohol or consume fatty, salty or protein-rich foods.

3. Never drink sea water or urine. Use a solar still or jerry can still to convert these into fresh drinking water.

4. Carry large clear plastic bags to procure water through transpiration. Practise using the bags before your trip.

5. Keep clothes on in the heat, but loosen for ventilation. Wear a wide-brimmed hat and roll down your sleeves.

6. Collect rain in any suitable receptacle. Mop up dew from leaves and damp grass at dawn.

7. Boil water at least five minutes to purify. Remove sedi-ment with an improvised filter (sand in a clean sock, etc.)

8. If possible, melt ice rather than snow - it is more dense.

9. Seek underground water at low points such as creek beds, cliff bases and just above the beach high water mark.

10. When deciding on a water procurement method try to evaluate possible gains against sweat expended.

11. Be alert for signs of water - bees, seed-eating birds, green vegetation and fresh grasses.

12. If you must travel or exert yourself, save these activi-ties for the cool of the night.

Water

You can live for weeks without food, but with no water in hot conditions the body starts to suffer on the first day. People have perished in the Australian outback after only three days without water. In our arid regions temperatures can hover over the 40 degree mark during the daytime. In such heat you would live no more than a week without water, even if you spent the daylight hours lying motionless in shade. With physical exertion this survival time is cut at least in half.

Water constitutes about two-thirds of our body weight, so a person weighing 75 kilograms contains roughly 50 litres of water. Have a look at a 50-litre aquarium - that's a lot of water. Circulation, respiration, digestion and other vital functions depend upon adequate maintenance of fluid levels. In the bush you must be conscious not only of how much you're taking in, but also the rate at which existing water is being lost. Perspiration and urination are not the only causes of water depletion. A great deal is exhaled as vapour, especially during times of exertion. Medical ailments such as vomiting, diarrhoea, weeping blisters and sunburn accelerate fluid loss. Death normally occurs when you lose seven or eight litres of water from the body without replacement.

Even when doing nothing in cold weather your body should have at least two litres per day. In an unshaded dinghy off the coast, six litres would be a minimum daily requirement. On treks with a heavy load in the tropical north the author has gone through 15 litres in one day. Moisture in food constitutes 35 - 40% of our total water intake and we drink the rest. Many wild creatures are adept at storing water within their bodies, but humans are not.

"Ration your sweat, not your water", the old adage goes. The less you lose the less you must replace. You can reduce daily water loss in several ways. If you must travel, do so at night when it is cooler. Lie in the shade when the sun is up. Move slowly and as little as possible. A person in full sun needs *three times the water* as someone resting in shade. Don't smoke or drink alcohol - both rob the body of water. Loosen clothing to encourage ventilation but do not remove it. Clothing prevents sunburn and slows down the rate at which sweat is lost through evaporation. Always wear a head covering in the sun. If adrift at sea, keep clothing wet to stay cool and take seasickness medication to limit vomiting.

Eat minimally when water is scarce, avoiding foods containing a lot of salt, fat and protein. These require extra water to digest. Don't talk. Cut down water loss through exhalation by breathing through the nose, keeping the mouth closed. Avoid lying directly on hot ground if you can. Use a hammock or rig up some sort of platform to rest on. This allows breezes to circulate around and beneath you.

Sometimes water should be filtered. This is especially true when digging for water in dried creek beds. To filter the muddy sludge seeping into your scooped hole, put some clean sand, grass or charcoal into a knotted shirt, trouser leg, clean sock or bandanna. Pour the dirty water through it, catching the filtered liquid in a billy. This filtering removes much of the sediment and increases palatability. If doubts remain about its bacterial content, boil the filtered water or use purification tablets before drinking. Boil at least five minutes to be safe.

Stay fully hydrated so body and mind function at their best. Always carry water when leaving your vehicle or base camp to explore on foot. Strap on a belt bag containing survival kit, map, compass and built-in pouches for two water bottles.

WARNING

Any waterholes showing signs of alkaline encrustation or lacking fringing vegetation should be viewed with great suspicion. They may be dangerously polluted.

Never drink sea water or urine - this rapidly accelerates the dehydration process. The same goes for the salt water found in many inland Australian lakes. Water showing obvious evidence of pollution is likely to cause vomiting and is not worth the risk.

FINDING WATER

Fresh water is often well hidden in the bush. It may be just under the ground, buried in a tree hollow, lying in a fissure at the base of a cliff or stored in plant roots. An empty but still muddy waterhole is a good place to dig for water. Start at the lowest point using your hands or any suitable stick or tool. Lightweight plastic trowels work well in mud. Don't waste time digging unless there is some evidence that water is likely to be found (moist ground, water plants, green grass, etc.). A lot of energy and sweat is used in digging so make the effort only where signs suggest a fruitful outcome. In riverbeds the lowest spot on the outside of the bend is the most likely place to find water.

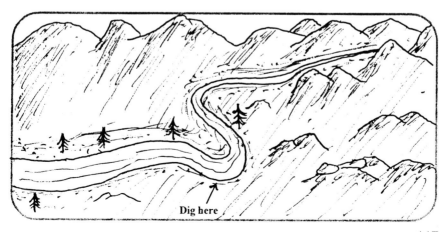

Dig here

In coastal areas search for water at the bottom of cliffs or dig in the dunes just above the high water mark. Rain falling in these areas is trapped by the sand and 'floats' above the denser sea water. Some delicacy is required in the digging. Go too deep and you'll pass the thin layer of fresh water, find the salt and end up with an undrinkable brackish mix. One trick is to prop twigs around the edges of the digging site to minimise the sand falling back into the hole.

On rocky coastlines look for fissures in the rock which may hold fresh water or indicate its presence just above the high water mark. Dark discoloration on the rock is an obvious sign. The vertical crack leading down to the sand (at left) was bone dry but led the author to a freshwater soak hidden metres away in the shrubbery above.

Be alert for animal signs indicating water nearby. Dragonflies and bees are normally not far from water. Following the flight path of parrots, finches and other seed-eating birds may reward the careful observer. A column of ants crawling up a tree trunk and disappearing into a hollow may indicate a hidden water source. To detect water in a tree hollow poke a long sapling as far down into the hole as you can. Pull it out and see if the end is wet. If so, tie a wad of grass or some absorbent cloth to the end of the stick and lower it back down. Soak up the water and squeeze it out, repeating the process as often as needed.

118

Don't assume a hollow is dry merely because the area hasn't seen rain for months. Cracks situated at the lowest forks of trees act as a natural catchment for dew which runs down from upper branches to collect in the hollow. She-oaks, paperbarks and old smooth-barked eucalypts can hold enormous quantities of water within these natural reservoirs in their trunks. A two-metre length of aquarium tubing is a handy item in dry country. Use it to suck water from otherwise unreachable tree hollows or narrow cracks in rocks.

The saying 'all animal tracks lead to water' is often heard. Unfortunately you may die of thirst before working out which are heading toward the water and which are going away. Many animals receive moisture from creatures they prey upon and drink infrequently. By following kangaroo or other herbivore tracks downhill you might be lucky to strike water, but you're more likely to use up precious energy and find nothing.

Carefully observe wild pigeons before dusk. Pigeons are one of the more dependable indicators of water in the bush. By watching their behaviour you can tell if they are moving toward a waterhole or away from it. Slow flying from tree to tree normally indicates they have drunk their fill and are returning to nesting areas. A straight, speedy flight low to the ground tells you they are on course for the nightly drink.

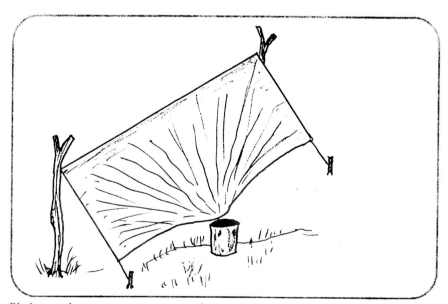

Shelter and water procurement at the same time - A lean-to shelter provides a convenient catchment surface for rain and dew. Pull down the centre of the tarp to direct the water into a large plastic bag or other container underneath.

119

Collect falling rain in any receptacle you can find. Use a groundsheet, plastic bags, curled sheets of bark or clothing (from which the water can be squeezed). Morning dew can be gathered. It's most plentiful when days are hot and the nights much cooler. A tarp spread on grass overnight will collect dew on the bottom or any rain on top. Tie some cloth around your lower legs and walk through long moist grass or low-lying shrubs; do this before the sun rises and sucks all the moisture away. Remove the cloths when soaked and squeeze the water into a billy. Small 'pack towels' are ideal for this and absorb an amazing amount of water for their weight. Over a litre of water can be collected in less than an hour with this method.

Wrap absorbent cloth around your legs to collect dew at dawn.

OBTAINING WATER FROM PLANTS

Water can be extracted from some tree roots, saplings and climbing vines. In arid areas select a tree with roots branching out from the trunk at or near ground level. Get water from surface roots before dawn. Trees store up much of their water during the night.

Cut radiating roots close to where they join the trunk at ground level. By scratching the soil away along their length they can gradually be pulled free of the ground. The root must then be cut into lengths of a metre or so. Prop them up with one end in a billy to collect the seepage. The water will not flow freely unless the root is cut into these short sections - this is an important step. Drain half a dozen root sections into the billy at a time for maximum effect and drink it within twenty-four hours. If left longer it ferments and is not drinkable.

In rainforests, lianas (climbing vines) may also be cut into metre-long sections and left to drain into a container. Rainforest vines often hang down in a 'U' shape starting from the treetop, extending nearly to the ground and then turning around to stretch up into the canopy again. To obtain water make a small notch-cut as high as you can reach and then a full cut through the vine at its lowest point. Have your container ready at the full cut. The volume and speed of flow may catch you by surprise and you won't want to waste a drop. If drinking directly from a cut vine don't touch it with your lips. Let the water trickle into your mouth to avoid contact with any irritant sap.

Extracting water from saplings is most successful in temperate regions with reasonable rainfall. A densely foliated sapling is best, around 12 cm in diameter and 4 to 7 metres tall. Cut it off at the ground, then make another cut diagonally across the upper trunk where it meets the lower branches. Lean the sapling against a nearby tree with the diagonally cut narrow end propped into a container to collect the water, as shown below.

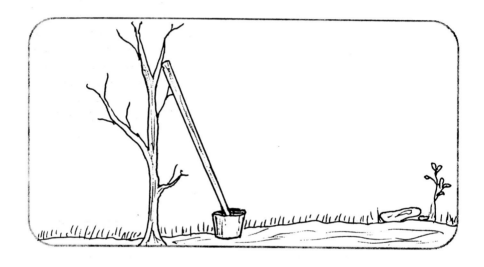

These methods of extracting water from roots, saplings and vines can be very harmful to the plants and may destroy them. Consequently they should only be used in desperate, life-threatening situations. Always try to measure what you'll derive from the plant versus how much sweat will be used in the process. Yanking a dozen roots out of the ground for a cup of water is pointless if you sweat out half a litre doing it. The same applies to digging up dry creek beds. If you must dig, wait until the sun goes down. The most efficient way to procure water from plants is with large, clear plastic condensation bags. Get into the habit of carrying several transpiration bags and use them in preference to any of the above techniques.

FRESH WATER FROM OCEAN FISH

A well-known yachtie survival trick can also be used by land explorers on lonely coasts. It involves squeezing moisture from freshly caught sea fish. Eating the fish would only use up more of the body's water for digestion but if you cut the flesh into small cubes, place it in a bandanna or shirt sleeve and squeeze hard, the moisture in the flesh can be wrung out into a container. Hold the fish-filled cloth at each end directly above the billy and use a twisting motion (like wringing out a wet shirt). This liquid is perfectly drinkable and virtually devoid of saltiness. In the absence of an alternative water source it will help keep you alive where there are plenty of fish.

A small amount of fresh water resides within the backbones of ocean fish. This is useful knowledge, especially if you are in a position to catch larger specimens. To obtain this water gut the fish and remove the backbone carefully so the fluid doesn't tip out. Fish eyeballs also contain moisture which can be sucked out. Don't consume fluids from other parts of the fish such as the digestive tract - these are high in protein and will rob the body of moisture. *DO NOT DRINK FISH OR SEA BIRD BLOOD* - it is very high in Vitamin A. Too much Vitamin A is poisonous and can harm the kidneys.

TRANSPIRATION BAGS

Since the 1940s it has been widely accepted that constructing a solar still is the most effective way to obtain water in arid regions. *This is not the case.* Solar stills are useful for distilling urine, sea water or contaminated water into safe drinking water, but as a collection method they are substantially inferior to transpiration bags. It is vital that the reader understand this point. If you want to distil water, think solar still. If you want to achieve maximum water extraction using plastic, think transpiration bag.

A transpiration (or condensation) bag is nothing more than a large, clear plastic bag used to extract water from vegetation. Typical size is two metres long, a metre wide and 150 microns thick (thinner bags are more prone to punctures). It can be positioned to cover the entire shrub or just a single branch, and is then tied off to seal it from the air. A catchment hollow (or 'sump') is created at the plastic's lowest point to collect water which is transpired from the foliage. This condenses and trickles down the sides of the plastic. The process is simple but must be performed properly.

Methods of using transpiration bags to best effect are summarised as follows:

ENCLOSING THE ENTIRE SHRUB

For someone trying to stay alive in arid regions (in other words, 80% of Australia), this is the best way to use plastic to get water from plants. Its advantage is that the small tree or bush acts as a pump to pull moisture directly from the ground. Every drop drawn up from the soil into the leaves has nowhere to go but into your carefully tied off bag. None is wasted. Compare this with a solar still which can only extract water from the soil itself, or any crushed plants you have previously placed in the hole.

TRANSPIRATION BAGS FOR SURVIVAL

Nick Vroomans is a former Chief Instructor for the Australian Defence Force Survival School and currently operates Staying Alive Survival Services, Australia's most comprehensive survival training organisation. Nick is probably the world's leading expert on water procurement by transpiration. Over the years he has dug over a thousand solar stills and tested transpiration bags under all types of Australian conditions. In a 12 hour period the most water he has ever obtained from a solar still is 300 millilitres. By contrast, transpiration bags encircling single saplings regularly produce outputs averaging 800 ml. The least amount of water he has ever obtained with a single transpiration bag is 250 ml. One bag left from dawn to dusk on a tea tree sapling yielded an impressive 6 litres.

The best procedure with transpiration bags is to attach them to the shrub in the morning and leave them alone until dusk. The temptation to raid the bag at midday and seal it up again must be resisted, as much of the advantages of the process are then lost. Similarly the idea of attaching a plastic drinking tube or 'tap' (such as a wine cask pour spout) may sound good, but in practice interferes with proper sealing.

Type of tree, climate, location and the amount of time the bag is in the sun all affect the yield. Site selection is important. Pick vegetation close to your stranded vehicle to save on sweat. If it's midday and you can get the bag (or bags) organised within an hour, do so immediately. From then on get them up at first light and remove them at sunset. They need sunshine to work. The ideal tree for transpiration has low, unshaded branches with plenty of foliage. Trees in dry creek beds and other low-lying areas offer the best yields but any healthy tree will produce. Select trees with a northerly aspect for maximum sunshine.

Don't use the same tree or section of branches on consecutive days as this increases the risk of toxins leaching out of the leaves to taint the water. A new tree is always more productive.

The following method is best when using the bag with a single small tree (say 2-4 metres tall).

1. Maximise sun on the bag. Select a tree that won't be shaded by other trees or cliffs nearby. It needs plenty of clear space around it.

2. Bend the top of the tree down and tie it off to the ground or to the base of the trunk.

3. Prune away any dead leaves and twigs. If necessary bind the branches together with cord so the bag fits over them easily.

4. Place the clear plastic bag over as much foliage as you can and tie off the opening, ensuring the bag is completely airtight.

5. Create a sump (collection point) at one of the bag's corners, big enough to hold around two litres. Adjust the bag so the sump is at its lowest point. Leave the sump hanging free - don't tie it to anything. The idea of the sump is to provide a water collection point free of foliage. Don't let branch tips get into the sump. A piece of cord tied *loosely* at the sump 'mouth' will help keep the two areas separate.

6. Leave the bag alone until sunset, then untie it and collect the water. During the night the same bag can be put to other survival uses - as a dew collector, windproof and waterproof clothing or in the making of shelter. With a thickness of 150 microns a transpiration bag is pretty sturdy, but care must still be taken to avoid punctures.

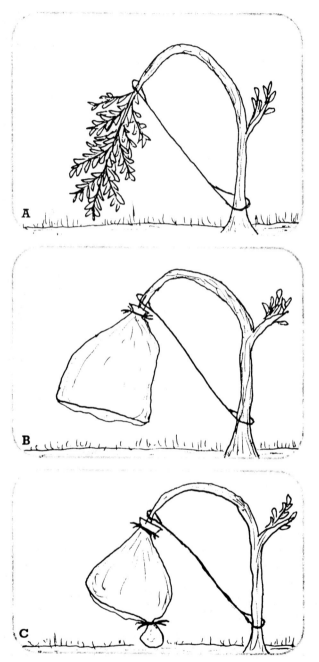

A - Bend the sapling over and tie it off to its trunk. B - Place the bag over the branch and seal the end with cord. C - Make the sump at the lowest point.

Along arid coastlines, distilling salt water can be a labour-intensive process whether you are digging a solar still or building a fire to make steam. A transpiration bag used on fresh plants above the high water mark is a much easier way to keep hydrated. Always carry transpiration bags in such areas.

ENCLOSING ONE OR MORE BRANCHES

On the rare occasions when transpiration bags are shown on a television documentary or in an old survival manual, the depiction is normally of a large bag tied over the end of a single extended branch or group of branches. This works adequately but is less productive than enveloping the whole plant. You're still pumping water from ground to foliage, but instead of trapping all the moisture you trap only that small portion encased by the bag. The remainder is released into the air and goes to waste. Where large trees are the only choice, tying the bag over a clump of well-leafed branches is certainly the way to go. In practice, smaller saplings suitable for total enclosure are more prevalent in arid environments than large trees.

COLLECTED FOLIAGE METHOD

If saplings are too small or covered with thorns which might puncture the bag, your next best option is to break off the foliage and stuff as much of it into the transpiration bag as you can. Select leaves that look relatively moist. Although there's no pumping effect with this method there is also no wastage; every drop of moisture drawn out of the leaves by the sun is collected. Even the most expertly constructed solar still loses part of its haul because not every condensation droplet reaches the container.

Practise using transpiration bags before you visit an arid region. When testing bags bring suitable cord for tying them off and a clear plastic container to measure output. Aside from their value in a survival situation, transpiration bags are also one of the least damaging methods of water procurement. Unless you leave the bag on for several days (which is not recommended) the plant will recover fully.

THE SOLAR STILL

Because they are less productive and more labour-intensive than transpiration bags, solar stills are not the first option for water procurement. Their main function in survival is in the distillation of otherwise undrinkable water. With a still you can convert salt water (either from the sea or from inland salt lakes), polluted water or urine into fresh pure water that's safe to drink. Basic requirements for a solar still are a water catchment container and a plastic sheet. Thin clear plastic works better than opaque material. A transpiration bag cut at two of its edges to form a single 2 metre by 2 metre sheet is ideal. A poncho, tarp or groundsheet will do if you have nothing else. As with transpiration bags, airtightness is paramount. If your plastic sheet has holes in it (even patched ones) your results will be far less productive.

Your catchment receptacle could be a billy, large cup or cooking pot. You could even form a piece of tarpaulin, some alfoil or a section of tree bark into a bowl shape. To capture maximum droplets use the widest container you have. Plastic containers are preferable to metal ones which can get very hot and 'burn off' some of their collected water.

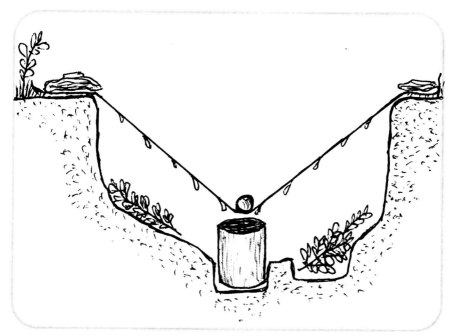

The Solar Still. Building one is hard work - save the job for the cool of the night.

As with transpiration bags, the hotter it gets the better it works. More sun makes more water. In drier parts of Australia the materials to make a solar still should be standard gear carried on every journey.

Construction is simple. Dig a hole about a metre wide and half a metre deep. The sides of the hole start off vertically then taper toward the bottom. A small cavity is dug in the centre at the lowest point to accommodate the container (see diagram). A shovel or bushwalker's trowel makes the job easier than with a digging stick or your hands. If you must use your hands, wear gloves or other protection. Stretch the plastic sheet across the finished hole and anchor the edges with soil or sand. *The edge must be totally sealed off from the air.* Push the centre of the sheet downward so it forms an inverted cone shape with the sides at a 30 to 40 degree angle. The angle is important. If too vertical the condensation droplets pick up too much speed and fall before they reach the container. If too horizontal the opposite occurs and they drop where they form, far from the centre of the sheet.

Weigh down the centre of the sheet with a small smooth rock to maintain the conical shape and cut down on wind flutter. Position the rock directly over the centre of the container. The sheet must not touch either the sides of the hole or any part of the container.

With just your container in a dry hole you'll only extract the moisture present in the soil itself, which is virtually nil in desert regions. The sweat used in making the still would exceed the water obtained from it. For maximum yield add as much urine, salt water or contaminated water as you have, so long as the resulting level stays below the rim of the billy. You can pour this 'bad water' into the bottom of the hole away from the container, but it's more efficient to dig an extra trough inside your hole, line it with a scrap of plastic and fill that up. The salts and impurities are removed by the distillation process. Add to the hole any fresh leafy plant material you can find to further enhance water production just before you position the container in the hole and seal up the edges.

The sun heats the foliage and the liquid inside the hole, evaporating the water which condenses on the plastic. This moisture runs down the sides of the smooth plastic to the lowest point (weighted by the rock) to drop into the container.

The plant material must not touch any part of the plastic. If necessary add a couple of extra depressions in your hole to accommodate it. Any portion of a plant that looks like it might yield moisture is worth a try. Succulents such as pigface and prickly pear are ideal, but any fresh looking greenery will do. Cut it up to expose the moist innards before adding it to the hole.

A creek bed or low point in the landscape is the best place to position the still, to take advantage of underground moisture. Coastal dunes just above the high water mark are another top location, making use of the underlying water table. Ensure your still is not in the shade; it needs full sun to do its job properly. It's easy to forget that a still placed in full sun in the morning may be totally in the shadow of trees or cliffs by late afternoon. Take note of your surroundings and position the still for continuous sunshine.

Build your still in the cool hours before dawn. It will be at least a couple of hours before it starts to produce water. Keep in mind that every time you remove the plastic to check the container you may lose up to an hour's worth of water production. A partial solution to this wastage is a two-metre length of flexible plastic aquarium tubing. One end is taped to the inside rim of the container while the other extends up from under the edge of the plastic at ground level. When you need a drink you suck it up out of the protruding end like a straw. However, a better option is simply to rest in the shade during the day and leave the thing alone until nightfall, only then removing whatever water has been produced. In theory, adding a drinking tube should not compromise the airtight seal but in practice the still works best when not disturbed.

If you need more water, building a second still is better than enlarging the existing one. The metre - wide size is optimum for water production. Smaller and larger ones don't work as well. You'll need more than one still to supply enough water to live on. After three or four days the yield falls sharply and you must replace the foliage or move the still to a new location.

FRESH WATER FROM SEA WATER

Arid coasts present special difficulties when it comes to finding water, but by using condensation you can extract fresh water from the ocean. If these methods are kept going throughout the day you can get enough fresh water to keep you alive indefinitely.

MINIMAL GEAR METHOD

Dig or scrape a wide, shallow hole in the ground or find a natural depression in the rocks above the high water mark. Fill this with clean sea water. The hole needn't be deeper than 10 or 15 centimetres, and about a metre wide. If you have dug a depression in earth or sand, line it with a tarp or plastic poncho to hold the water in. Use a wide strip of paperbark or a waterproof jacket as a liner if there's nothing else. The transpiration bags in your vehicle survival kit are ideal.

You'll also need matches (or other fire-lighting devices), stones, some firewood and an appropriately sized cloth for absorbing rising steam. For bushwalkers this can be a towel, track suit top or large T-shirt. Drivers may have something larger such as a picnic blanket, tablecloth or bed sheets. Have more than one cloth at the ready so you can replace them one after the other.

Build a fire and heat several stones in it. Don't use rocks from a creek bed or any found below the high water mark. These contain moisture and can explode dangerously when heated. Place the red-hot stones in the sea water, using one or more pronged sticks as tongs if nothing else is handy. Add enough stones to bring the water to a boil. The resulting water vapour gets soaked up by the cloth stretched immediately above (but not touching) the simmering surface. This is wrung out when saturated to give pure fresh water.

Once you have a good steam going, ensure that as little as possible is escaping around the edges of the cloth. This steam is precious - do all you can to get as much as possible onto the cloth, which should be wrung out only after it has cooled. If several cloths are handy use them in sequence, constantly wringing and replacing. Hold the cloth edges in place with stones, branches or even fishing line tied to trees. If using the latter method, save time and steam loss by having a second cloth already tied in place above the one to be removed.

COOKING POT AND TRIPOD METHOD

Distilling sea water with hot rocks in the ground is labour inten-
sive but viable if you can protect yourself from the sun and collect enough
firewood to keep things going. A less tedious variation on this theme is
possible with a camp oven or large cooking pot. The wider the container the better, but even a standard billy will suffice.

First build a tripod from three stout branches, each two metres long.
Lash these together at the top and space the base of each pole so they
are about a metre apart. Dig a 5 cm depression for each pole tip for
stability. From the top of the tripod suspend your cooking pot with cord
or wire so its bottom is roughly 30 cm above the ground. Fill it 2/3 full
with sea water and cover the open top with an absorbent cloth. Build
the fire directly underneath. The fire's size and the height of the hanging pot is arranged so you achieve steady heat without scorching the
cloth. Don't try to maintain a rolling boil - a steady simmer is sufficient
and conserves fuel. Keep the fire going as long as needed, replacing
the sea water before it boils dry and substituting dry cloths for soaked
ones. *Always* lift hot cloths with a stick and let them cool before squeezing out the water.

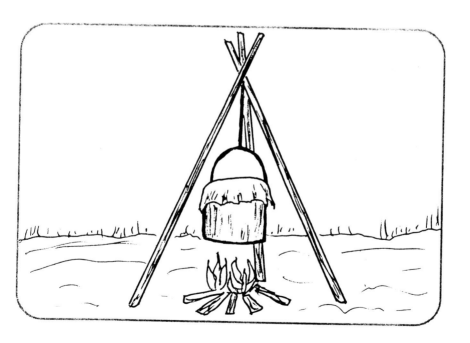

JERRY CAN, PLASTIC BAG AND HOSE METHOD

Outback drivers normally carry a spare jerry can, at least 2 metres of siphon hose and a plastic bag. Combine these items to create a salt water evaporation still far superior to the methods already outlined.

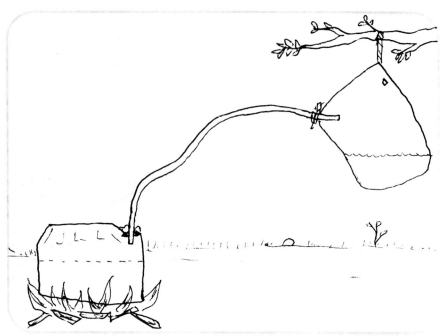

The jerry can still supplies enough fresh water for survival.

Fill the jerry can 2/3 full with sea water and insert one end of the hose or tubing into the spout. Wedge it in securely with a piece of cloth or other material to form an airtight seal. Suspend the plastic bag from a nearby branch at a height above the top of the jerry can. The elevated end of the hose is inserted in the bag and tied on with cord or tape to ensure a tight seal. A thicker hose works better than a narrow one. Next, puncture a tiny hole near the highest part of the plastic bag to let air escape. This needn't be bigger than a centimetre or two in diameter - any wider and you'll lose too much steam.

Light a fire underneath the jerry can to bring the water to a boil, then immediately scrape away some of the fuel to reduce it to a simmer. With the right amount of heat the steam coming off the water will rise, enter the hose and end up in the plastic bag where it condenses and rolls down the sides to collect at the bottom. If the fire is too hot much of the steam will go shooting out the tiny vent hole.

The advantage of this technique is that it virtually maintains itself as long as you keep the water at a simmer. You need only pour more sea water into the can as it gets low and empty the plastic collection bag occasionally. If kept going all day this system will supply more than enough drinking water for your needs. In the absence of a jerry can other containers can be tried.

AVOIDING DEHYDRATION

We lose water from our bodies through perspiration, urination and breathing and this must be constantly replaced. In cool conditions at rest you might lose only two or three litres a day. During strenuous exertion in hot humid weather this increases dramatically - over ten litres a day may be lost.

Neither the body nor the brain functions at its best during periods of extreme thirst. People stranded in deserts who run out of water tend to do irrational things that worsen an already perilous situation. It is hard to think straight when dehydrated.

When hiking, develop the habit of taking a ten minute break at least every hour. Drink at each stop whether thirsty or not. Beside a river, attach a drinking cup to your belt to dip in the water. You make steadier progress when fully hydrated. Take small amounts of water at frequent intervals.

Squeeze and drink - in desert areas, the Water-Holding Frog (Cyclorana platycephala) *is used by Aboriginal people as an emergency water source.*

Photo courtesy of Brad Maryan, WASAH.

135

Symptoms of dehydration include thirst, mental and physical lethargy and dry skin. Urination becomes concentrated, dark yellow in colour and infrequent (normal urine is clear or light yellow). Headache is common. Extreme cases result in loss of consciousness and death.

When sweating profusely you must replace at least as much water as you're losing. Once the body's water level is back on track some thought can be given to replacing lost glucose and salt. Help this along with rehydration products such as Powerade, Gastrolyte or similar. Alternatively, you can mix a tablespoon of sugar and 1/4 teaspoon of table salt into a litre of water and drink that.

In Australia it can be a long way between waterholes. In these circumstances avoid salty, fatty and protein-rich foods as they only increase thirst. By walking during the night and resting in shade during the day your water will last at least twice as long. This method of travel is a strange concept to those who have never hiked at night, but in flat hot country with sparse shade it is the only way to go. Moonlit treks in the desert offer a unique experience. Provided you go slowly and keep an eye out for rabbit warrens, wombat holes and other perils it is reasonably safe.

WATER CARRIERS

These should be light but not so flimsy that they spring a leak at the slightest provocation. Be wary of putting plastic water carriers directly down on the ground. Many grasses found in Australia's arid regions are needle-sharp and make pincushions out of cheap containers.

Most clear collapsible containers sold by camping and department stores are better suited to car camping than serious trekking. Fully rigid plastic containers are the best choice for car trips.

On foot the practical option is a water bag, available from bushwalking shops. The author carries two water containers on most explorations: a ten litre Ortlieb water bag and a six-litre Sea To Summit bag with spare liner. Both are well-made and feather light.

Carrying two or more bags is better than just one because you can distribute the weight more evenly within your pack. The spare container is necessary in case one leaks.

Keep water bags away from sharp objects to avoid punctures. When taking the pack off to stop for a drink put the water bag on top of the pack, not on the ground. If sitting with your back resting against a tree, hold the bag on your lap. With care a good water bag should last many years.

Non-lubricated condoms make handy emergency water carriers, as do the inner bladders from standard four-litre wine casks. A plastic bag

136

knotted or tied at the top is another choice. Of course these flimsier water holders need extra protection from abrasions when stored in the pack. Bark containers, animal bladders and hollow vines (carried in a 'U' shape) are possible alternative water carriers.

Isolated rock outcrops in an otherwise flat landscape tend to attract clouds (just like lone islands at sea). Rainwater may often be found at the base of the rocks or in well shaded cracks and hollows.

Survival Priorities
FOOD

1. Food is one of the last things to think about in a survival situation. Protection from the elements, water, medical self-help and preparations to signal rescuers are more urgent.

2. Carry foods offering the most nutritional value for weight.

3. If short of water avoid fatty, salty and protein-rich foods.

4. Animal foods are generally more important to long-term survival than plant foods. Insects are often the easiest type of protein to obtain.

5. Avoid mushrooms and large nuts - many are very toxic.

6. Use the Plant Edibility Test before eating unknown plants.

7. Don't eat too much of one plant at a time or rely too much on one food source. A balanced diet is necessary to maintain health.

8. Many Australian animals are protected by law. Even where this is not the case the taking of native wildlife is a last resort for dire circumstances only. In a non-emergency, snares, night-line fishing, netting and other survival methods may be illegal. Pack sufficient food so there is no need to deplete the bush.

9. In the short term it may be wiser to rest and conserve existing calories than to spend energy on hunting.

10. In the bush, waste no part of a food animal. Practise cooking methods that retain maximum nutrients. Preserve any surplus food for later - you may need it.

Food

For many people the word survival conjures up images of living off the land, dining on berries, fish and snared animals. In Australia there is growing interest in the subject of bush tucker and traditional Aboriginal cooking methods. Snacking on wild tucker is one of the pleasures of the outdoors, but foraging should be a rare treat rather than a survival necessity. *Always carry enough food for your needs, plus some extra for the unexpected.* Areas near human habitation are often denuded of bush foods to the detriment of local wildlife that depend on them. Although this isn't such a problem in remote areas, enthusiasm for foraging should always be tempered with conservation and restraint.

Food is way down the priority list in a survival situation. Without water the problem of food is largely irrelevant. Protecting yourself from the weather and preparing for rescue usually takes precedence over stomach needs as well.

Food for bush travel must be sustaining and provide basic requirements of protein, fat, carbohydrates, vitamins, fibre, minerals and trace elements. It must give you energy to keep going. A hiker in reasonably smooth terrain might burn 5000 calories per day. Around half these calories would be consumed by the walking itself - the remainder are taken up by other activities and normal metabolism. Even at rest your breathing, circulation and other 'automatics' burn 60-80 calories every hour. Just as it's important to conserve the body's existing water it is equally wise not to waste calories. Don't squander energy when you don't have to. Anxiety and fear also devour calories. A stressed person needs more food than a calm one.

A gram of protein produces 4 calories - the same as a gram of carbohydrate. A gram of fat produces 9 calories. While high fat consumption is unhealthy in the long term, bodily needs in a survival scenario differ from those in urban life. In physically demanding bush emergencies fat is a desirable energy producer.

When selecting foods consider nutritional value, perishability, weight, palatability and simplicity of preparation. An important aspect is the packaging - you must be able to take all litter out with you.

Dehydrated food is the obvious choice for bush travel. Its compactness means walkers can carry up to three weeks' worth of food on their backs, and four-wheel drivers can be self-sustaining for two months or more.

Camping and mountaineering shops sell an array of freeze-dried foods vacuum-packed in foil. Many are complete meals. Though convenient they are expensive. Another problem is that the foil packaging doesn't burn. Supermarkets stock a range of dried products suitable for camping so specialist camping foods are not necessary.

Many outdoor travellers dry their own foods before a trip. Quality food dehydrators will dry just about any foods. The only real exceptions are eggs, avocados and foods containing a lot of fat or oil. Spaghetti bolognaise dehydrates well but you must use lean beef. By drying your own foods you avoid preservatives found in store-bought items, especially dried fruit. Another point is that you can dry foods otherwise too perishable, bulky or inconvenient to carry on long trips. Dehydrators use an accelerated air drying process over a 10-12 hour period. The food is placed on trays at night and removed in the morning.

If food is nutritious and balanced it will see you through the most physically challenging circumstances. If not, it is wasting space and money. In many areas bush tucker will be scarce. *Do not rely on it.* If injured you might be physically unable to forage, fish or hunt, in which case the food you carry in will be all there is. Make it count.

The amount you'll need depends on weather, terrain and activity level. Weight-wise, 700-800 grams of food per person per day is a good average for walkers to work on, since dried foods make up the bulk of provisions. 4WD explorers will have a higher weight per person/per day because tinned and perishable foods contain more water. Drivers are also more likely to store food in its original (heavier) packaging.

Always soak dried foods for hours or overnight before using them. Serious digestive blockages can occur if too much dehydrated food is consumed 'as is'. Show restraint with trail snacks. Eating a whole packet of dried banana chips and washing it down with a litre of water is equivalent to consuming over a dozen bananas. It's far better to pre-soak items in a bowl than to have the expansion take place in your stomach.

Keep bush meals simple. Breakfast must be substantial enough to keep you going all morning. Home-made muesli combined with powdered milk is a proven performer on gruelling trips. Porridge is a hearty choice for chilly weather. Oats keep almost indefinitely and offer good food value for weight.

BUSH MUESLI

To make your own muesli combine any or all of the following ingredients. Store in heavy-duty plastic bags and keep out of the sun.

Rolled oats	Dates	Figs
Bran	Dried pears	Currants
Wheat germ	Dried apricots	Sultanas
Wheat biscuit cereal	Pine nuts	Dried apples
Sesame seeds	Pitted prunes	Slivered almonds
Sunflower seed kernels	Macadamia nuts	Dried peaches

Walkers like lunch to be quick and light so it doesn't slow progress, but if taken to extremes this can lead to low blood sugar toward the end of the day. In colder conditions a cooked lunch is justified. With a portable stove a hearty soup is quick to prepare and recharges you for the afternoon. The hottest part of the day is also a good time for a salt and mineral replacement drink.

Dinner replenishes the body's energy stores. Centre it around pasta or rice for maximum carbohydrate intake. If using the 'cook it all in one billy' method, add dried packet soups to the boiling pasta. This creates a sauce as it thickens. Add lentils and beans to keep protein levels up in the absence of meat or fish.

Snack throughout the day on high-energy foods. Don't let blood sugar levels deplete during exercise. There's a big difference between recreational bushwalking on well-kept trails and slogging across trackless terrain. A varied diet helps stave off fatigue that leads to carelessness and accidents. Sultanas, nuts, hard-shelled chocolate, salami sticks and high-energy food bars are typical snack items.

Damper cooked in the coals is a great morale lifter. Use stone ground wholemeal flour instead of white flour to get the most nutrition from your efforts.

Staple dinner items include long-grain or brown rice, pasta, dried soup mixes, lentils and soy beans. A time-saving way to cook rice is to bring it to a boil, cover and set it aside; then you can use the fire or stove for something else. In a half hour or so the rice cooks itself. In cold weather you'll need to insulate the covered rice pot with a towel and put it in your sleeping bag to keep the wind from cooling it.

Dehydrated vegetables such as peas, corn, carrots and green beans keep vitamin levels up. By far the most carbohydrate-packed of all vegies is the potato, with over ten times the carbohydrate content per weight of carrots or green beans. Dried instant mashed potato is always worth including. Tomato paste is also available in dehydrated form (flakes). Packet parmesan cheese is hard to beat for high protein and fat content. Egg white powder (available from health food shops) isn't cheap but is very protein-rich and easily added to meals.

Other essentials include olive oil, raw sugar, herbs, spices and plenty of tea.

BUSH TUCKER

It is satisfying to be able to identify, locate and prepare bush foods. If stranded somewhere, a basic knowledge of bush foods may keep you alive until rescue arrives or until you can make your own way out.

Aborigines have sought bush foods for centuries, moving from place to place in response to seasonal availability of fruits, nuts, tubers and game. They've learned which plants harbour irritant toxins and how some can be made safe to eat with special preparation or cooking methods.

Some excellent publications are available on Australian bush tucker. The Northern Territory Conservation Commission produces a pocket-sized Bush Tucker Identikit that covers the more common Top End bush food plants. Colour photos and plant descriptions are combined with charts showing the flowering and fruiting seasons for each plant. Bush Food (*Jennifer Isaacs, Ure Smith Press 1987*) is too large for trekkers to lug around but is ideal for vehicle travel or home reference. It covers the range of traditional Aboriginal foods from shellfish and seed damper to fruits and insects. Herbal medicines and an appendix table of plant foods are also featured.

ANIMAL FOODS

Virtually every type of Australian animal may be eaten. In the bush, protein and fat are much easier to obtain from animal flesh than plants. The idea of chomping on grasshoppers, lizards, worms and ants has little appeal for most of us, though more 'acceptable' bush treats such as barramundi, yabbies or mud crabs don't attract the same level of revulsion. When survival is at stake the bush is no place for a discerning palate. You must get sustenance from any available source.

Traditional Aboriginal methods of hunting game and collecting animal foods are not indiscriminate. Strict codes and century-old customs govern the capture, preparation and cooking of animals. Some animal species are considered special totems, and these species are rarely eaten. Traditional food laws ensure a future food supply by regulating hunting and taking seasonal availability into consideration.

WARNING

Most native animal species are protected by law. Techniques for obtaining animal food outlined in this book are for use in desperate, life-threatening situations only. Under normal (non-survival) circumstances some methods would be ethically inexcusable, wasteful or contravene wildlife laws.

Smaller food items (insects, oysters, yabbies, etc.) are easier to obtain than larger animals such as kangaroos or emus. If present in sufficient quantity smaller animals provide just as much protein value.

MAMMALS

Kangaroo flesh tastes similar to lean beef and is a very acceptable bush food. Traditional Aboriginal hunting methods involve driving kangaroos toward a line of hunters waiting behind rocks or scrub along the expected route of escape. Bush fires are sometimes lit to force the animals in the preferred direction. This drive and ambush method works best with a large group of people. Aboriginal-style kangaroo hunts use up enormous amounts of energy. A thorough understanding of the animals moving, eating and drinking habits is necessary for success.

Without a firearm, kangaroo hunting isn't easy. In a survival scenario, waiting quietly in a hide near where the animals drink is the best bet. Build the hide out of branches or grass and position it downwind of the anticipated path to the water's edge. Success depends upon total stillness and quiet until the prey is close. A bow and arrow, spear, club or catapult is used to stun or kill the animal. Approach larger wounded kangaroos cautiously. They can deliver a serious blow with their feet.

Smaller mammals are easier to catch. Hollow logs are a favoured daytime resting place. Beware of snakes in residence. A long stick, hooked at one end, is pushed into the hole to drag the animal out. Tying a small noose to the end of the probe is another idea.

The Aboriginal habit of consuming the heart, liver and other offal of hunted game adds to the nutritional intake. In a survival situation as little as possible should be wasted.

Digging small animals out of burrows is hard work. An alternative is to place a snare at the burrow opening. Fishing line or slender rope can be used but brass or copper wire is best, thick enough to hold its shape when formed into a loop. Use a slip knot so the snare tightens when pulled.

The effectiveness of snares in survival situations is overrated, especially for Australian conditions. In controlled tests to determine capture rates it was found that on average you would need to rig at least 27 snares to catch one small animal - not a good energy output for input ratio. Percentages improve at burrows known to be inhabited, but reductions in rabbit numbers from the Calicivirus now make snares a largely impractical survival option.

BIRDS

Emus, ducks, pigeons and other birds offer sustaining meat. Aborigines traditionally hunt emus by digging pits covered over by scrub, then driving the birds into the well-disguised pits.

Magpie geese and other waterfowl may be ambushed from cover and killed with a catapult before or after they take flight. Bicycle tyre innertube attached to a strong (but slightly flexible) forked stick makes an effective slingshot. Aborigines hunt waterfowl by throwing boomerangs into large flocks or by swimming underwater until directly beneath a swimming duck or goose. The unsuspecting bird is then dragged under by its feet.

Trap seed-eating birds with a simple deadfall - a large flat stone propped up at one edge by a stick. Place seed bait under the rock and wait some distance away. A length of fishing line is attached to the stick while you hold the other end. When a bird is in position below the rock, pull the line sharply to drop the rock.

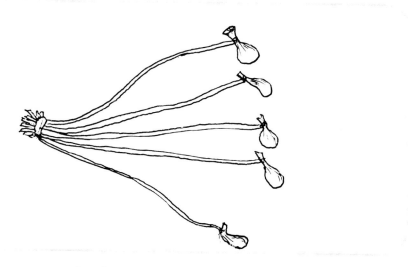

One weapon worth trying in a survival scenario is the bola. South American gauchos use it to catch rheas, a flightless bird similar to the emu; eskimos hunt birds in flight with the same weapon. It consists of half a dozen lengths of cord tied together at one end; the other ends are weighted with rocks encased in cloth pouches. Hold it by the joined end and swing in an arc above the head. When sufficient momentum is achieved the bola is released, twirling through the air toward the quarry and entangling its legs so it can be dispatched.

145

REPTILES

Lizards are an important survival food source. In desert regions they may be the easiest protein to find. Goannas are sometimes docile or curious enough to be approached and clubbed with a branch. You can also try digging them out of their burrows but this takes energy, skill, luck and a metal digging tool. The taste of goanna is similar to chicken but more oily and rubbery. Water dragons and smaller lizards must also be considered fair game in desperate times. Cook slowly over an even layer of hot coals and skin before eating. Be careful not to overcook.

Goannas have long been an important traditional protein source for Central Australian Aborigines, who use an elongated iron crowbar to dig them out of their burrows. **Photo courtesy of Brad Maryan, WASAH.**

Long-necked turtles are common throughout northern Australia. Catch them by hand in shallow creeks or on a fishing line using fish or insects as bait. Shrinking waterholes will often turn up a few turtles buried in mud. Prod the mud with a stick to find them or use the Aboriginal method, pressing down with bare feet against the ooze until resistance (in the form of a hibernating turtle) is felt.

Turtle meat is tasty and nourishing. Cook whole in the fire, belly side up for ten minutes. Then pull out the intestines via a hole cut in the neck. Clean out the large intestine well and cook separately in the coals until crispy - the result is like pork crackling. Cook the turtle in the embers for about twenty minutes on each side. Slower cooking with minimal flame gives better results than a hasty scorching. Once cooked the plastron (belly shell) is taken off in one piece by cutting around the edge. The meat then stays intact in the carapace, which serves as a handy bowl. The juices left in the bottom of the shell may also be drunk.

Sea turtles and their eggs are a potential survival food. Victims of ocean capsizes often tell of sea turtles coming alongside floating rafts, close enough to be grabbed. On remote tropical beaches during egg-laying season they are also found. If chasing a small turtle through the shallows, flip it onto its back at once rather than trying to grab at a flipper.

To cook a large sea turtle, make a slit in the underside of the neck and remove the liver, intestines and any fat through the hole. Heat several stones (about tennis ball size) in a large fire and stuff them into the body cavity through the neck hole. Tie up the neck cavity with fishing line or pack it with leaves. Leave the turtle to roast from the inside for a couple of hours. In the meantime the previously removed offal and any eggs are cooked on the coals, along with the legs which are sliced off.

Detect turtle eggs along the beach by probing a long stick into the sand where tracks and obvious digging activity are evident. Eggs may be up to a metre below the surface of the sand. The raw soft-shelled eggs are very thirst-quenching.

Snakes are perfectly good bush food in an emergency. Australia is home to several potentially deadly species so extreme caution is needed when killing any snake for food. A long, springy branch enables you to club it to death without getting too close. When in doubt always assume a snake is poisonous. Hundreds of people are bitten on the hand by snakes each year in Australia while trying to harass, move or handle these creatures, so never try to pin a snake to the ground with your hand. Use a lengthy branch with a small fork at one end. Even venomous snakes are edible - just cut off the head and poison glands before cooking. Cook snakes whole on the coals and skin before eating.

Some pythons grow to large size and provide plenty of meat, though the numerous bones are a drawback. File snakes are meaty and surprisingly abundant in many northern waterholes. Aboriginal women on bush tucker trips in Arnhem Land locate them by feeling around in the mud with their feet. The snake is then yanked out of the water and quickly killed, a process accomplished by holding the reptile's head in the mouth and giving the body a sharp tug. This breaks its neck.

Once again, the killing and eating of reptiles should be confined to a true survival predicament. *All native Australian reptiles are protected species and some are endangered.*

FISH

In coastal and river areas fish are normally the most reliable protein source. The emergency hooks and line in your survival kit become precious when you're stranded near a body of water. In the tropics a wire trace is desirable so fewer hooks are lost to small sharks and other predators.

There is no need to lose hope if you're without fishing gear. Hand-spun fishing line made from plant fibres will substitute for store-bought monofilament. Improvise hooks from carved pieces of wood, bits of shell, large thorns, bones or catfish barbs. Safety pins don't work as well as you might expect but are better than nothing. Add some barbs for extra grip if carving a hook out of wood.

For best results use bait from the local area. The soft flesh of hermit crabs, mangrove snails and other tidal creatures is good bait. Earthworms, live insects, spiders and yabbies perform well in fresh water. Capture bait fish in the shallows using a knotted shirt, stuff sack or your hat's fly net.

Make artificial lures from aluminium foil, coloured cloth or shiny metal. Anything you can find that glitters, spins, wobbles or resembles natural prey is worth trying. Even torn scraps of white plastic bag dragged through the water have hooked big fish.

In a survival situation rig a night line, a length of fishing line with half a dozen hooks spaced evenly along its length. A rock tied to the end anchors it to the bottom. The top end is secured to a branch on the bank. Put the line out before bedtime and check it first thing in the morning. If you're stuck in an area for awhile and have enough fresh bait, leave the line out during the day as well.

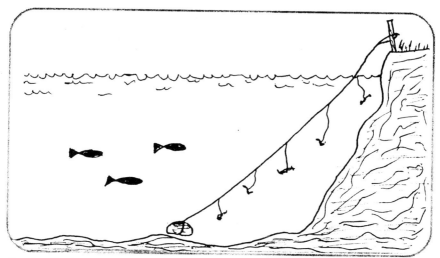

Passive fishing with a night-line is possible when bait is plentiful, though sharks sometimes get to the catch before you do.

Aside from hook and line fishing you can also make a fish spear or fish traps. A knife lashed tightly to the end of a branch makes a serviceable spear, though there's always a chance the knife may come off and be lost in murky water. Spears should be lightweight and as straight as possible. A pronged spear is best. Bind three or four shorter sticks to the business end of the spear shaft. Sharpen the tips to a fine point and harden them in the fire. Barbed spear points give maximum holding power.

Spearing is easiest at low tide when fish get trapped in rock pools or reefs by receding water. Probing your spear into holes on a shallow reef can often bring results. With moving fish try to get directly above the prey and spear downward. If spearing at an angle, aim slightly low to compensate for water refraction. Fishing with a spear takes practice but is effective in the hands of experts. Numerous instances are documented from early settlement where Aboriginal spearmen easily out-fished settlers using conventional fishing methods in the same location.

In clear inland waterholes a combination of swimming and spearing is worth a try. Species such as sooty grunter are curious and will approach a swimmer to within a metre.

Practising survival skills in the Top End has its rewards.

Traps work on the basic principle that fish enter a narrow opening and are trapped by the falling tide or an inability to find their way back out. They can be time-consuming to build, but certainly worth the effort if no other fishing method is available.

Make fish nets from natural plant fibre, parachute cord or twine. Fishing line makes a very strong net. Net-making is a handy survival skill that's easy to learn.

If fish aren't biting near the edge of a waterhole try your luck in deeper water with a sail float. This is made from any sort of buoyant wood. In the tropics old palm frond bases are suitable. A miniature mast, keel and sail are attached and a line is tied to the 'stern' to feed it out into deep water from an upwind position. Three or four baited hooks dangle a metre or so below the float. It sounds fiddly but it works.

Always fish from a ledge in crocodile country.

A light above the water attracts fish at night. Another trick is to place a mirror or weighted square of alfoil in shallow water - fish are drawn to the reflected sun or moonlight.

Don't discount the value of tiny fish. If captured in quantity, fingerlings are useful food. The tiniest fish (under 6 cm) can be cooked in hot ashes and swallowed whole, or boiled and crushed into a paste. If boiling fish, drink the leftover fluid - it too has food value.

Cook smaller fish by gutting them and placing in the coals of the fire. Don't throw the innards away - they make ideal bait. Bake larger fish in a ground oven. In most cases scaling is unnecessary. Fish skin is nutritious so don't waste it. Don't eat triggerfish, pufferfish or porcupine fish and be wary of sharp spines prevalent on many species, especially catfish. Avoid the razor-sharp bony plates near the gills of barramundi.

SHELLFISH

Australia's aquatic environments are rich in edible bivalves, crustaceans and gastropods. Mangrove areas are especially bountiful, though collection is a muddy experience.

Rock oysters are excellent food. Pry them open with a knife and eat raw or harvest them the Aboriginal way. At low tide, pile dry grass on top of the oysters and set it alight. The fire should be quick and hot, burning out in three or four minutes. This brief steaming opens the shells but doesn't allow the flesh to toughen.

Mud oysters (*Batissa violacea*) live just below the surface of the mangrove mud. Locate them by poking a stick in the mud near the roots. Mud crabs are another mangrove delicacy, detected by their burrows. When these are found the surrounding mud is tapped with a strong stick until it 'clunks'. The crab is then dug out at once.

Black nerites (*Nerita lineata*) look like small grey snails that cling to the lower roots of mangrove trees, often in great numbers. The raw flesh inside makes good bait and can also be boiled and eaten. The clam-like flavour is bland. Dozens are needed for a decent feed but in the tropics they are an easily collected protein source.

Mangrove worms (shipworms) live in the wood of tidal mangroves. Cut mangrove roots open with a knife or break them to extract the worms, which are actually molluscs. Remove the tail and the hard plates at the head end. Their stomach contents should be milked out to reduce the unpleasant woody flavour. The larger pinkish-grey ones can grow over 25 centimetres long and may be eaten raw. The smaller white ones irritate the throat unless cooked.

Away from the coast, freshwater mussels, yabbies and jungle land snails (*Xanthomelon pachystylum*) can be collected, cooked and eaten. Catch yabbies by tying a small piece of meat to the end of a string, dropping it into the river and pulling it out slowly when the yabbie clings to it. Some will escape just as you're making a grab for them. Very slow hand movements are crucial for success. Yabbie traps are more effective. One of the simplest is an old billy with several holes punched into the bottom. Tie a length of fishing line to the handle, tie a scrap of meat (such as a tiny lizard or frog) to the inside of the billy and lower it into the water. When yabbies go after the bait you sharply yank the billy straight out of the water. The holes in the bottom reduce drag so you can pull it up quickly before the yabbies react.

If you have no billy you can make a trap out of reeds, weaving them into a rough bottle shape so the yabbies must enter through one small opening in search of the bait tied inside. Leave the trap underwater and check it every half hour.

INSECTS

Insects comprise a huge segment of the animal kingdom but are largely ignored by humans as food. They are often the most reliable source of animal food for the survivor. Most insects are edible. You get more food value by eating them raw, but cooking in the ashes or boiling removes the possibility of harmful parasites and increases palatability.

Termites are tasty and nutritious; chunks of their mounds can be broken off with a rock and submerged in water to flush out the insects. This is also a good way to attract fish. Poke a reed or small twig into ant or termite holes, then slowly draw it out with the insects attached. The eggs are good food too. Clumps of termite nest added to your campfire produce a long-lasting smoke that deters mosquitoes.

Collect grasshoppers or crickets by hand, swat them with a branch or use a net made from a shirt. Remove the spiky legs, wings and antennae and roast in the ashes. Grasshoppers are high in food value, especially protein.

Grind large numbers of ants or termites into a paste. Eat this on its own or add to other foods. Bite off the large abdomens of green ants; they have a refreshing lemon taste. Beware - they sting if you don't get them first. Honey ants (*Melophorus*) which store a sweet nectar in their bloated abdomens always rate a mention in survival books, which seem to suggest they're easy to obtain and found all over Central Australia. In reality their distribution is very limited and a foraging survivor (even in the right spot) is unlikely to locate them. An organised bush tucker tour out of Alice Springs is your best chance of seeing these unique insects.

Australia's best known insect food is the witchetty grub, found in the roots of the witchetty bush (*Acacia kempeana*). Most other wood-dwelling grubs are edible as well, but avoid hairy caterpillars as the hairs may be irritant. Any brightly coloured insects should be ignored. Their appearance is a warning that they are unpalatable or poisonous. Insects exuding an unpleasant smell should also be left alone.

March flies, dragonflies, moths and other flying insects make good food if you can capture enough of them. A white sheet strung between trees at night attracts flying insects when a torch is shined on it. Even the introduced honey bee may be eaten. Hold a lighted bundle of grass near their nest entrance to fill it with smoke. Do this at night when the bees are inactive inside. After filling the nest with smoke, plug the entrance. This traps the bees inside and kills them. *Before eating bees remove the legs, wings, stinger and poison sac.* Taste is enhanced by boiling or roasting in the fire. Bees' honey is the finest emergency bush food available, providing instant energy. It is excellent for reviving victims of physical exhaustion.

Native bees are stingless and resemble small black flies. They are often attracted to human sweat. Capture one and tie a tiny piece of spider web or coloured thread to its body. Then track it visually to its nest in a hollow tree or old termite mound. The honey is a high-energy snack and the bees themselves may also be eaten. This is hard to avoid anyway since they always get mixed in with handfuls of honey pulled from the nest. The yellow balls of pollen and beeswax are edible too.

In addition to insects, another source of protein is the earthworm. Collect a supply and keep them in a container overnight to allow their insides to clean out. Worms can be sun-dried on a rock and kept for days.

PLANT FOODS

To identify plants, Wild Food Plants of Australia (*Tim Low, Angus & Robertson*) is a useful field guide. It's small enough for the rucksack and well worth packing on any wilderness trip.

Many Australian plants are edible but others are highly poisonous. Of the safe varieties there are varying levels of palatability. Some plant foods cherished by Aboriginal people will seem overly tart, stringy or sour to non-Aboriginal foragers. This is nothing more than palate conditioning.

Research on the vitamin content of indigenous plants has brought to light the exceptional food value of many species. The nutrition stored in

154

some native seeds and tubers in many cases exceeds that of closely related cultivated foods. For example, wattle seed damper compares very favourably with any store-bought wholemeal bread in protein and fat content.

Surviving in the bush on plant foods alone is difficult. A survivor's aim is maximum calories with plenty of protein, fat and carbohydrates. Therefore fish, insects, reptiles and other animal foods are a more sustaining choice than plant material. Wild plants will often benefit the survivor more as bush medicine than food.

Because medical help isn't readily accessible in a survival situation, *extreme caution is necessary when trying any new plants*. Toxin levels in many Australian species are formidable. The rule with any wild plant is simple - if in doubt, leave it alone.

TUBERS

Aside from animal food, tubers are probably the most useful source of energy for bush survival. Being hidden underground they are more difficult to locate than other plant foods but are well worth the effort. Tubers store water, starch and sugar and are often found where vines, lilies, ground orchids or water plants are visible. Native tubers vary from long and stringy to tiny and bulbous. Though botanists differentiate between tubers, corms, bulbs and rhizomes, any swollen extension of a plant found underground can be viewed as a tuber for survival purposes.

It's more practical to unearth lots of small tubers than to dig deeply for one large one, which may be a full metre underground. Some larger tropical yams also contain bitter toxins, which Aboriginal women are skilled at leaching out in a lengthy process. The 'Cheeky' Yam *Dioscorea bulbifera* is finely grated, soaked overnight in a fast-flowing stream and baked before it is considered safe to eat. Its yellow flesh and rounded shape distinguish it from the white-fleshed Long Yam *Dioscorea transversa*, frequently found near tropical beaches. Smaller long yams may be eaten raw while larger ones are better cooked. Clean but don't peel them. Both these species have thin vines and heart-shaped leaves.

Freshwater billabongs are the place to seek out the tubers of sedges and other aquatic species that are edible raw. Bulrushes, spike rushes (*Eliocharus dulcis*), water ribbons, clubrushes and water lilies are common water plants yielding tubers. All parts of a water lily may be eaten - pods, stalks, flowers, seeds and bulbs.

Tubers to avoid include those of the large-leafed lilies: cunjevoi, black arum, Polynesian arrowroot, taro and similar. The toxins in the roots of these plants are extremely irritating to the throat.

SEEDS AND NUTS

Seeds are the most energy-packed of all plant foods but the collecting, winnowing, grinding, baking and other work needed to render smaller seeds edible is time consuming. Virtually any type of grass seed may be ground up between rocks and baked into a damper.

Kurrajong seed pods contain about half a dozen tasty and nutritious yellow seeds. Damper made from the crushed seeds has a nutty flavour and is high in fat. The hairy 'packing material' in the pods is highly poisonous, however, and must be completely removed. The Aboriginal method of preparation involves baking the seeds and hairy pith together in the fire. The roasted seeds are then rubbed between the palms to allow the toxic hairs to blow away in the wind. This is performed upwind so no irritant material blows into the eyes. Wash hands well after handling the material inside kurrajong pods.

The quandong is best known as an edible fruit but its dry seeds also yield food. Crack them open to reveal an edible, oil-rich kernel. Other plants with edible seeds include common pigweed (*Portulaca oleracea*), woolybutt (*Eragrostis eriopoda*), Mitchell grass (*Astrelba pectinata*) and wild millet (*Panicum decompositum*).

Wild nuts (as well as native beans and peas) are best avoided. Most species need extensive pulverising, soaking and other toxin-leaching techniques to make them safe to eat. The energy used in preparing the nuts will normally exceed that derived from them. Many are dangerously poisonous. An exception is the bush peanut (*Sterculia quadrifida*) which can be eaten raw straight from the pod. In northwestern Australia the mineral-rich pith and seeds of boabs are also edible raw. Collect the mature nuts before they dry out and become too hard.

FRUIT

A variety of native bush fruits may be eaten. Only a few (such as the native raspberry) resemble their cultivated counterparts in flavour and appearance. Most taste tart, acidic, dry or bitter to European palates. Juicier varieties serve as thirst quenchers while on the move.

Because some fruits are poisonous it's wise to carry a field guide illustrating the safe varieties. Some well-known native fruits include bush tomatoes (*Solanum*), wild figs, desert bananas (*Leichhardtia australis*), lillipillies, quandongs, bush peaches (*Terminalia carpentariae*), cocky apples (*Planchonia careya*) and emu berries (*Grewia retusifolia*).

The small berries of the common dodder laurel (*Cassytha melantha*) are tangy and plentiful in season. Geebungs are easily recognised, resembling a grape with a single spike extending from the bottom of the smooth, greenish fruit. Cheese fruit (*Morinda citrifolia*) tastes and smells like rotten cheese so calling it palatable is generous, but is has good food value and is used in many ways as Aboriginal bush medicine.

Coastal areas provide ample opportunities for fruit foraging. The midyim shrub (*Austromyrtus dulcis*) found in southeastern Queensland produces delicious speckled berries. Western Victoria and South Australia are home to muntari (*Kunzea pomifera*), a creeper bearing a profusion of tasty fruits in late summer. In the Top End the tasty red fruits of the lady apple (*Syzygium suborbiculare*) are found both in coastal dunes and further inland.

Many introduced plants are useful survival tucker. Wild passionfruit, guavas and blackberries are prolific in many areas, even far from settlement. The fruit of the prickly pear is edible but covered with irritating hairs. It shouldn't be handled with bare hands. Chop the purplish-red fruit from the plant with a knife and let it fall to the ground. Slice it in half and scoop out the sticky inner pulp. This way you never touch the well-armed fruit's exterior.

As with many other types of bush tucker, fruits are subject to seasonal fluctuations in availability. You must know not only where the fruit is likely to be found but the time of year that it ripens. Even then the weather may thwart your foraging efforts - too much (or too little) rain can make certain fruits unavailable during their normal season.

LEAVES AND SHOOTS

Early explorers sampled the greenery of many native plants, mostly with disappointing results. Foliage is a less significant emergency food than fruits, seeds or tubers. Only a handful of indigenous greens are of interest to the survivor. Among these are pigweed (*Portulaca oleracea*), New Zealand spinach (*Tetragonia tetragonoides*) and various water lily species.

The mat-rush *Lomandra longifolia* is a common plant along watercourses. The white inner base of the stems has a pleasant snow pea flavour when eaten raw. New shoots of the common bulrush are also good food. Several varieties of saltbush are edible as a cooked vegetable. Boil the leaves to take away the saltiness. Other plants used as cooked greens are pigface, sea purslane, watercress and sea celery. The tender white tips of newly sprouted grasses provide tangible nutrition and may be eaten raw.

The starchy 'heart' at the top of tree ferns (*Dicksonia antarctica*) and some palm trees is edible either raw or cooked. Unfortunately removing it also kills the tree, so this should never be done except in an emergency.

Suburban weeds sometimes find their way into remote bush. Species safe to eat raw or cooked include chickweed, dandelion, dock, sowthistle, peppercress, cats-ear, amaranth and wood-sorrel. Tender young plants picked when the ground is moist are best. Older dried-out plants tend to be bitter. Cook them with a brief steaming. Overcooking destroys vitamin content.

Don't ignore seaweed and algae. Seaweed is rich in minerals and vitamins. Use fresh growing seaweed, not decaying material washed up on the beach. Most seaweed is best when boiled but may be nibbled raw. Sea lettuce (*Ulva lactuca*) is a widespread edible variety in Australia. Avoid seaweed that smells bad and just eat small amounts at a time. Don't eat seaweed if you're low on water - it increases thirst.

Bright green algae (*Spirogyra*) clinging to rocks in shallow fresh water is edible, though its flavour is negligible and its slimy consistency unappealing. Eat it raw after a good rinsing. *Only healthy green algae should ever be eaten.* The infamous blue-green algae that periodically infests some waterways is highly toxic. It is identified by its bluish green tinge, unpleasant gaseous odour and the fact that it floats in stagnant water. Bright green algae attaches to rocks.

OTHER PLANT FOODS

Suck nectar directly from flowers or make a drink by soaking blossoms in water. Grevilleas, banksias, tea-trees, mat-rushes and eucalypts yield ample nectar at the right times of year. Silky oak and banksia flowers become so saturated with nectar that it drips to the ground.

The best plan with wild fungi is to ignore them. Nutritive benefits of unknown bush mushrooms are far outweighed by the danger of poisoning from one of the toxic varieties. Cooking poisonous wild mushrooms does nothing to remove their toxins.

The gum that exudes from some trees and shrubs provides a useful snack. Softer gums are eaten like toffee and harder ones baked in the ashes, crushed to a powder and mixed with water. Unfortunately the vast majority of Australian tree gums aren't palatable. Only a few plants yield the sweet, lighter-coloured gums. These include casuarina, kurrajong, bauhinia and terminalia trees, as well as several types of wattle.

Lerps (also called manna) are sweet, white encrustations left behind by insect activity on gum leaves. Scrape as much as you can into a container to mix with water or nibble directly from leaves. In arid regions the round, grey-coloured insect galls found on bloodwood trees contain an edible grub as well as a small amount of refreshing liquid. Some of these galls are nearly as large as a tennis ball. Only the fresh, greyish-tan galls (not the old, dried-up brown ones) are edible.

158

PLANT EDIBILITY TEST

With survival at stake you may decide to sample unfamiliar plants. The abundance of poisonous, irritant or otherwise harmful plants in Australia makes this risky. Minimize risk by following the steps listed below in precise order. DO NOT take short cuts with this edibility test.

1. Select a fresh-looking plant free from obvious disease. When selecting greenery, younger leaves and shoots are preferable to older specimens which may be bitter or toxic.

2. Crush a piece of the plant and hold it to your nose. Reject any with the odour of peaches or bitter almonds.

3. Rub a little of the crushed plant on the skin of your arm. Wait two minutes. If swelling, rash or other irritation occurs, reject the plant. If not, go to steps 4-7 in order, *waiting a full minute between each step* to see if any ill effects occur. If throat soreness, burning sensation or any other discomfort is experienced, reject the plant.

4. Touch a small portion to your lips. Wait one minute.

5. Touch a tiny portion to your tongue. Wait one minute.

6. Chew a small piece *without* swallowing. Wait one minute.

7. If all is well so far, chew and swallow a small portion. It is then wise to wait a couple of hours (at least) to see how your stomach handles matters. Eat or drink nothing else during this wait. If there's no sign of trouble, then eat five times the amount previously consumed and wait a full eight hours. If you're still okay after this you may assume the part of the plant which you've eaten is safe. Do not assume *all* parts of the plant are safe just because you have tested one section. Some plants have edible seeds but poisonous leaves. Others may have poisonous milky sap but edible fruit, etc.

General foraging rules: Avoid native beans and peas, cycads, wild mushrooms and large seeds. Don't eat too much of a plant at one time. Some are fine in small doses but cause stomach upset if consumed in bulk. Tropical rainforests are home to an array of irritant and toxic plants so take care in these areas. Trust your nose and taste buds. Reject plants which smell or taste bitter or unpleasant.

FOOD PRESERVATION

Waste nothing in a survival situation. Make tools or fish hooks with animal bones. Dried hides can become clothing or containers. Meat is precious in the bush so make the most of it. Preserve what you don't eat for later use. This also applies to fish and plant foods.

Store preserved foods in plastic bags or other waterproof, airtight containers. Exposure to heat, dampness or direct sunlight speeds up deterioration of stored foods.

Preservation Methods

Climate, circumstances and available materials determine the ways in which extra food is preserved in a survival situation:

Sun Drying	Heat Drying
Smoking	Salting
Freezing	Keeping the animal alive

Sun dried fish has kept life raft survivors alive on many occasions. The same process can be used in the bush, provided the breeze is sufficient to keep flies at bay. Strong sunshine and sustained winds are the best conditions for sun drying. Thin strips of kangaroo meat may take up to two weeks to sun dry. Fattier meats (such as duck) are very hard to dry and are better preserved by rubbing salt into the flesh.

Dry fish fillets on a rack made of branches. Get the rack up and ready before you start catching fish. Leave plenty of space between the poles for air circulation. When the fillets are brittle and devoid of moisture they are ready for storage. Don't rush the process. Over-drying is preferable to pulling them off the rack too soon.

Earthworms, termite eggs, fruits and herbs can be dried by spreading them out on a hot rock in the sun. Crush dried foods into a powder and add to soups or rice.

Drying food over a fire is quicker than using the sun. Suspend the items on a spit above the fire. You want to dry the food rather than cook it, so ensure the fire doesn't get too hot. Slice meat, fish or fruit as thinly as you can without it falling apart.

A tripod rack is a convenient way to smoke meat or fish.

Smoking dries out food and provides a protective seal against bacteria. Use green leaves rather than grass to increase smoke on the fire. Reduce the fire to hot embers for use with a smoking rack. Avoid flames. Not only do they cook food instead of smoking it, but they may reach high enough to ignite the rack itself.

Freezing is a viable preservation method in parts of Australia where temperatures get low enough. Ensure the item is completely frozen. Food that partially thaws and then re-freezes can cause serious stomach upsets from bacteria thriving in the temperature changes.

Station stockmen in the Top End preserve large chunks of beef by rubbing salt generously into the flesh. This works best when excess fat is trimmed away first. Another option is to boil the meat and then keep it in very salty water until needed. This keeps bacteria from getting to it.

The final method of preservation is simple - keep the animal alive until you need it. If you've eaten your fill in a survival situation and then encounter a goanna, snake, crab or small mammal, don't let the opportunity for a later meal go by. Capture the creature and keep it alive for future use.

Survival Priorities
Navigation

1. Learn how to use maps and compass before you go bush. Orienteering, bushwalking and scouting associations run very worthwhile courses in direction-finding.

2. If you are lost, STOP! Relax and drink some water. Panic can kill - don't start crashing through the bush. Think before moving again. Retrace steps if possible. Choose the safest route to backtrack to known landmarks.

3. Always inform someone of your intended route, anticipated return time and the sort of gear you're carrying. If rescuers know you have a signal reflector, blue tarp or red rucksack for example, such facts will be helpful if a search has to be initiated.

4. Trust your compass. Take bearings several metres away from your vehicle - its metal can affect the reading.

5. Small variations between true north and grid north can be ignored for most bush navigation, but the difference in grid north and magnetic north can be over 10 degrees. This magnetic variation is displayed on your map. Use it to convert map bearings to compass bearings.

6. Use map and compass to monitor your course regularly. Straying off course results in wasted fuel (vehicles) or wasted energy (trekkers).

7. When bushwalking, periodically look behind you as you travel. If you ever need to backtrack the route will then appear more familiar.

8. You may have map but no compass, compass but no map or neither. Use all available direction-finding indicators: sun, moon, stars, wristwatch and wind direction.

Finding Your Way

Bush navigation is more than just using map and compass. Sensible judgement, careful observation of surroundings and ability to interpret the position of sun and stars are all part of direction-finding.

Aiming the compass in the direction you want to travel is the easy part; following the desired bearing may not be. Detours around rock outcrops, thorny vegetation, impassable cliffs and flooded swamps are common once you stray from walking tracks. In these instances a compass is reduced to a mere indicator of general direction. Fog, snowstorms and heavy rain also play havoc with compass navigation by reducing visibility.

With maps the problem lies in what they do *not* tell you: that the tiny creek ahead has turned into a swirling torrent from recent rains; that the landscape is choked with prickly shrubs or ankle-wrenching boulders; that the thick, head-high grass hides a network of deep holes, invisible until you are nearly on top of them.

Sometimes a waterway can be followed downstream to civilisation, but not always. A creek bank can be a demanding place to walk, with thick vegetation, oozy mud and rocky gorges. Sticking to higher ground may be faster and offers a better chance to see distant landmarks. On a ridge you have a clearer view of the bends of the river ahead and can take short-cuts between them to save time.

In northern Australia many waterways lead to remote, mangrove-fringed coasts and nothing more, though from a survival standpoint this is not always a bad result. The mouth of a tropical river offers reasonable chances of being spotted by passing fishing boats or aircraft, and bush tucker is generally more plentiful in such areas than further inland.

MAPS

For outdoor purposes topographic maps are the best choice. The 1:100,000 scale is detailed enough for most bushwalking, inland kayaking or 4WD trips. At this scale one centimetre on the map equals one kilometre in the bush. The 1:250,000 scale shows a larger area in less detail but is suitable for general outback driving. Anything less detailed than 1:100,000 or 1:250,000 is inadequate for bush navigation. Tourist maps are useful for local information on specific areas but not for serious bush travel. Topographical maps are available from AUSLIG (the national mapping agency in Canberra) as well as most map stores.

Maps are full of information which assists survival. The brown contour lines show the layout of the landscape in regard to relative elevation. This helps in selecting the safest and least arduous route through difficult terrain. Contour lines indicate steep terrain when close together and more level ground when spaced apart.

Contour lines on a topographic map show you the shape of the land. To navigate you must correlate this information with the terrain around you.

Whether heading toward water or searching for a spot to await rescue, proper interpretation of map features cuts down time and energy in getting there. Maps can show you the easiest route for medical evacuations, the most promising campsite locations or the best way to escape from thick vegetation or swampy ground.

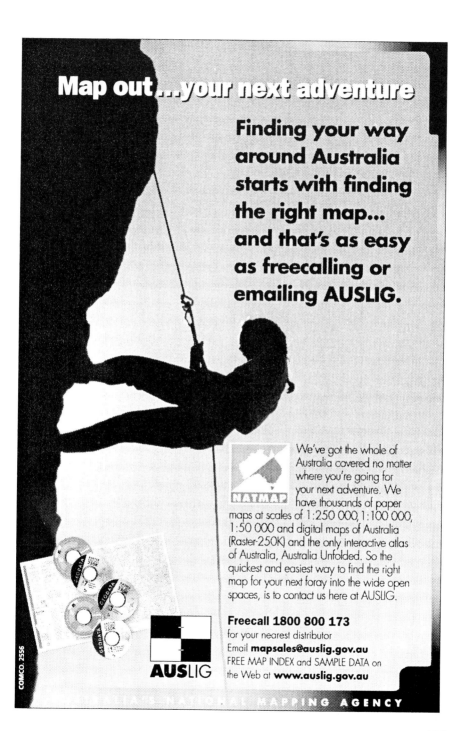

Map out ...your next adventure

Finding your way around Australia starts with finding the right map... and that's as easy as freecalling or emailing AUSLIG.

We've got the whole of Australia covered no matter where you're going for your next adventure. We have thousands of paper maps at scales of 1:250 000, 1:100 000, 1:50 000 and digital maps of Australia (Raster-250K) and the only interactive atlas of Australia, Australia Unfolded. So the quickest and easiest way to find the right map for your next foray into the wide open spaces, is to contact us here at AUSLIG.

Freecall 1800 800 173
for your nearest distributor
Email **mapsales@auslig.gov.au**
FREE MAP INDEX and SAMPLE DATA on the Web at **www.auslig.gov.au**

AUSLIG

COMCO. 2556

AUSTRALIA'S NATIONAL MAPPING AGENCY

FIRST, ORIENT YOUR MAP

To use a map you must first orient it, turning it so that features on the map correspond with the terrain in front of you. Keep the map oriented as you travel. This is easy with a compass, but even without one you can keep a degree of control by paying close attention to changes in slope and the position of the sun and known landmarks. Being able to estimate your speed accurately over the ground in varied terrain will also help you get a fix on your position.

Grid lines on a map are spaced both horizontally and vertically, essentially dividing the map into numerous small squares. These are handy for measuring distances and pinpointing locations. Vertical grid lines are aligned north to south. There is a marginal difference between 'grid north' and 'true north' but this is so minor in Australia that it can virtually be ignored. The difference between the two stems from the fact that the earth is round and maps are flat. It's easier to portray the lines as straight rather than curved. 'Magnetic north' is also shown on the map and may be several degrees different from true north. The red needle on your compass points to magnetic north.

At the bottom of the topographical map is a key to the various symbols used. These indicate man-made features (buildings, dams, roads, etc.) and natural features (types of vegetation, swamps, whether a beach is sandy or muddy, etc.). There is a certain amount of standardisation on maps. Creeks are normally shown as a single blue line, though the real width of the stream will of course vary depending on recent rainfall. Larger rivers (especially in the tropics) are displayed at both dry season levels (solid blue) and wet season flood levels (added dotted lines). Man-made features are generally represented as black, vegetation as a shade of green, waterways as blue and surface features (cliff edges, roads, elevation changes) as brown.

Check the map's date. For some parts of the country the most recent map available in the scale desired may be twenty years old. Natural features don't change much in that time but man-made features do. Roads are altered, tracks obliterated by vegetation, rivers diverted and outback settlements abandoned. Seek local advice when concerned about an older map.

Measuring distance on a map is a simple matter of using the scale bar and a straight edge (such as the edge of your compass). A piece of thread can be placed on the map to measure meandering routes, then stretched out against the scale for the total distance. Small map measurers are available that do the same job.

Gradients must be taken into account. For example, climbing up a 45 degree slope for one kilometre adds an extra 41 metres to the actual walking distance. The contour interval (distance between contour lines) is shown at the bottom of your map.

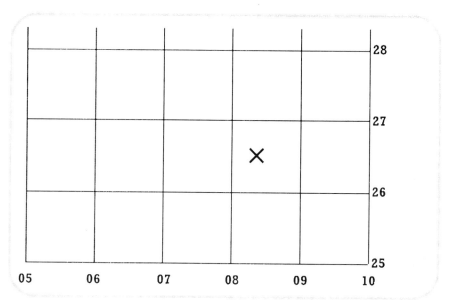

If you ever have to radio your position to someone (such as the Royal Flying Doctor Service) the most accurate way is with a map grid reference. A six digit reference is the most precise. The first three digits give your vertical position (this is always quoted first in any grid reference) and the last three give the horizontal. In the example above you are to the right of the 08 vertical grid line, and (dividing the grid square into tenths) you estimate your position to be about three tenths from the 08 line. Therefore the first three digits of your grid reference are 083. Moving to the horizontal grid, you are above the 26 line by five tenths so your last three digits are 265. Your complete grid reference would therefore be given as 083265. This tells people exactly where you are on the specified topographic map.

When survival depends upon getting somewhere within a certain time it helps to know how fast you're travelling so you can predict pace over the landscape. How far in one day can a person walk in trackless bush? There are too many variables for a simple answer. In flat open country a fit person might trek over thirty kilometres if rest stops are brief. In Tasmanian rainforests the tangle of undergrowth, fallen trees and uneven ground can slow progress right down; six kilometres a day may be all that's possible. Scrambling up and down sandstone escarpments in the Northern Territory is also snail-paced, with more time spent moving vertically than horizontally. Shirt-catching thorns and dense, tall grass all reduce pace over the course of a full day.

Most walkers overestimate off-trail speed when planning trips. A tight schedule from A to B leaves little room for the unexpected. *Always give yourself time to spare.* Haste works in the city but leads to trouble in the bush. A sore knee, worsening blister or maze of ankle-grabbing vines can cut foot speed in half. Allow for unforeseen problems.

If you're heading some distance from camp but have no map you should make your own. Take pen and paper and mark down distinguishing landmarks as you go - distinctive cliffs, big boulders, waterways, lone trees or bushes recognisable from any direction. Making a bush map improves observation skills and prevents confusion when returning to camp. More than one bushwalker has put down a pack in rough country, wandered off a hundred metres or so and then been unable to find the pack for hours after taking one wrong turn.

COMPASS

A hand-held compass is a reliable and indispensable tool for bush navigation. The compass is divided into 360 degrees. North is at zero, east at 090, south at 180 and west at 270. The compass is a simple instrument when used simply. Practise the basics in familiar surroundings before venturing into the bush.

Attach a loop of sturdy cord to the compass and suspend it from your neck. This is the best place for it. In open woodland the 'tree to tree method' is used to stay precisely on a bearing. If, for example, the desired bearing is 190, raise the compass to the horizon and scan ahead to find a distant tree top at exactly 190 degrees. Tuck the compass out of sight and walk until you reach the base of that tree. Pull out the compass again and repeat the process with another treetop, etc. This is far more efficient than the 'rubberneck method' where the compass is clutched constantly and progress checked every twenty seconds or so.

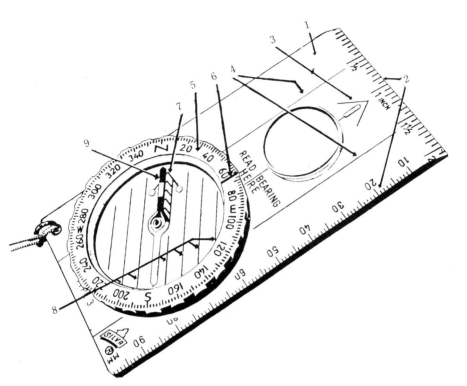

*PARTS OF A COMPASS - 1. Base plate 2. Base plate edge 3. Travel arrow
4. Aid lines 5. Rotating dial (zero to 360 degrees) 6. Index marker (which
lines up with the travel arrow) 7. Orienting arrow 8. Parallel orienting lines
9. Magnetic compass needle (the red end always points to magnetic north).*

It's possible to improvise a crude compass by magnetising a sewing
needle and suspending it in the air by a thread, so it hangs horizontally
from its middle. It will then swing around to align itself to north and south.
Another way is to fill a nonmetallic container with water and float the magnet-
ised needle on the surface on top of a small piece of paper or blade of
grass. The problem with a makeshift needle compass is how to magnetise it:
You must stroke it repeatedly in one direction against a piece of silk or (much
better) a pocket magnet, two items not normally found in the average rucksack. Also, a slight breeze or the presence of ferrous rock nearby may give a
totally false reading. Even when the needle aligns perfectly with magnetic
north and south it's up to you to determine which end points where, using
other indicators such as the sun's direction. Needle compasses are a favourite of survival manuals but the alternatives are simpler - *always* carry a
spare compass and learn to tell direction from sun, moon and stars.

TOO MANY NORTHS

For navigation novices the confusing part of the exercise is working out which north to use. Topographic maps normally display a diagram showing directions of True North, Grid North and Magnetic North. Others may only have a little notice saying something like "Magnetic variation is approximately 3 degrees (50 mm) easterly over the entire area". True North is where the geographic North Pole is, but for most navigation purposes it's an irrelevance - forget about it. What's important is Grid North (the vertical grid lines shown on your map) and Magnetic North (where your compass always points). For purposes of explanation the difference between Grid North and Magnetic North will be referred to in this book as the 'magnetic variation'.

To be accurate with map and compass you have to compensate for this magnetic variation. One convenient way to do this is to draw your own magnetic meridians on the map at home before you go. First, determine the variation between Grid North and Magnetic North from the diagram on your map. Then, using a ruler and a protractor, draw a line from the bottom edge of the map (where it meets a vertical grid line) to the top border of the map at the angle of variation. In other words, if Magnetic North is to the east of Grid North by 9 degrees your freshly drawn magnetic meridian line will angle away to the right of the vertical grid line at a 9 degree angle. Once you've drawn one magnetic meridian it's a simple process to add parallel lines across the entire map at the same angle, 4 cm (or the width of your ruler) apart.

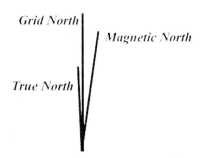

Now all your newly created lines point toward Magnetic North - the same as your compass. Having forgotten about True North, you can now forget about Grid North - the north on the compass now matches the north on the map. Now orient your map so it corresponds with the surrounding landscape by rotating it so the north-south magnetic meridian lines align with your compass needle.

Magnetic variation is not a constant because the earth's magnetic field is always changing. For this reason maps also tell you the annual change in magnetic variation. This is usually only a tiny fraction of one degree and isn't really significant unless you have a very old map. If, for example, the annual variation change is 1/10th of one degree to the east per year and your map is twenty years old, you'll need to add two full degrees to your magnetic variation.

DETERMINING YOUR POSITION

Confirming your location is the first step in compass navigation. You must know your starting point. To do this you check visible landmarks against information on your map, taking bearings on recognisable features of the terrain. Let's say that from where you're standing on a ridge you can see a peak, a jutting cliff and a small waterhole in the distance, which you recognise from your map. Take a bearing on the peak as follows:

1. Holding the compass in a horizontal position in front of you, take a bearing on the peak by sighting it along the direction of travel arrow.

2. Keeping the peak and the direction of travel arrow lined up, rotate the compass housing (without moving the base plate) until the orienting arrow (inside the housing underneath the needle) points in the same direction as north on the compass needle. Now read the peak's bearing.

3. Orient your map by placing it on the ground and rotating it so the top edge points to north.

4. Now place the compass on the map so that one front corner of the base plate touches the peak. If you have previously drawn your own magnetic meridian lines on the map, the magnetic needle, orienting arrow and your meridian lines should now all be aligned. Holding the base plate firmly on the map, draw a line from the peak back along the edge of the compass, continuing until you reach the map edge.

5. Now repeat the process with the cliff, then the waterhole. If there are other visible landmarks, take another bearing. Two is the minimum for an accurate fix but three or four are even better.

6. Where the three drawn lines intersect is your current position.

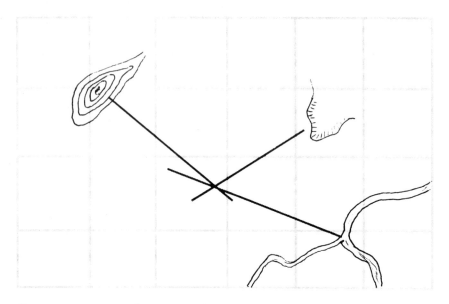

To get an accurate fix on your location, take bearings on three distinctive landmarks. Draw straight lines along those bearings on your map - your position is where all three lines meet.

FOLLOWING A BEARING

Once you know where you are you can decide the best route to reach your destination. Maps will tell you if a particular route is too steep, swampy or covered in rainforest, but 'terrain awareness' is needed to assess other route selection factors. Study the map to make initial decisions about obstacles in your path. Should they be waded through, clambered over or detoured around? Are there recognisable landmarks along the way to confirm your progress? Is there drinking water along the route? Choosing the best route is a combination of map and compass skills, observation and an understanding of your physical limitations. Don't choose the quickest route; choose the safest. To plan a course from point A to point B on the map:

1. Put the edge of the compass base plate along a line drawn between the two points, with the travel arrow pointed toward the destination.

172

2. Hold the base plate firmly and turn the circular housing until the orienting arrow beneath the compass needle is parallel with the magnetic meridian lines you've drawn on your map. The red (north) end of the needle will also be aligned with these, pointing north. Read the bearing where the dial meets the direction of travel arrow.

3. Now pick up the compass and hold it horizontally in front of you. Rotate your body until the orienting arrow lines up directly under the needle (as it did on the map).

4. The direction of travel arrow at the front edge of your compass now points to your destination.

Now let's say you haven't put hand-drawn meridian lines on your map as previously suggested (or you're using someone else's map). If that's the case you can use the Grid North lines instead, but you must then convert your grid bearings to magnetic bearings.

There are two ways to do this. If your grid bearing (the bearing using the map's Grid North lines as a north reference) is, say 120 degrees, to convert this to a magnetic bearing (which is what you want for compass use), look at the magnetic variation diagram on your map. If it tells you that magnetic north is five degrees to the east (or to the 'right') of Grid North, then *subtract* five degrees from 120. Your magnetic bearing is then 115. The rule to remember is that when the magnetic variation is to the west (or 'left') of Grid North, you need to *add* it. If it is to the east (right) you *subtract* it. Just remember the saying "East is Least".

If all this adding, subtracting and rule remembering seems far too much to bear there is a less mathematical way of adjusting for magnetic variation. Once you've got your grid bearing, place your compass on top of the map's magnetic variation diagram. Line up the orienting arrow with the Grid North line. Hold the base plate steady and turn the housing slightly until the orienting arrow now lines up with the magnetic north line. Your compass is now oriented to magnetic north, and your Grid Bearing has been converted to a magnetic bearing that reconciles with your compass.

It's not a bad idea to write down bearings and distances as you go and record how long it takes to traverse each straight leg. This helps you estimate future pace and is invaluable if you ever have to backtrack.

Precision navigation isn't always possible in a survival situation. Difficult terrain may make it necessary to purposely angle away from a desired course, sometimes for hours at a time. In the bush the straightest course is not necessarily the most sensible one.

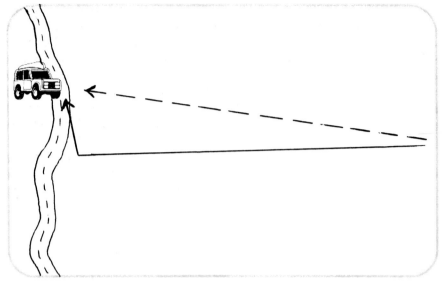

'Aiming off' is a useful method of ensuring you don't miss a destination such as a campsite along a creek or a vehicle parked on an isolated track. Suppose you've left your vehicle to hike to a waterhole 5 km away from the vehicle track. Your bearing to the waterhole is 110. You go and have your swim. Now to get back to the car you could set your compass for the opposite bearing (290) and backtrack until you reach the road again. But what if when you arrive the vehicle isn't there? Obviously you have strayed to the left or right of the bearing, but which? The best way to avoid this situation is to aim off to one side of the bearing (say 20 degrees to the left) on purpose. Then when you reach the track you know you need to turn right to get to the car.

TAKING A BACK BEARING

In theory, humans should be able to walk in a straight line. In practice we tend to walk around in circles. Even with a compass you can get sidetracked by several degrees while circling obstacles and fighting through vegetation. If the way ahead offers poorer visibility or less prominent landmarks than terrain behind you, take a back bearing to verify you're still on course.

Let's say you're trekking in a vast treeless plain with no distinguishing features on the horizon. You've spent the night beside a small hill, the only distinctive landmark visible in any direction. You want to reach a waterhole which your map says is thirteen kilometres away at a bearing of 260 from your hill. Since the terrain is flat, you decide 13 km is within your capabilities and you aim to reach the waterhole some time in the afternoon. You hoist the pack, set the compass on a bearing of 260 and head away from the hill. You soon discover the terrain is a collection of boggy mud patches caused by recent heavy rain. You make small detours around these obstacles, and this unavoidably takes you off your compass course for up to fifteen minutes at a time.

The way to make sure you are still on course after all these detours is to take a back bearing. Turn around and face the hill behind you in the distance. You know the bearing from hill to waterhole is 260; therefore the back bearing from waterhole to hill is exactly the opposite (or different by 180 degrees). On the opposite side of the compass dial from 260 is 080. Pointing your compass at the hill, it should be exactly at 080. If it is not you have strayed to the left or the right of your bearing, and need to get back on course.

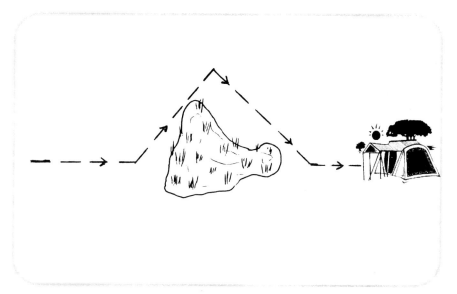

Using a controlled zigzag you can maintain your compass bearing around obstacles which prevent a straight line course. For example, if your camp is due east (090) but there's a swamp directly in your path, angle 45 degrees to the left of your course (now your new bearing is 045) and count paces until you reach the widest point of the swamp. Let's say you've walked 714 paces. Now, set your compass for 45 degrees to the <u>right</u> of your original 090 bearing (your new course is now 135). Walk until you have counted 714 paces again. Stop and reset the compass for 090. You are back on course for camp, minus the leeches.

IF YOU GET LOST

Being lost is a state of mind rather than a physical condition. Knowing where you are is simply a matter of using available information to narrow down the options until you can pinpoint your location on a map. You might then decide you don't like where you are, but you are still not 'lost'. If you have no idea where you are and have no map, make your own 'mud map' as you travel. Mark down prominent land features and measure distances in minutes from your watch or by counting steps taken between marked points. That way you can always backtrack to locate previously found water supplies or campsites again.

Statistically people are more likely to get lost when travelling alone, perhaps because panic tends to cloud reason more quickly. Two or more people can sit down and calmly reason out where they might have lost their way.

If you decide you're lost the thing to do is *stop, take a seat and calm down*. The situation is unlikely to worsen in the ten minutes used to take a few deep breaths, analyse the options and abate your tension. Check the map and find your last known position. If possible, try to slowly, carefully retrace your steps to get there. If it's getting dark, the weather is closing in or you're not physically up to it , don't try to backtrack - stay put to wait for better travelling conditions or rescue. Don't start crashing through the bush. Concentrate on conserving precious energy and making yourself visible to searchers. Hang bright clothing from trees. Have materials for a signal fire in readiness and break out the reflecting mirror. Relax, protect yourself from the elements and evaluate your water supply. If you've told people where you're going you shouldn't have to wait more than two or three days before someone comes looking. Anxiety and panic are your enemies - fight them.

NAVIGATING WITHOUT A COMPASS

USING THE SUN

Without a compass you can use the positions of sun, moon or stars to find your way. The sun always rises in the east and sets in the west. Time of year determines the exact position on the horizon where the sun rises and sets. In midwinter (around June 21 in Australia) the sun is further away from us to the north. In midsummer (about December 21) it is directly over the Tropic of Capricorn (roughly the latitude of Rockhampton and Alice Springs).

What this means is that if you place a stick upright in the ground at noon (anywhere in Australia in winter or south of the Tropic of Capricorn in summer) its shadow will point due south. It doesn't matter if you don't have a watch - the shadow stick also tells you if it is before noon or after. Scratch a line along the shadow's length and mark the end with a cross. Wait fifteen minutes and do this again. If the shadow is shrinking it is before noon; if it's getting longer it's afternoon. At noon (disregarding any daylight savings time) the shadow length is shortest. Shadows move anticlockwise in the Southern Hemisphere.

There are two ways to use a shadow stick to determine east-west.

1. This quick method works any time of day and regardless of whether you are north or south of the Tropic of Capricorn. The ground must be flat and clear of bushes. Impale a metre-long stick into the ground as upright as possible. Mark the tip of the shadow (1) with a cross. Wait fifteen or twenty minutes and mark the new shadow tip (2). Draw a line between the two to get an west-east line. Your first mark is west, the second east. North-south is therefore at right angles to the line. This is a handy way to quickly check direction when on the move.

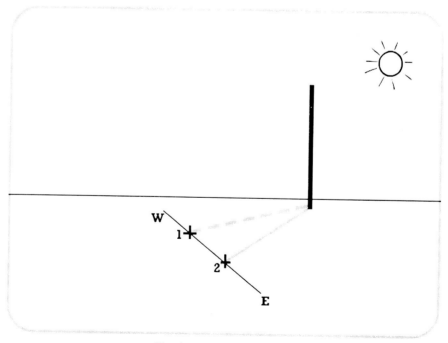

Shadow stick technique 1

2. The above method is more than adequate for most survival scenarios. If you are going to spend a whole day in one spot you can use the following process, which is a bit more precise. Put your upright stick in the ground and mark the shadow tip in the morning (1). Now draw an arc from this point, using a piece of string tied to the base of the stick. Keep an eye on the shadow throughout the day. It will shrink until noon then lengthen in the afternoon. At the *precise* point where its tip again touches your arc, mark the spot (2). Now draw a straight line from the morning mark to the afternoon mark - this line points from west to east.

It doesn't matter what time in the morning you make the first mark, but at least two hours before noon gives better accuracy.

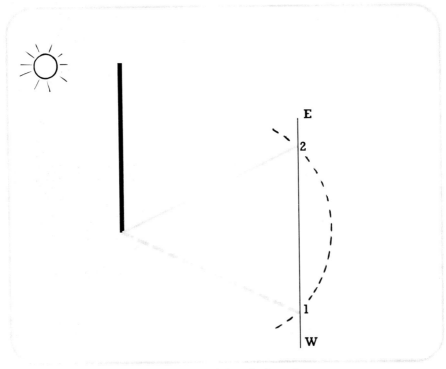

Shadow stick technique 2

If you have a watch with hands (not a digital) there is an easy way to determine north-south. Hold the watch horizontally in front of you and point 12 toward the sun. Now look at the hour hand. Your north-south line lies exactly halfway between the hour hand and the 12.

FRIGHTENED YOU MIGHT GET LOST?

Lowrance Electronics makes state of the art portable position finders, so light and compact they will fit in your pocket or back pack without problems. Powered by replaceable AA torch batteries, backed up by an internal lithium battery that protects information for up to 10 years, these hand held GPS sets make everyone a great navigator.

Just turn them on and take off, and your Lowrance hand held GPS will record your path and save the location of any position you ask it to; where you parked the car, fresh water, camp sites and so on. You can even use icons to indicate the nature of the position saved.

When it's time to go home you just follow your track back to the car, or request the direction and distance to a previously saved point.

FOR FURTHER INFORMATION, PHONE, FAX OR WRITE TO

LOWRANCE AUSTRALIA

42/9 Powells Road, Brookvale, NSW 2100
Phone: (02) 9905 9700, Fax (02) 9905 5220
http://www.lowrance.com.au
Email: aust@lowrance.com.au

Name _____

Address _____

Town _____ P/C _____ LNF/1

MOON AND STARS

Like the sun, the moon and stars also rise in the east and set in the west. If the moon rises after midnight the bright side points toward the east. If it comes out before sunset the bright side points west. Periodically checking the moon is not the most precise method of getting an east-west direction but it can certainly help when cloud cover obscures stars but lets a faint moon shine through.

In Australia the Southern Cross is a handy navigational guide; it's always in an approximate southerly direction. It is distinguished from other cross-shaped constellations by two nearby pointer stars and its proximity to the Coal Sack, a black spot in the milky way which lies roughly between the pointer stars and the Cross.

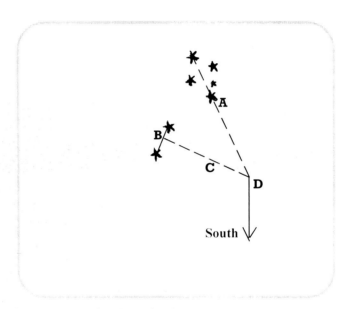

To find south using the Southern Cross, extend an imaginary line along the axis of the cross (A). Now connect the two pointers with another imaginary line (B). Bisect this line with another at right angles to it (C), and extend that until it meets up with the Southern Cross line (point D). From that point drop a line straight down to the horizon to find due south.

Other groups of stars can aid night navigation as well. In the summer the Seven Sisters is a clearly visible group of stars lying low in the sky to the north. It looks like an upside-down saucepan. When the 'handle' is horizontal the Seven Sisters are at due north. If you were heading up the Cape York track the Seven Sisters would be visible through your windscreen on a clear night.

Another useful aid is The Saucepan in the Orion group, which passes overhead and sets in the west. Its handle always points south.

In the warmer months (October to March) you can navigate at night using the Saucepan, Southern Cross and Seven Sisters. Between March and October, use the Southern Cross and a group called the Frying Pan, which rises in the east as soon as the sun sets.

City dwellers don't see as much of the stars because there is so much artificial light around. If you want to increase your celestial knowledge you can buy hand-held star finders that rotate to show the locations of major constellations.

Bush Survival Skills Course

Ever got lost in thick bush with a hungry stomach?
Or in torrential rain without a rain coat (which wouldn't have improved the situation anyway)? Bush survival skills are essential for all those who venture out there, be it alone or with friends.

Learn with the bush survival specialists: navigation, bush foods and medicine plants, bush cooking, fire lighting, water conservation, survival shelters, hunting and trapping, rescue signalling, survival psychology. For further information please contact:

HIGH 'n WILD Mountain Adventures
Ph (02) 4782 6224, Fax (02) 4782 6143
3/5 Katoomba Street
KATOOMBA NSW 2780
info@high-n-wild.com.au
www.high-n-wild.com.au

Survival Priorities
Bush Travel

IN A VEHICLE

1. Have your vehicle checked out before you go bush.

2. If with a stranded vehicle, DON'T LEAVE IT unless you absolutely have to. It is an aid to survival and signalling.

3. Carry a MINIMUM of 9 litres of water per person, plus 18 litres for the radiator. In arid areas you may need more.

4. Carry appropriate tools, spares and recovery equipment. In more remote areas carry an HF radio or other method of communicating with the outside world.

5. Take a course in 4WD driving skills, de-bogging and/or roadside maintenance before going bush.

6. Most bush accidents stem from speed or inexperience in handling the vehicle in different conditions.

ON FOOT

1. Ridges paralleling a creek may offer easier terrain than the bank itself, and offer better views of the surrounds.

2. A slow but steady pace is the safest and most energy-efficient way to traverse rugged terrain on foot.

3. The safety of night walking depends upon the terrain. In hot regions it may be a survival necessity.

4. Cross rivers carefully. Avoid obstructions, high banks and fast currents. For group crossings use a safety rope.

Bush Travel

Planning is the key to a safe bush journey. The one item you leave behind is inevitably the one you need most in an emergency, so pack your vehicle, boat or rucksack very carefully. A desolate stretch of wilderness is no place to suddenly realise you've left the vehicle jack, blister pads or compass at home.

Learn as much as you can about the area before you go. Checking on road conditions, availability of fuel and other details can save a lot of difficulties later on. A leisurely bush experience is always more pleasant than a rushed one, so give yourself plenty of time.

VEHICLES IN THE BUSH

Driving in remote regions demands careful preparation. Choose the right time of year to go. Midsummer driving in the Centre is uncomfortably hot while the Top End is best explored in the dry season between April and October. Check average temperatures and rainfall in the area for the time you plan to travel, taking note of night-time minimums too. In arid Australia the difference between the hottest part of the day and the cold hours before dawn can exceed 30 degrees.

A good way to learn the ins and outs of outback driving is to enrol in a course through your State Association of Four Wheel Drive Clubs or Motoring Association. A basic vehicle maintenance course is advisable before going too far afield. Four wheel drive clubs put on regular trips for drivers of all proficiency levels, where you can learn from experienced drivers in the safety of an organised convoy.

A range of publications offer valuable detailed advice on 4WD bush travel. Four that can be highly recommended are Explore Australia by Four Wheel Drive (*Viking 1998*), Safe Outback Travel (*Jack Absalom, Five Mile Press 1992*), Gregory's 4WD Survival Guide (*1998*) and Explore Wild Australia with the Bush Tucker Man (*Les Hiddens, Penguin Books 1999*).

Choosing a vehicle for the bush is a personal matter. People have different ideas about 'the ideal 4WD', but from a safety and survival aspect there are some obvious considerations. Manuals are superior to automatics when it comes to hill work and towing. Automatics are handy when ploughing through deep sand, where manual gears can't be changed quite as quickly. When choosing a 4WD make or model the most relevant questions are "What will I be using the vehicle for?" and "How readily can I get spare parts in remote towns?"

Diesel is the fuel of choice in the outback. Diesel engines are less prone to electrical failures when they get wet. Minimal electrics means there is less to go wrong. However, if you get water in the air intake of a diesel engine it's bad news - you're looking at a complete engine replacement or overhaul. This is why snorkels are a common sight on diesel vehicles. Petrol 4WDs are popular among city drivers who occasionally venture off road.

One point that relates directly to survival is power windows. People have drowned in flooded cars when the electrics got wet and failed, locking the windows closed and preventing escape. Manually operated windows are preferable for serious bush driving, but these are increasingly hard to find on newer 4WD models.

VEHICLE EXTRAS

Every accessory you add to a 4WD has some effect on the vehicle's performance. A heavy bull bar weighs down the front end, a long-range fuel tank changes the centre of gravity and an electric winch puts extra strain on battery power. It's not hard to spend over $10,000 to outfit a 4WD for outback use so talk to those who live and work in the bush before you splash out on something you can easily do without. A 4WD is heavy enough on an expedition with all the food, water and extra fuel supplies; the last thing you need is superfluous weight dragging you into every bog along the route. Be selective with accessories.

A dual battery system is advisable if you have extra electrical gear to run: radios, electric winches, mini-fridges, etc. A small fire extinguisher (specifically designed for vehicle use) is also a good idea. A well shaken can of lemonade, cola or beer makes a good emergency substitute - just shake, pop the top slightly so the foam shoots out and point it at the fire.

Long-range fuel or water tanks are popular with some travellers, but their drawback is that if they spring a leak you can lose all the contents as you're bumping down the track. A number of separate water containers is safer than just one or two - if one breaks it's not such a drama. Store water upright in sturdy plastic containers, packed to prevent jostling. Metal jerry cans of spare fuel *should not* be stored inside the vehicle - this is very dangerous. Store fuel cans on the outside of the 4WD on metal racks fitted at the rear bumper.

WINCHES AND RECOVERY EQUIPMENT

Getting bogged in sand or mud is usually avoidable with caution and an understanding of how your vehicle handles various conditions. When you get stuck you should have the gear to get yourself out: a winch, approved D-shackles, snatch strap and large diameter pulley block.

Winches come in four types:

1. Hydraulic: The winch motor is powered by your vehicle's engine through a pressure pump.

2. Electric: Permanently mounted on the front of the vehicle and runs off the car battery.

3. PTO (Power Takeoff): Runs off the engine via the gearbox or transfer case.

4. Manual: Operated by hand.

Each type has its pros and cons. An electric winch puts added load on your battery, but this can be offset by installing a dual battery system. PTO and hydraulic winches are heavier than electric winches and don't work if your engine fails.

Hand-operated winches are the cheapest and simplest option. They work even if both motor or battery are dead and can be attached to the rear of a vehicle to pull it out backwards. This is an advantage in many de-bogging operations. Physically they are more demanding than other types but the effort is reduced with a pulley block.

A pulley block (snatch block) is used to multiply a winch's pulling power. With power-operated winches they slow down winching speed but provide more power.

Snatch straps are used between a bogged vehicle and a towing vehicle. They are made from sturdy webbing that stretches to supply extra pulling power when the towing vehicle accelerates. Always attach the snatch strap to a solid part of the bogged vehicle's chassis and the other end to a towbar solid enough for the job. Serious injury or death is possible if a snatch strap breaks free from either end and you're standing nearby. *Never use a snatch strap with a pulley block.*

It may seem a bit extreme to think of getting bogged as the start of a survival situation, but that's the best way to approach it. You need to devise a safe strategy, avoid injury, ensure protection from sunburn and temperature extremes. You have to think about keeping up fluid levels during strenuous work such as digging out tyres. If the de-bogging process takes longer than expected, stop for a rest. Rig up a tarp for shade, boil the billy and give yourself a breather.

WINCHING BASICS

* Wear sturdy gloves for all winching.
* Always pull straight rather than at an angle from the vehicle.
* Keep winch cables and straps clean.
* Don't let the winch cable cross over itself on the drum.
* Keep everybody well clear of cables during winching.
* Drape a blanket or similar covering over the cable to dull the recoil if it should snap.
* To slow battery drain when using electric winches, increase your engine's idle speed.
* Trees used as winching anchor points should be protected from damage. Use wide webbing straps rather than cable, and pad if necessary.
* Vehicle recovery can be difficult and dangerous when improperly performed. Learn how it's done before you go bush. 4WD clubs offer useful practical courses on winching, towing etc.

SPARE PARTS

Before any trip always make a list of spare parts to carry, appropriate for the type of journey being undertaken. Some spare items that should be carried on serious 4WD adventures include:

* Drive belts for radiator fan, alternator, water pump, power steering or air conditioning.
* Spare wheel(s). Over-inflate slightly to allow for air loss.
* All essential hoses and hose clips: heater, radiator, bypass, power steering, plus a plastic syphon hose.
* Spare battery, spark plugs and distributor points.
* Puncture kit with spare inner tube and valves.

186

* Full set of fuses for vehicle and radio.
* Set of relevant tools. Don't go overboard but take what you need.
* Fuel, air and water filters (one of each).
* Light globes (several of each) for all lights in and on the vehicle.
* Fluids (brake and clutch fluid, radiator coolant, distilled water etc.).
* Lubricants (engine oil, gearbox oil etc.).
* Durable trouble-light. Sturdy torch with spare batteries and globe.
* Heavy duty jumper leads.
* Spare fuel in jerry cans.

This is by no means a comprehensive list. Four wheel drive clubs can advise you on the spare parts you should carry for a planned journey in a specific vehicle. One of the most important items to have along is the vehicle's maintenance manual. This is a must regardless of your mechanical ability.

Think of your vehicle as an aid to survival. You can shelter inside it while a bushfire passes. A tarp can be suspended from it to create shade on a treeless plain. It presents air searchers with a distinctive object to look for. In a survival situation the items that matter most are your HF radio, first aid kit, water supply, signalling gear and survival kit.

Minimum water requirements for a vehicle in remote country are 9 litres per person plus 18 litres for the vehicle. Radiator problems, air conditioning breakdowns and other difficulties can increase water needs dramatically. In arid regions err on the surplus side when it comes to water. In an emergency you may need every drop.

COMMUNICATION

Effective communication saves lives. In an isolated area a two-way radio or other communication device ensures you can contact the outside world when needed. At present, mobile phone networks are fine for settled regions but not reliable for remote areas, which are normally out of their range. Do not depend upon a mobile for bush communication. New-technology satellite telephones are a more expensive but very effective alternative, allowing communication to and from virtually anywhere in Australia (and for that matter, the world).

An HF radio lets you talk to other vehicles or contact the Royal Flying Doctor Service in an emergency. The RFDS hires out HF radios from some of their bases if you don't want to buy one. To operate an HF radio you must obtain a license and be allocated a registered call sign (contact the Australian Communications Authority, (02 6256 5555). When calling the RFDS, leave the set open so they can relay messages or tell you if you need to switch to another channel. It cannot be stressed enough that the Flying Doctor Service is for *real emergencies*. Minor injuries that can be dealt with by driving the patient to the nearest town do not constitute an emergency. They also tie up a plane that may be needed by someone in a more serious situation.

Citizen Band (CB) radios are useful for inter-vehicle communication within a range of 25 km or so (depending on terrain) and are not overly expensive. As with HF radios, an operating license and call sign allocation is required.

MAINTENANCE

In urban areas a vehicle breakdown is an inconvenience, but in the bush it can be a real problem. If you have plenty of water you can just wait for another vehicle to come along - maybe they can help you then and there, maybe not. A flat battery 200 km from the nearest town on a desolate track is serious. Your mobile phone won't work out there, assistance is unlikely and your HF radio (which operates off the battery too) is no help. If you have let people know your plans and stuck to them a search should get under way in a few days. Whether or not rescue is expected, take stock of water and other essential supplies and start thinking about survival priorities. If you have packed transpiration bags, a tarp for shade, a reasonable food supply and suitable clothing then you're not in any immediate danger. Get your signalling devices ready and stay calm. Save any strenuous activity for the cool of the night.

Avoid such situations through preparation. Have your vehicle checked out by a mechanic prior to any long trips. A more conscientious approach to maintenance is needed in the bush than in the city - you must constantly check all aspects of your vehicle to keep one step ahead of potential problems. Each time you approach the vehicle have a quick look underneath to check for leaks. Daily monitoring of oil, fuel, water, tyres and fan-belt should become a habit. Keep an eye out for loose wheel nuts, cracked hoses, corrosion on battery terminals, worn parts and anything out of the ordinary. Listen for unusual rattles and noises coming from any part of the car. Stop to periodically remove spinifex that accumulates in the exhaust pipe - it catches fire easily. Have a thorough read of your vehicle manual before you go away, especially the troubleshooting section.

An adult education course on vehicle maintenance is much cheaper than paying thousands of dollars to get a 4WD towed out of the bush and repaired. Small mechanical faults can become major if they are not detected and rectified in time on the road. Know your vehicle, drive at a safe speed for the conditions, carry essential spare parts and tools and take the time to inspect the engine regularly as you travel.

The P.E.T.R.O.L. Check

A basic daily maintenance routine is essential for safe outback driving. An easy way to remember what to check is the acronym P-E-T-R-O-L. This check only takes a few minutes - do it at least once a day.

P - for Petrol. Check fuel level.
E - for Electrical. Check battery terminals and levels.
T - for Tyres. Check pressure; check sidewalls for cuts.
R - for Radiator. Check coolant level.
O - for Oil. Check oil level.
L - for Lights. Check all vehicle lights are functioning.

TYRES

In the bush, always mend punctures as soon as they happen. On rough tracks it is not uncommon to get two or more punctures within a short time, even with new tyres. Having a flat tyre hanging off the back of the vehicle doesn't help you. Always carry at least two spare tyres, one spare inner tube and a puncture kit which includes an inner-sleeve.

Damaged tyres that are too far gone for driving still have survival uses. A cut section can be used as a temporary tyre gaiter; pieces can be soaked in oil and set alight to signal air searchers with black smoke; appropriately sized pieces can be cut and tied to the feet to make emergency footwear.

Getting the Tyre off the Rim

Pack a large rubber mallet and a quality tyre lever. To break the bead a 'tyre-plier' or similar tool is very handy. When replacing the rim a bit of liquid detergent on the tyre bead and rim makes it slippery so it goes back on more easily.

A high-lift jack (in addition to your normal jack) should be standard gear on bush journeys. You can use it to separate the rim from the tyre. Put the tyre underneath the front end of the vehicle and the base of the high-lift jack on top of the rubber of the tyre. As you jack up the front end the weight presses down on the tyre, separating it from the metal rim.

You can also break the bead by placing the tyre flat on the ground and having another vehicle drive over the edge of it as close to the rim as possible; you may have to do this at a few points around the tyre.

Experienced four wheel drivers carry at least two spare wheels in remote country.

Photo: Colin & Georgina Wright

Select tyres suited to the conditions. For example, wide tyres aren't a good idea on wet roads but work well in sand. Keep records of the air pressure that works best in different conditions. You can buy electric air pumps these days which are quick and easy and fit under the bonnet, but a hand pump should also be packed just in case. Carry a plank base (at least three centimetres thick) to put underneath the jack when changing tyres.

BUSH DRIVING

Safe driving in the bush is simply knowing where to put your wheels and using the correct revs, speed and gears for the right situation. Most bush 4WD accidents are related to speed or not knowing enough about what the vehicle can and can't do in certain situations. Corrugations, cattle, protruding rocks, fallen branches, sudden washouts and other hazards are the rule rather than the exception on bush tracks. The best advice is to *slow down*.

The Art of Waiting

In the bush it's dangerous to try to keep to tight schedules, either on foot or in a vehicle. The author once came upon a 4WD stuck right in the middle of a Top End river just after the wet season. Instead of waiting two or three days for the water level to drop, the couple had tried to cross. The driver (an older gentleman with a heart condition) set off on foot to get help at a nearby station, leaving his panicking wife sitting on top of the flooded car, wondering whether she would be swept downstream at any moment.

This episode could easily have ended in tragedy. These people were travelling too early in the dry season for their level of experience and should never have attempted the crossing. Had they simply waited, a more experienced driver would have come along in a matter of hours (or the following morning) to give them a hand. In the modern world we are used to having things happen instantaneously, but in bush situations the best plan is sometimes to do nothing at all. *Patience is a wilderness survival skill*. Waiting for weather to clear, swollen creeks to abate or assistance to arrive can save your life.

With creek crossings, standard practice is to slowly walk through the crossing first to gauge depth and work out the best places for tyre grip. Obviously this isn't advisable in crocodile habitats. Have a good look at the vehicle before going across - check that the tyre pressure is right, the exhaust pipe isn't hanging down, etc. If the walk-through tells you the water is going to be up over the tops of your tyres you should consider if crossing there is worth the risk. For all deep crossings a tarp should be wrapped right around the radiator area at the front of the vehicle to keep water from flowing onto the engine and drenching it. Disconnecting the fan belt is also a good idea to protect the radiator and reduce splash on the engine. Use low-range second gear or high-range first gear to get through and keep going until you are well clear of the opposite bank.

Difficult vehicle recoveries must be planned very carefully.
Photo: Bill & Barbara Brooker, Toyota Landcruiser Club QLD

Deep sand is common on some back roads. The key to getting through is to keep up a decent (but not excessive) speed in the highest gear you have. Reducing tyre pressure to about 15-20 psi gives better traction, but *remember to re-inflate to normal pressure once you're back on hard roads.*

Other bush road hazards include corrugations, road trains and bulldust. Corrugations are handled simply - by slowing down. The prudent thing to do if a big road train is heading toward you is to get right off the track, stop and let it pass. When trying to pass a road train in front of you, wait for the driver to give you a signal to pass.

Bulldust is a fine, powdery road dust. It can be kept out of the car to some extent by rolling up windows and turning up air-conditioning. Take care in bulldust areas - a deep pothole filled with the dust is well disguised and can do serious damage if you plough into it too fast. In bulldust country, check your air filter regularly. If it's getting blocked, remove it and give it a few knocks against a tree to shake the dust out. Then blow through it from the centre toward the outside, rotating it to clean out the entire circle. *Never clean air filters by washing them with water*. The combination of dust and water will dry like concrete, ruining the filter.

There are times when you get bogged with no tree or other suitable winch anchor in sight. The answer is a Portable Tree. This works on the same principle as a boat anchor. You attach the end of the winch cable to it, set it on the mud or sand at the proper angle and slowly start winching. The 'anchor' digs in deeper and deeper until it stops dead and then pulls the vehicle out of the bog. It is an invaluable aid in beach, mangrove and swampy areas.

If you don't carry a Portable Tree, dig a 70 cm deep hole straight ahead of the vehicle. Put a thick log or your spare tyre into it to serve as the anchor. It is important to angle the hole away from the vehicle (see below) so the anchoring object isn't pulled straight out when the winching starts.

On difficult stretches of track it helps to have a spotter to watch where your wheels are going and direct you over the terrain. Photo: Colin & Georgina Wright

*Being familiar with your vehicle and knowing what it can do in different
conditions is fundamental to your survival.*   Photo: Colin & Georgina Wright

ON FOOT

With bush mishaps it is almost always best to remain with your vehicle, beached boat or disabled aircraft. This makes it easier for searchers to find you. In any landscape a lone walker is very difficult to spot from the air. People have perished after walking away from a vehicle that contained all their survival requirements. If you need to find food or water there may be no choice but to set off on foot, but don't abandon the vehicle before you have to. If you do, leave a note behind detailing the date, time, direction of travel, amount of food and water carried and physical condition of the travellers.

Plan walking routes so minimum energy is expended. Follow watercourses downstream where practical. Even when 'lost' you should have some idea whether civilisation is likely to be found downstream. If you can maintain your direction up on high ground, do so. A ridge parallelling a river's course may offer faster going than the bank. In the north, cattle and donkey trails along creek banks provide a handy path. Use binoculars to check the terrain ahead - they are a real help in rugged country. Seeing what's up ahead is especially important in rocky areas and swamp. If you leave the vehicle, take the binoculars with you.

When travelling in a group each individual should have a specific responsibility. One person could be the lead scout, selecting the safest and easiest route. Another might work with the scout to ensure proper compass direction is maintained. Others can look for signs of water or handy shelter. More importantly each person must be responsible for keeping track of at least one other member of the party. Travel in pairs and maintain a pace that makes allowance for slower walkers. Groups must not spread too far apart, especially in rough country. Over the course of a full day a slower, steady pace always works better than the 'sprint and rest' method.

Walking overland at night is best avoided unless the terrain is fairly flat and free of obstacles, or unless daytime heat makes night travel a survival necessity. Move slowly in the dark, avoid slopes and use your forward foot to check the ground before putting full weight down. Even flat terrain can be riddled with rabbit warrens and other surprises. Stop frequently to listen and smell the surroundings. Ears and nose can tell you things about the surroundings than your eyes cannot, such as proximity of water or presence of specific vegetation. Keep away from trees. A wide-brimmed hat will deflect some branches from your eyes, but holding an arm in front of your face is better protection.

It takes the human eye a good half hour to become properly adjusted to the dark, so give yourself some time away from artificial lights or fire before setting off into the darkness. Close one eye when looking at your map or compass with the torch. This way you can recover your night vision more quickly and keep moving.

Travel in mountainous rainforest demands patience. In temperate, moss-covered rainforests it may be difficult to know if you're walking on the ground or treading on a tangled network of vegetation suspended a metre or more above it. In tropical jungle the hazards include spiky plant life. The 'wait-a-while' vine is one of the worst, and aptly named. If you blunder into it there is no choice but to back up and disengage clothes (or skin) from the barbs. Trying to push through only results in more torn flesh and fabric. The vine isn't all bad, however - in a food emergency you can use it to snag small fish or yabbies or extract grubs from rotten logs.

RIVER CROSSINGS

Rivers must be respected. In northern regions they may be home to saltwater crocodiles and sharks. In inland areas there may be unpredictable currents, hidden obstacles and unseen snags. Secure pack contents in plastic bags whenever crossing rivers or waterholes. Use a large rubbish bag as a liner for the main rucksack compartment and smaller bags for the remainder. Tie the tops well or twist and knot. Your water transpiration bags may even be big enough to surround the whole pack; your gear stays dry and the air trapped in the bag adds buoyancy.

A sturdy walking staff is handy for crossings up to waist deep, especially on rocky bottoms. A stout, two-metre tree branch becomes a third leg, providing a stable tripod effect to improve balance. Snags, rocks and hidden holes are avoided by using the walking stick as a forward probe. In shallow creeks it's tempting to try to keep dry by jumping from one boulder to the next, but it may be safer to wade across - many broken limbs have resulted from hikers leaping onto slippery rocks.

Unfortunately straight, stout, two metre branches aren't always around when you need them. Some experienced walkers never go bush without their adjustable aluminium walking pole (or two, one for each hand). They're lightweight, add stability over rough ground and take some of the strain off legs when climbing. *Trezeta* is a popular brand in Australia. Staffs have other survival functions too. Poke them into prospective natural shelters to check for snakes. Turn them into a leg splint or fishing pole. Use them to prop up the groundsheet when making a quick shelter.

Face the current as you start across the river and proceed slowly. Use a shuffling motion rather than a series of big steps. Leave boots on. Bare feet do not grip as well and offer little protection against sharp stones. Submerged branches are another hazard, capable of breaking limbs if you become tangled in them. *ALWAYS* undo the backpack's belt strap before crossing. If you fall in and are swept downstream you can easily slip out of one of the shoulder straps, swing the pack around and grip it tightly in front of you until you regain control. Don't let go of the pack; it provides flotation as well as cushioning against collisions with rocks.

Study a river thoroughly before deciding on the best place and method for crossing. Toss in a twig to check speed and direction of current. Current is usually strongest on the outside bends of a river. Steer clear of steep banks, submerged trees and weed-choked sections.

If the water is above waist deep you must swim across. Hold the pack in front of you and kick with the legs. Clothes should be removed and stored inside the waterproofed pack. In strong current select a landing spot well downstream to allow for the inevitable drift. When crossing without a pack make use of any extra flotation. An empty jerry can, buoyant log or large plastic bag filled with air will help.

With the right natural materials it's possible to build a raft to cross large calm bodies of water. Traditional Aboriginal rafts in the Top End are made from pandanus, paperbark and bush string. A frame of pandanus poles is lashed together with plant fibres and large metre-wide slabs of paperbark are placed on top to sit on.

For group crossings of dangerous rivers a safety rope is advisable. The strongest swimmer in the group should initially take one end of the rope to the opposite bank.

Quicksand is more prevalent in old Hollywood movies than the Australian bush but it does occur. Soft oozy mud is no less dangerous, and a common obstacle for explorers of lowland swamps and mangrove coasts. The weight of a full pack is no help and it's alarming how quickly mud can change from a nuisance to a real problem. Remove the pack immediately if you start sinking deep into a mud bog. Work yourself into a horizontal spread-eagled position (face up) to distribute body weight evenly along the surface. Adopt a slithering motion incorporating a kind of backstroke to move across the mud to solid ground. Retrieve the pack later from a safe distance with a long hooked branch.

READING THE WEATHER

Anticipating the weather is an important survival skill. To be at home in the wild you must become attuned to changes in the environment. Every year people get trapped by bad weather somewhere in the Australian bush. With better preparation this could largely be avoided. Before venturing into any wilderness, learn what you can about local weather patterns. Consult the weather bureau, local farmers, park rangers and other sources of information. You should have a good idea of expected weather before heading off. Most importantly, check on recent rainfall.

Obviously a lengthy trek would not be on the cards in an area that has seen no rain in four years. Recent heavy rainfall can also make walking difficult, with increased mud and detours around temporary swamps. Thick grass and prolific ground vines also increase dramatically after rain, impeding progress.

The planning of river kayaking journeys is hugely affected by recent rainfall. A river that's too dry means many tiring portages over rough terrain. Big rains increase a river's current, making it unpredictable and more hazardous for navigation.

"Red sky in morning, sailor's warning. Red sky at night, sailor's delight". This is perhaps the best known weather adage, but nature provides many other indicators. In extreme circumstances knowing how to read them could save your life. At the very least they make time spent travelling the bush more comfortable.

When wind comes first and is quickly followed by rain, fine conditions can usually be expected soon after the rain. When the rain comes first (with no wind) a long spell of bad weather may be in the offing. Check for a greenish light in the sky just before a thunderstorm. This indicates that hail is on the way, and shelter should be sought at once. A rainbow late in the afternoon denotes fine weather, while one appearing in the morning is generally the sign of a wet day ahead.

Animals are of little use as long-range weather forecasters but their actions say a lot about the immediate climate. Insects don't fly as high when bad weather is brewing, and species that store their eggs underground (especially ants) are very active before a storm, relocating their precious cargo to higher ground. If bees are swarming, fine weather can be expected to last for the next eight hours at least.

Spiders are useful predictors of the day's weather. With a fine and windless day ahead they spin long and intricate webs and show persistent activity across them. When rain is on the way, webs are spun tighter and shorter and the spider stays more passive in the centre. A multitude of webs strung across high grass after dawn is a good sign of fine weather to come.

Survival Priorities
Hazardous Creatures

1. Be crocodile-wise: stand well back from the bank when fishing, heed crocodile warning signs and seek local advice regarding safe swimming areas. Don't collect water from the same section of river twice. Most crocodile attacks have occurred in the tropical wet season.

2. Leather boots and gaiters offer good protection against snakebite. Carry a crepe roller bandage in your pocket when walking in snake country so any bites can be bandaged without delay (see first aid chapter).

3. Treat fish stings with heat. Treat jellyfish stings by neutralising the poison with vinegar *before* attempting to remove the stinging tentacles.

4. Proper identification is important with any hazardous animal. Learn to recognise Australia's most dangerous snakes, spiders and shore creatures.

5. Unless extremely desperate for food, cut the line if any sharks are caught while fishing.

6. Feral cattle and wild pigs can be aggressive in some circumstances and should be given plenty of room. Cook feral pig meat thoroughly to avoid parasites.

7. Inspect your body thoroughly in tick country on a daily basis - the quicker they are detected the better.

8. The best way to avoid contact with hazardous creatures is to wear suitable protective clothing, understand their habits and know where they live. If contact occurs you should be aware of the right first aid treatment.

Hazardous Creatures

Australia boasts an array of creatures which can cause discomfort, injury or even death to humans, but most are easily avoided by taking simple precautions and being aware of their preferred habitats. Compared to many other countries Australia's animal hazards are relatively few. Even so, some of our most appealing creatures harbour hidden surprises. Picking up a male platypus can result in a nasty sting from the spurs located on its back legs. Attractiveness is no insurance against danger - the blue-ringed octopus, butterfly cod and geographer cone shell are all beautiful to look at but potentially fatal to touch.

For most bites and stings the standard first aid technique is the Pressure and Immobilisation Method (PIM). This involves applying a firm (but not tight) roller bandage over the bite and along the entire limb. This compression slows the flow of venom toward the heart and keeps it largely confined to the local bite area. A splint is then applied if practical. The victim is kept as still as possible while medical attention is sought. In serious cases you might need to give mouth-to-mouth resuscitation or heart massage as symptoms worsen, and this may have to be kept up for several hours.

There are some special cases where the pressure/immobilisation method shouldn't be used. Red-back spider bites are treated with a cold compress only. A plastic bag filled with ice from the esky does the job. The victim should then be taken to a hospital as soon as possible for a dose of red-back antivenene. Do *not* apply a restrictive bandage to red-back bites. It only makes the pain worse. Red-backs aren't much of a bush hazard - you're more likely to encounter them in your garden than in the wild.

With bee, wasp and ant stings an ice pack or iced water is applied, unless a severe allergic reaction occurs. In that case use pressure/immobilisation until you can get to a doctor. With tick bites the first priority is to carefully remove the tick. With bee stings the stinger and poison sac must be removed before you do anything else.

The other major exception to the pressure/immobilisation method is poisonous fish stings, which are treated with heat to neutralise the venom.

MARINE ANIMALS

SHARKS

Several dangerous species are found in Australian waters. These include white pointers, tiger sharks, whalers and a few others. Some sharks will venture far up into rivers. Large species may come in close to shore, even in water under a metre deep. Blood and vibrations in the water can attract sharks.

Basic precautions reduce the possibility of shark attack. Fish speared in the shallows should be taken ashore immediately. Don't swim at night or thrash around in the water. If a shark is inadvertently hooked while fishing, cut the line rather than pull it in. A struggling shark can inflict a nasty bite if allowed within range.

With shark attack the main aim is to remove the victim from the water and stem the flow of blood from the bitten area. Do not delay - every second counts. Apply direct pressure with a bandage, tee-shirt or similar and elevate the affected area.

SALT WATER CROCODILES

These powerful animals typify the northern bush at its most primeval. Crocodiles can become territorial and aggressive during the breeding season. There are a great many myths about 'salties': that they always roll their bodies when they attack, that their habitat is confined to muddy mangrove regions, that they only attack from the water or that they prefer to store their prey underwater to let it rot for a few days.

Here are some facts:

1. They may be found far out to sea and near coral reefs. In the wet season they can travel overland and up rivers for great distances. They may be present in fresh water billabongs a hundred miles or more inland at any time of year.

2. They can outrun a man over very short distances on land.

3. Females guarding their nests in the breeding season (October to March) will aggressively defend the area against human intrusion. The majority of attacks on humans occur during these warmer wet season months when crocodiles are more active. Attacks on boats and propellers are usually the work of large males exercising territorial aggression.

204

Human carelessness has played a part in most of the crocodile attacks in Australia during the past thirty years. Alcohol consumption has had a role in some cases too. Swimming at night or in known crocodile areas is *not* a good idea. Brief naps on sandy river banks or coastlines can turn out to be very brief indeed. A kayak, canoe or small tinny offers little protection against a determined crocodile.

When camped in croc country collect your fresh water from a different section of the river each time - don't be predictable. Stand well back from the water's edge when fishing, or better yet find a three-metre high rock ledge to fish from. Clean fish and cut bait away from the water's edge.

The author encountered this 5 metre crocodile in the lower Ord River in Western Australia. The white floating object in front of it is a full-grown cow it had recently pulled into the water.

BLUE-RINGED OCTOPUS

The bite from this small, attractive octopus is often painless and may go unnoticed by the victim. Its venom can cause death in under two hours and symptoms develop within minutes after the bite. These include blurred vision, muscular paralysis, nausea, difficulty in swallowing and loss of tactile sensation. No antivenene exists so the only chance is to treat the bite as you would snakebite and give cardiac massage and mouth-to-mouth resuscitation until the poison's effects subside. This may take hours and by no means guarantees survival, but there is no other way.

The blue-ringed octopus lives in rock pools along our coasts in all states. When threatened its blue rings become brighter in colour while its brown body bands darken. Do not handle these creatures. Active at night, they hide in rock crevices during the day and may take up residence in large abandoned seashells.

Though their venom is highly toxic, sea snakes are not aggressive. The few bites that do occur are usually related to net fishing, often at night when a snake is grabbed by accident. If sea snakes are not handled there is nothing to fear.

Photo: Courtesy of Brad Maryan, WASAH

JELLYFISH

Jellyfish inhabit all Australian coastlines. Several species are a danger to humans, especially the deadly box jellyfish and the *Chiropsalmus* of northern waters. The tentacles (and occasionally the bells) of some types of jellyfish stick to the skin and sting vigorously, often with excruciating results. The natural reaction to this acute pain is to frantically try to remove the tentacles. This unfortunately leads to a fresh injection of more poison. The hand tugging at the tentacles gets a good stinging as well.

The proper way to treat jellyfish stings is to flood the stung area with vinegar to neutralise the poison. Then carefully remove the tentacles with tweezers. The old idea of rubbing sand (or metho, or ammonia) over the stings only makes it worse. Seek medical attention at once and resuscitate the patient if necessary.

OTHER MARINE DANGERS

Stingrays are common inhabitants of estuaries and shorelines. The barbed spike along their tail flicks up vertically to impale the victim. This is a purely defensive reaction, generally occurring when the ray is unwittingly trod upon. Humans are usually stung on the legs, but swimmers or divers skimming along the sandy bottom risk being stung in the heart or other vital organ. Such a wound could be fatal.

Pain and the likelihood of infection are present with all stingray wounds. Stingrays should not be handled. Some species are flexible enough to swing the tail up and over their body to sting a human hand grasping their head. They can be encountered in very shallow water.

A number of fish species are armed with poisonous spines, such as stonefish, butterfly cod, scorpionfish and catfish. There is a good chance of infection with fish stings. Severe pain may result in shock. Poisonous spines are found along the back of some species and around the head or underside of others. The surgeon fish houses its weapon just in front of its tail - when danger nears it flicks this out like a switchblade.

The pressure/immobilisation method should *not* be used with fish stings. Remove any remaining spines or foreign matter from the wound. Spines buried deep in the flesh may have to be left in until the victim can reach a doctor. Immerse the affected area in hot water. This should be as hot as the patient can stand but not scalding. Heat neutralises the poison and should be applied as soon as possible after the sting.

The author witnessed an interesting variation to this first aid technique in Queensland when a stockman sustained a nasty catfish sting to his forearm. He walked straight to his vehicle and pressed his arm hard against the hot metal of the bonnet, which was in the sun. When it got too hot he would lift it off for a few seconds, then press the arm down again. This process was repeated several times, after which he calmly walked back down to the river to continue fishing.

While some species have nasty spines, others are poisonous to eat. Puffer fish, porcupine fish and trigger fish should be rejected as potential survival food.

Cone shells are beautiful but should not be touched. If picked up, a miniature barbed harpoon is injected into the skin and a powerful venom pumped in. Numbness around the lips and mouth, muscle paralysis, lack of consciousness and even death may follow. There is a widespread but mistaken belief that no danger exists as long as you pick up a cone shell by its broad end. This is not so - the snout which houses the venomous dart can move along the entire opening of the shell. Treatment for cone shell stings is essentially the same as for snakebite.

SNAKES

Fear of snakes is near the top of the list of human phobias. Mostly this fear is without foundation. We are far more afraid of snakes in the bush than our fellow motorists in the city, though the latter are statistically hundreds of times more likely to cause us serious harm. Snakes are inoffensive creatures that go out of their way to avoid us. Bites to humans are a defensive rather than offensive reaction. Of Australia's many venomous species only a few pose a serious threat to a healthy adult.

Unless you are 100% positive about a snake's identification, treat it as poisonous. Also remember that even nonvenomous snakes (such as pythons) have sizeable teeth and may bite if provoked. Snakes are protected by law in all states and must not be killed. In a desperate survival situation you may need to dispatch one for food, but do this only when there is no personal risk. Hunger is temporary; death by snakebite is not.

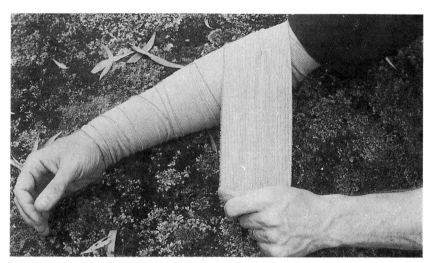

Always carry a roller bandage in snake country - just in case.

Several Australian species are quite dangerous to humans. The more troublesome include the taipan, fierce snake, tiger snake, rough-scaled snake, eastern small-eyed snake, king brown, death adder and copperhead.

Snake venom enters the lymphatic system first before being released into the bloodstream. Venom contains substances that coagulate blood, destroy blood cells and damage blood vessels. The neurotoxins in the venom go to work to cause muscle paralysis. There is not always sharp pain at the bite site - some people don't even realise they have been bitten until they start showing symptoms. Puncture marks are not always easy to see. Once bitten, the effects of the venom may not be felt for several minutes or even a couple of hours. Often one of the first signs is paralysis of the jaw or tongue muscles. This may be followed by a tightening in the diaphragm and rib cage muscles as the paralysis spreads. Further symptoms include headache, nausea, vomiting, blurred vision, light-headedness, profuse sweating and discoloured urine. In severe cases unconsciousness and death may result.

Treatment for snakebite is described in detail in the first aid chapter. One or two 75 mm crepe roller bandages should always be carried in the rucksack in snake country. Prevention is always better than cure, so wear boots that reach above the ankles when bush-bashing. Long trousers or heavy gaiters offer extra protection. Keep an eye out for snakes near waterholes and in swampy area. Wherever there are plenty of frogs there are likely to be snakes preying upon them.

FRESHWATER CROCODILES

The smaller Johnstone River crocodile (found only in fresh water) is a fish-eater and poses little threat to humans unless harassed. In crowded shrinking waterholes they can be territorial and cranky, but this aggression is mostly directed toward other crocodiles. These reptiles move surprisingly quickly on land.

Freshwater crocs are not really a danger, but teeth like these deserve respect.

INSECTS

Some ants give a very painful bite. The main culprits are bull ants, jumping ants and the green ants of northern regions. An acquired allergy to repeated bites is an extra danger, and potentially quite serious. Severe reactions to ant bites (and bee stings) often respond to an antihistamine. This should only be administered to a conscious victim.

Beware of green ant nests in rainforests and vine thickets. They look like a fist-sized ball of leaves suspended from a branch. Bump into one accidentally and you're covered in an army of stinging ants in no time.

Of the many bee species found in Australia only the European honey bee is a danger to man. If you're stung the poison gland and attached stinger should be immediately removed. Scrape it away sideways with the blade of a knife or your fingernail. Avoid squeezing more poison into the wound - tweezers should not be used. Apply an ice pack or cold compress once the stinger is out. If a serious allergic reaction to the sting occurs seek medical attention immediately.

A bee stings once and dies soon afterwards but wasps can sting repeatedly. The most troublesome is the European wasp, thought to have arrived in Australia via New Zealand.

Bloodsucking horseflies are more nuisance than danger. They hover slowly for awhile before alighting on the skin. Spot them in time and you can swat them before they bite.

Around two hundred species of mosquito call Australia home. Most are harmless to man but others carry a variety of diseases spread through their bites. Ross River fever, malaria, dengue fever, encephalitis, filariasis and epidemic polyarthritis are all carried by mossies. Global statistics on human fatalities show the mosquito to be by far the most dangerous insect in the world. Though mosquitoes tend to be associated with tropical areas, they can be just as voracious in temperate zones.

Reduce biting attacks by wearing long-sleeve shirts and trousers. Sleep under a mosquito net at night. Cover exposed areas of skin with repellent. Dusk is their prime time, especially when it's still warm and the breeze has dropped. Campfire smoke keeps them away but only if you are in the thick of it. Sit upwind a metre from the fire and you may still be devoured. Throwing chunks of termite nest on the fire seems to deter them.

LEECHES, SCORPIONS AND CENTIPEDES

Explorers' journals abound with accounts of 'leech-infested swamps' but these blood-sucking creatures are more a bother than a threat. Usually encountered when swimming in quiet, reedy pools or bushwalking through damp rainforest, they are easily removed. Some bushwalkers just pull them off, but this may add to the bleeding. Instead, touch them with a lighted match and they drop off. Let the wound bleed a little before applying some antiseptic to prevent infection (the wound will continue to bleed anyway because leech saliva contains an anti-clotting agent). The initial bite is not usually painful and you may not even realise you've been bitten until you take off your boots.

Australian scorpions are not considered a mortal threat to humans, unlike their brethren in Mexico and other parts of the world. They can still give an intensely painful sting accompanied by swelling. Shaking boots out before putting them on in the morning is always wise.

Centipedes, like scorpions, are not generally viewed as life-threatening in Australia although their bite can be very painful. Inflammation and swelling are common and some blistering may occur. Discomfort can last for days after the bite. Though no deaths have been recorded from centipede bites in this country, this is a creature to treat with respect.

SPIDERS AND TICKS

Out in the bush every spider bite should be taken seriously. Our rich spider fauna includes several species that give a very painful bite and at least three that are potentially lethal. Funnel-webs and red-backs are responsible for over a dozen deaths each year in Australia, with the Funnel-web considered the more dangerous of the two. The sheer power of a funnel-web's fangs is impressive. Fortunately antivenenes are available for both species.

Pressure/immobilisation treatment is suitable for funnel-web bites and should be initiated without delay. For red-backs apply a cold compress only. In both cases seek medical attention as soon as you can.

Many of us wouldn't know a wolf spider from an orb-weaver, but identification of spiders is paramount when a bite occurs. *If it can be done safely,* capture the offending spider and take it along to the hospital.

Two other dangerous species are the fiddleback and the black house spider. The fiddleback's distribution is not fully understood but it is known to exist in Sydney and much of South Australia. It probably also occurs in other areas. The black house spider is common throughout Australia.

Learn to identify these four dangerous species. Contact with them usually occurs in garden sheds, dark garages and in the home rather than in the bush, where most spider encounters stem from scrub-bashing through dense undergrowth.

Mouse spiders and wolf spiders can provide a nasty bite but are not in the same league as the species already mentioned. The hunstsman is large and formidable looking but harmless to man.

Ticks are carriers of a multitude of diseases worldwide. In Australia the most troublesome species is the scrub tick found in eastern Australia between the mountains and the coast. Also called the paralysis tick, its saliva contains a poison that causes muscular paralysis. If left untreated symptoms may worsen to affect breathing and circulation. Scrub ticks and other species are responsible for spreading other ailments such as Q fever.

Ticks should be removed as soon as they are detected. Their preference for burrowing into soft, hidden areas such as the groin or armpit makes it a good idea to have regular tick inspections during and after visiting problem regions. The earlier you get to them the easier they are to remove and the less they will affect health. Don't squeeze them - use tweezers to *carefully* pull them off. Ensure the entire creature is removed, mouth parts and all. Use pressure/immobilisation after the tick is removed.

FERAL ANIMALS

Give feral cattle and pigs a wide berth. On rare occasions they may show aggression toward humans. Try to make sure a tree is handy, either to hide behind or to climb if things turn ugly. Don't camp near regularly used cattle trails, especially near waterways. The animals' noisy complaining will not only keep you awake, but a cranky bull may want to take matters further.

Feral pigs carry parasites harmful to humans, so if circumstances necessitate the eating of wild pig meat, cook it very thoroughly.

The introduced cane toad is a common sight in Queensland and has now spread into parts of New South Wales and the Northern Territory. When irritated, a milky venom is released from the skin on its back. Most of this comes from two swollen glands behind its eyes. An extremely agitated toad can squirt this venom up to a metre away.

Cane toads should not be handled without gloves. Even their eggs are highly poisonous. The venom is cardioactive (affecting the heart) and one of its major ingredients is adrenaline. Getting some on your skin is not a problem in itself. To work the poison must enter the body through a cut or via the eyes, nose or mouth. Cane toads have no use to the survivor so there is no need to go near them.

In certain Australian environments the likelihood of running into a hazardous creature is very remote indeed.

Photo: Gary Tischer

213

Survival Priorities
Equipment

1. The right equipment can save your life. Quality gear provides a safety margin in rugged terrain, harsh weather and stressful situations. Buy the best you can afford - there is no such thing as bargain survival equipment.

2. Think of *all* your gear as survival equipment. Choose gear on the basis of how it can help you stay alive.

3. Equipment is an aid to basic survival skills, not a substitute for them. In an emergency your most prized gear may be lost or broken.

4. Hiring equipment for a single trip is a good way to test gear out - everything from tents and HF radios to fully outfitted 4WD vehicles can be hired.

5. The ultimate survival challenge is to be stranded with minimal clothing and no equipment. In such situations you must be able to improvise gear from natural materials. Especially useful is the making of cordage from plant fibres. 'Bush string' used to lash or bind sticks or branches can help create a variety of handmade survival aids.

6. Make checklists of equipment before every trip, and check each item off as it is packed. Only one person should do the packing to avoid confusion or omissions.

7. Safety equipment that hasn't been used for some time should be checked for signs of deterioration.

Equipment for Survival

One of the first tasks when planning a journey is to list the gear needed. It's easier to break this up into three lists: general equipment, first aid gear and food supplies. Over time you'll evolve your own ideas about what constitutes essential gear. Use what works best for you. Trial and error will make some of the choices for you but seek out expert advice before you start spending money. Get the very best gear you can afford. Cheap boots, tents, packs and sleeping bags are no bargain if they don't hold up to sustained use. In an emergency your life may depend on having quality, dependable gear.

Outdoor equipment continues to improve each year. It is more activity-specific and user-friendly than ever before and manufacturers are increasingly able to combine efficient design, lightweight materials and enhanced durability.

Think of all your gear as survival equipment. In extreme circumstances its eventual function may be to keep you alive. In a survival situation the right gear and the ability to use it can make all the difference. A single match, compass or plastic bag may be all that separates you from death when things go wrong. If you have compiled an appropriate survival kit and chosen the rest of your gear with survival in mind you are way ahead if the unexpected strikes.

RUCKSACKS

Pack selection can be whittled down to three main factors: purpose, capacity and fit. The purpose which the pack is meant to serve is the first consideration. There are basically four types of full-size packs: travel, expedition, alpine and hybrid.

For global backpackers coping with airport luggage carousels and European hostel hopping, the travel pack is ideal. It features hide-away straps, convenient carry handles, suitcase-like zips and plenty of extra compartments. Virtually all have a detachable day pack on the front and you can get to the main pack through the front as well as the top. Straps and hip belts on some travel packs may be of a lower standard than on expedition packs, which are specially designed to carry heavier loads closer to the back.

Expedition packs are made for serious bush trekking, with extra reinforcing along all seams and extremely tough abrasion-resistant fabrics. The harness systems in these packs have improved a lot over the years and the innovations keep coming. One of the best features is the lumbar pad. This is attached to the pack where it meets the small of your back, providing improved cushioning and allowing a bit of air to get between back and pack. The comfort and stability of modern internal frame rucksacks is a far cry from the aluminium packs of yesteryear with their unwieldy weight distribution, fragile frames and tendency to snag on every passing branch.

Another specialised rucksack type is the alpine pack made for mountaineering journeys. It is smaller, lighter and more streamlined than a conventional full-size trek pack. It has fewer compartments and fits more neatly to the curvatures of the climber's body. Meant for speed rather than maximum carrying capacity, it's not really roomy enough for full-scale self-sufficient explorations of lengthy duration.

There are optional extras (called 'module options') that can be attached with webbing to some packs for those who combine hiking with other pursuits. Detachable day packs are the most popular option, but climbers could instead attach a module for carrying crampons, snow-shovel, ice-axe and climbing ropes. Yet another module is designed to securely hold cross-country skis or a snowboard.

The fourth type of rucksack is known as the hybrid pack. It contains features of different pack types in the one pack. Examples are an expedition rucksack with carrying handles, an alpine pack with a detachable day pack (a la hostellers pack) or a travel pack that comes in a narrower alpine-pack shape.

From a survival standpoint one of the more useful pack accessories is the hydration system. This features an easy-access plastic tube attached externally at shoulder height which allows water to be sucked up from a hidden water bag. The idea is that you drink more regularly if water is easily accessible rather than having to stop and drag out a water bottle at every stop. Hydration systems are as much a safety feature as a convenience. It has been shown that drinking small amounts of water regularly (rather than gulping it down at distant intervals) is the best way to keep your body hydrated.

Rucksack capacity must be measured against body size and shape. Pack size is measured by litre capacity; the standard is 60-65 litres for

Pack design technology has made great strides in the past decade. The Cirque 70 Rucksack is one of the most durable expedition packs made. A detachable day pack, snowboard module or crag and ice module can also be attached to the main pack. The hood may be converted into a belt bag when detached and combined with the removable hip belt. The Cirque Rucksack System incorporates a BAR Harness for optimum load-bearing, comfort and fit. Photo: Andrew Kemp women and 70-75 for men. Don't be tempted to buy a larger pack so you can go further and cram in more. If your body is really meant for the smaller size you will sacrifice both comfort and efficiency - the load won't sit properly. Harnesses and straps on modern packs are very adjustable, so try on as many packs as it takes to find one that feels right.

Packs should be loaded with weight when you try them on in the shop. Fifteen kilos will give a good idea of the pack's balance, stability, fit and comfort. Load weight should be distributed between hips and shoulders, and it should be easy to adjust the straps to shift weight from one to the other. Centre of gravity is all-important. The top of a well-fitting rucksack will fit reasonably snugly against your shoulder blades. Some slight leaning forward is unavoidable with a heavy pack, but you should not feel you are about to topple over onto your back like a floundering turtle. Ideally 90% of the weight should rest on the hips and only 10% on the shoulders.

A vital factor in pack fit is the distance from hip to shoulder. A man and a woman of equal height and weight will not attain the same degree of comfort if they put on the same rucksack. This is because men are typically longer in the torso, whereas women tend toward shorter hip-to-neck distance and longer legs.

Choose your sleeping bag carefully. Its warmth can be significant in maintaining the most important survival priority - bodily protection. Try to find a sheltered spot for sleeping (such as this natural rock enclosure) where you are protected from wind and safe from falling branches. **Photo: Andrew Kemp**

SLEEPING BAGS

For lightweight camping, 'mummy-style' sleeping bags filled with down offer the best warmth-for-weight efficiency. These taper toward the foot of the bag to reduce bulk and weight and are suitable for all sorts of conditions. The many advantages of down sleeping bags are offset by their susceptibility to moisture. If they get wet they lose their insulation and take a long time to dry out. A number of synthetic bag fillings have been trying to emulate or improve upon down for years, with mixed results.

In the morning spread your bag out to air and to release accumulated moisture before packing it away. Some bags are made with a waterproof foot. This sidesteps the age-old problem of a bag getting damp at the foot end and the moisture creeping up towards the head. Compression storage bags are a handy item for compacting the sleeping bag down to a smaller size for stowing away. These incorporate tightening straps which reduce the size of a packed bag by about a third.

SLEEPING MATS AND GROUNDSHEETS

Sleeping mats provide an insulation and comfort barrier between ground and sleeping bag. They are normally used inside the tent or bivvy. In places where ground gets cold or damp there is no question of doing without one. Mats are equally necessary in hot conditions. Sandy banks of Top End waterholes stay very hot even after the sun has been down for a couple of hours. Retreating from mosquitoes into a hot tent is bad enough, but without a mat things are much worse - the stored heat in the sand goes straight through your back. The mat has a survival use during the day as well. If no other platform is available it helps separate you from the hot ground to conserve the body's moisture.

Thin, closed-cell foam mats have been around for years and are moisture-resistant, light and easy to roll up. Nylon-encased self-inflating mats are a pricier but more comfortable alternative. These are available in full size or hip length. You open the valve to fill the mattress with air. When you pack up the mat in the morning use your knees to push the air out again as you roll it up.

Self-inflating mats are very durable but air leaks can happen. After a trip the way to pinpoint a leak is to fill a bathtub with soapy water, submerge the entire inflated mat and wait for bubbles to surface from the leak. Mark the spot immediately, then repair. In the bush a quiet creek (minus the soap) does the same trick.

Most self-inflating mats can be converted into comfortable camp seats with the addition of a casing into which the mattress is folded. These converters weigh as little as 300 grams.

A plastic groundsheet protects the tent bottom from sharp stones and separates it from damp ground. It also performs other functions. You can use it as a windbreak, emergency shelter or flotation device (when crossing rivers, fill with air and tie up one end like a Santa sack). They can help in making a solar still. The edge of the groundsheet protruding from beneath the tent is a convenient place to put things so they don't get lost. Objects are more visible against the background of the groundsheet than the ground itself. Torches and eating utensils are less likely to be left behind.

STOVES AND COOKING GEAR

These days a cooking stove must be considered essential gear for overnight bush trips. It may be impractical, impossible or ecologically irresponsible to build a cooking fire. Most cooking fires are built too large and waste wood. It is disheartening to come upon the remains of a camper's raging bonfire, its presence betrayed by the pile of ugly charred remnants. A cooking fire needn't be wider than the circumference of a dinner plate. If you regularly feed it small twigs it will produce sufficient heat to cook even the most elaborate bush meal.

Aside from environmental advantages, stoves let you stop and cook anywhere, from barren deserts to snowcapped peaks. The flame on a stove is easier to control than any campfire, and everything from a cup of tea to a hearty stew is easy to prepare.

Simplicity is relative. The best stove is one you can use with minimal fuss. If it's too fiddly or you don't feel comfortable operating it in all conditions then you need a simpler stove. Two of the most widely used outdoor stoves in Australia are the Swedish-made Trangia and the American-made MSR brands. For both you can buy individual parts of the stove separately, which is a great help.

Trangias are popular because they are virtually foolproof and very easy to use. For straightforward simplicity they're unmatched. Trangia uses methylated spirits only, a fuel readily available in Australia but harder to find in third world countries (it is sometimes called white gas). The Trangia takes about 10 minutes to boil a litre of water. It requires no priming or pressurisation. The metho must be stored in a bottle designed for that purpose - *any old plastic bottle will not do.*

The MSR Whisperlite Internationale 600 is a rugged multi-fuel stove that will burn white gas, kerosene, petrol and even aviation fuel. With white gas it boils a litre of water in under four minutes. For alpine camping this is one of the quickest stoves for melting a pot of snow, and it also comes with a self-cleaning jet. This is a built-in wire which pushes out debris that might otherwise clog the works. As its name suggests, the Whisperlite weighs in at a mere 402 grams (minus the fuel bottle).

A stove that does its job and is simple to use makes camping in adverse conditions much more bearable.   Photo: Gary Tischer

The MSR Dragonfly is a similar high quality expedition stove. It burns diesel fuel as well as all the fuels used by the Whisperlite. This extra fuel option is handy if you are driving a diesel 4WD.

Each fuel has its quirks. Kerosene flame can be smoky. Metho stove burners won't run at full flame for more than about 35 minutes before they need refilling.

Compare using a stove with the time-consuming trauma of gathering dry tinder and wood (if there is any), piling it just right, lighting it and scorching your eyebrows trying to blow life into the flame. For time management there is no contest between a stove and a wood fire.

Keep it simple when it comes to cookware and utensils. For lone treks you can rely solely upon an aluminium billy, a folding knife, a spoon and a cup. The billy cooks dinner, is cleaned and then boils water for tea. A fork is redundant; the spoon handles everything. The large cup serves doubly as a bowl. In cases where a wide dinner plate is preferable (for eating freshly caught fish, for example) a level stone, palm frond base or slab of bark makes an adequate substitute.

OTHER REQUIREMENTS

It is worth carrying basic fishing gear so you can supplement rations with fresh fish. Some hikers carry telescopic fishing rods but a plastic hand reel will do for remote regions. Serious walking can lead you to pristine waterways that have never been fished; these practically guarantee success. In tropical estuaries you can even use a hand spool to fish with lures. You don't get the even retrieval that a rod provides but plenty of fish can be caught this way. Cast the lure by hand and wind it in quickly the second it hits the water.

Pack an assortment of hooks, swivels, sinkers, lures and wire traces in a small plastic box divided into compartments. In the tropics, 300 metres of 20 lb. test monofilament line will suffice. For rod fishing a lighter line is preferable, but for hand-casting the 20 lb. strain is best since the only drag control is your arm muscle. Wire traces are essential up north because anything from a trevally to a hammerhead shark may take your hook. Ultra-light tackle is fine for sportfishing, but in a survival situation you want gear that will hook and land as many fish as possible.

You can buy fishing gloves but cotton garden gloves with leather across the palm serve equally well. They protect against line friction and fish spines, and are also invaluable for handling crayfish or prying oysters from rocks.

The small netting sold as a replacement for prawn scoop nets is a useful survival item. Thread the top loops onto a green branch, bending the branch into a teardrop shape as you go. This do-it-yourself scoop net can be used on bait fish, crabs and yabbies.

A basic bush repair kit should include safety pins, small sewing kit, rubber bands and spare batteries for torch and camera. You might include a small wire saw, which is a piece of serrated wire with rings on each end. You wrap it around a branch, pull back and forth on each ring and saw through it with friction. The needle holder from the first aid kit can be used as needle-nosed pliers. Some duct tape is useful for emergency patch jobs. Take a look at all your equipment before a journey and ask yourself if you have the materials to make a decent temporary repair if there's a problem. If not you should revise what's in your repair kit. Tent seams may split, water bags may leak, tarps may get punctured, etc. Be ready.

On expeditions where a lot of steep gullies must be negotiated a length of climbing rope should be considered. On long walks where you carry a lot of food there may not be spare pack space for rope, in which case avoiding steep, rugged areas is the only option.

Descending a canyon wall on your own is accomplished by doubling the rope over a branch so both ends hang down evenly. Then grasp both strands firmly together and lower yourself hand over hand to the bottom. Several twists in the double rope reduce the chance that a strand will escape your grasp. Once at the bottom, simply untwist the rope and pull it down after you. Brief climbs can be accomplished by the same method, provided you can toss one end of the rope over a suitably strong branch above your head. Test the holding power of the anchoring branch before clambering up.

WARNING

Rock climbing, abseiling and wilderness rope work are not for the untrained. A series of courses in the relevant speciality are essential to ensure a suitable level of safety.

The best items for the bush are those with multiple uses. A shovel will dig holes, but you can also barbecue a slab of meat on the blade by holding it over the fire. A chemical glow light can signal rescuers, light up a cave or attract fish. A space blanket can conserve heat or repel it, and can be used as shade or a signal reflector. A self-inflating sleep mat provides insulation against hot or cold ground and could also be shaped into a full leg splint. A triangular bandage may serve as desert headwear, a sling or as an absorbent cloth for collecting dew. A jacket can become padding for a bruised hip, a signalling aid, a rain collector or a pillow. In a survival situation consider all the different ways a piece of gear can help you. For example, strong nylon cord has a range of uses:

1. Clothesline.

2. Extra tie-downs for tents and shelters in windy weather.

3. For lowering your pack down rock faces. Instead of wearing it and struggling for balance you send it down first.

4. Chin strap for your hat.

5. As a safety rope for group river crossings.

6. As a replacement for shoelaces, camera strap, belt, etc.

7. For capturing freshwater yabbies. Tie some meat or a piece of fish to one end, lower into the water and pull it up slowly when the yabbie grabs it. This is where that scoop net is useful.

8. For tying water bags, wet socks or drinking cup to the outside of the pack.

Modern technology has given us new clothing and pack fabrics, better boot design and a range of other improvements for bush travel. The role that electronics now plays in outdoor pursuits is no better illustrated than in the three-man Icetrek Expedition to the South Pole in November 1998. The explorers carried an Iridium, the world's first hand-held global satellite phone. This phone allows communication with anyone from virtually anywhere on earth. Though the cost is several thousand dollars, such a phone would be worth its weight in gold on journeys to harsh, remote parts of the planet.

Global Positioning Systems and Emergency Position Indicating Rescue Beacons (EPIRBs) are other examples of technological survival aids. It must be stressed that such gear is only as good as your understanding of how to use it, and it may not be available in certain survival situations. In a vehicle smash, boat capsize or fall down a gully, electronic gear can be broken or permanently lost.

Think of equipment as an aid to survival skills, not a substitute for them. We rely on many items more than we realise. Imagine being camped in the desert 100 kilometres from anywhere and a dingo walks off with your boots during the night. Could you cope? Is there a Plan B for such an occurrence? An HF radio is a great idea for vehicle travel in isolated areas, but suppose yours packs up just when you need it to contact the Flying Doctor? Does someone know where you are? Are you competent enough in first aid to look after the patient (or yourself) until someone comes looking for you?

When you're coping with a life-threatening situation your survival kit and safety gear become precious. Don't let them deteriorate from lack of use. Make periodic checks to see what needs replacing. Flares and EPIRBs, for example, have an expiry date after which they should not be used. Most flares have a three year shelf life, and it is unwise (and may also be illegal) to keep them longer than that. Other survival gear can rust or grow brittle with age. Items such as car jacks and 4WD winch cables must be kept clean to work properly.

Always make equipment lists before a trip. Don't rely on memory. Check everything off as it's packed into the rucksack or the vehicle.

IMPROVISED GEAR

When gear is broken or lost you may be able to make a substitute using wilderness materials, either on their own or combined with man-made objects. At other times you might need specific items such as a rack for smoking meat, a stretcher for an injured person or some cordage made from plant fibres. Makeshift gear can make a real difference to survival when no other options are available.

Something as simple as a hollow reed can be invaluable in the right circumstances. Water hidden deep in a tree trunk or rock crevice could be sucked out using the reed like a straw. Even a single stout stick has potential as a balancing staff for river crossings, a hunting club for reptiles or as a support for the billy. Collect two long branches, add a couple of large plastic bags and you have an emergency stretcher or camp bed.

In a primitive scenario (i.e. with no gear at all) it is important to be able to join poles or branches together. Any fresh, supple vine or inner tree bark can be made into 'bush string' which is used to lash sticks or branches together to make shelters, rafts, fish traps and a range of other survival aids.

It's a simple matter to spin (or plait) string, cord or thick rope from common plants. Longer grasses, inner bark, vines and sedges offer pliant, fibrous material. Virtually every species of palm tree has lengthy flexible fibres on some part of the plant that are perfect for bush cord-age. With grasses and rushes don't yank the whole plant out by the roots - this wastes energy and kills the plant. Harvest the material by cutting it off just above ground level so it can grow back. Test fibres for pliability and strength before harvesting.

While some fibres are used as they come off the plant, others should be spun or braided to increase strength. A plaited rope consisting of numerous narrow fibre strands is normally stronger than a single vine of the same thickness.

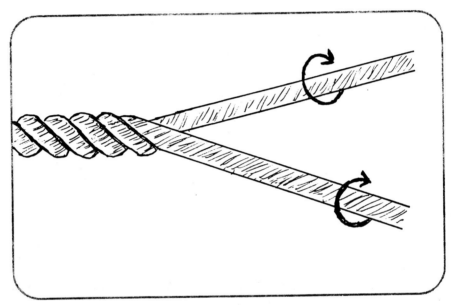

Two-strand spinning is a simple way to make strong cord. Collect plant fibres and separate them into two strands. Each strand should be of equal thickness and be made up of numerous individual fibres, which are spun clockwise to hold them together. The two strands are then twisted together anticlockwise. Spinning the cord is easiest when a second person holds the other end. If on your own you'll have to tie the end to a branch, hold it between your feet or weigh it down with a rock. Take your time and aim for uniform thickness.

Plaiting or braiding is another way. The standard three-strand plait is easy to learn and quick to complete. The end of one braided cord can be woven into the end of another to create any length you need.

With improvised survival gear it doesn't have to be pretty as long as it works. Trying to memorise dozens of different types of knots and

226

their specific uses is impractical. Instead, learn 5 or 6 that you can tie competently and that will see you through most situations. If you regularly practise survival skills you'll soon learn which knots are best for lashing poles, tying on fish hooks or making adjustable guy ropes for the tent.

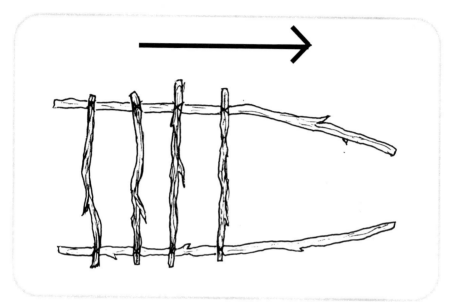

A travois (overhead view) is a wooden platform which you drag along the ground behind you. It can make carrying heavy gear or an injured person easier. Like so many other handmade survival aids, all that's needed are some cord (or plant fibres), a knife and some tree branches of appropriate size.

Survival Priorities
At Sea

1. Don't abandon your craft unless you're sure it will sink. Staying with the vessel provides flotation (which conserves energy) and makes you more visible to searchers.

2. Wear a life jacket.

3. Your first goals in an offshore survival situation are to protect yourself from the elements and attract rescue.

4. Store a watertight survival cache in your boat where it can be immediately grabbed in an emergency. Drinking water, EPIRBs and flares are the priorities.

5. If floating, save precious body heat by adopting the H.E.L.P. position (covering up wrists, groin and chest).

6. Your life raft won't help if you cannot detach it. Proper training in life raft procedures could save your life.

7. Try to establish where you are in relation to land.

8. Windburn, sunburn and saltwater sores are the most common health problems. Cover up and stay out of the sun. Don't waste energy. Keep the bottom of the life raft dry.

9. Flares, signal mirrors and emergency radio beacons (EPIRBs) save lives. Learn how to use them properly.

Survival At Sea

Survival at sea and survival in the bush are not mutually exclusive. Many isolated coastal areas are accessible only by boat. Boating mishaps on remote shores can develop into bush survival situations.

Most principles of survival on land also apply to exploring the coast by tinnie or cruising on a yacht at sea. The difference at sea is that problems of exposure, water procurement and signalling take on a greater urgency. For humans with minimal gear the ocean provides major survival challenges.

A capsize is always serious. Heavy seas, cold water and loss of vital supplies can spell disaster for the unprepared. Today's sailors rely on sophisticated navigational gear, expensive radio beacons and other modern equipment, but emergency beacons and other essentials may fail, get lost or become unusable. A boat floating upside down in rolling seas makes accessing gear in the cabin very tough. Life rafts can fail to inflate or be swept away in heavy seas as you try to climb aboard. A yacht can sink in less than a minute. To survive you must know where all emergency gear is stored and be able to reach it in those crucial few seconds before you hit the water.

Basic marine safety equipment must be carried by law, depending on the size of the vessel and where it's being used. Additional gear should be considered where applicable. Investment in reliable safety equipment is money well spent, and training in its proper use is equally vital. Certified courses in marine safety, navigation and sea survival are well worth the time. Telling someone where you're going and when you expect to return is important on land, but even more so at sea where survival resources may be scant.

Those who have clung for days to a capsized craft or survived weeks in a life raft all tend to say the same thing afterwards: "I wish I had tied more gear down". Put small items into lockers secured to the vessel. Latches must be strong enough so they don't fly open in a capsize. Sturdy net bags secured at the top are handy for storage. Tie them to something solid. Survival items such as fishing rods, gaffs, ropes and landing nets should be individually secured to the gunwale.

Everything that's not tied down...

Back in the 1970s a lone fisherman was exploring a Top End tidal river in an open tinnie. He bumped into an unseen object (probably a submerged log) which overturned his craft and flung him into the water. Nothing in the boat was tied down. Everything but his rifle, a single tin of food and a few other odds and ends sank out of sight. He had no maps or compass. In those few seconds a leisurely bush trip turned into a survival ordeal. He was stranded for two months in an isolated region until rescued (purely by luck) by some passing stockmen on horseback.

In 1989 a 12.65 metre trimaran was overturned by a huge wave off the coast of New Zealand, leaving four crew huddled in the aft cabin. Their vessel carried a functioning EPIRB which transmitted for the first eight days, but for some reason the signal was never picked up. The men spent 119 days floating at sea before reaching land. During the first days of their ordeal a number of vital pieces of gear floated away. Fortunately this situation was rectified before it destroyed their survival chances.

At sea no gear can afford to be wasted. Even seemingly inconsequential items may assist survival in some way. Stow all gear securely and know where to find essentials in a hurry.

GEAR TO SAVE YOUR LIFE

The gear you carry (or can salvage) on the water is far more significant than in land-based survival. In the bush a short piece of cord, a tarp or a single plastic bottle might be merely handy, but offshore such items can be the deciding factor in whether you live or die. In the water your exposure to the elements is more immediate and perilous so flotation and clothing become crucial. In the bush an individual on foot is hard to spot from the air, but a person floating in water is virtually invisible in an expanse of whitecaps and swells.

In addition to normal water and food supplies you should have a special survival food cache stored in double plastic bags in a locker near the hatch. Store tinned goods separately. Remove paper labels from tin cans and re-label with waterproof indelible marker. Emergency supplies could include rice (which can be eaten uncooked after soaking), freeze-dried foods, muesli mix, milk powder and high-energy foods such as chocolates, sweets, energy bars, etc. Foods that don't require cooking should be the mainstays. You won't be able to cook on a life raft, but it's remotely possible a small portable stove might be used in very calm seas on an overturned vessel.

A hand-held portable VHF radio can save your life. This should be stored in a waterproof plastic bag in a secure locker. Passing container ships may pick up your signal. Do not assume that passing ships will see you. A yacht sunk by a whale off the Costa Rican coast spent 66 days afloat before being rescued. During their life raft ordeal they counted 40 passing ships on the horizon before being spotted and rescued by the 41st.

MARINE SURVIVAL KIT

A sea survival kit should include the following items, individually wrapped in waterproof plastic and stored together in a secure but easily accessible locker.

1. **EPIRB (emergency rescue beacon)**
2. **Hand-held VHF radio**
3. **Water storage containers**
4. **First Aid Kit**
5. **Dried food**
6. **A manual on survival at sea**
7. **Fishing lines, hooks and lures**
8. **Gaff hooks/hand spears with extra spear tips**
9. **Waterproof matches**
10. **Space blanket/tarp**
11. **Hand-held saltwater desalinator (Pur Survivor 6 Watermaker)**
12. **High-energy snack foods (chocolate, boiled sweets)**
13. **Signal mirror and/or signalling torch**
14. **Floating stainless steel knives and sharpening stones**
15. **Plankton net/landing net**
16. **Full-body survival suits**
17. **Tin opener (and spare)**

18. **Spoons, plastic bowls and large cups with handles**
19. **Heavy-duty waterproof torch and spare batteries**
20. **Distress V-sheet to attract rescuers**
21. **Emergency flares/dye markers**
22. **Electronic flint lighter**

Use this list as a guide, to be adjusted according to your vessel and the type of trip. Long-distance racing yachts might carry three or four EPIRBs to be on the safe side because they sail so far from land. Even in coastal boating a spare beacon isn't a bad idea.

The first aid kit will include items not found in the normal bush kit such as sea sickness pills, saltwater soap and cream for sea sores. Ginger root powder capsules are a natural method of treating motion sickness and don't cause drowsiness like some medications. Sunburn and windburn are common problems when adrift without a canopy; plenty of sunblock is essential.

A gaff is a useful survival tool. It can spear fish, help lift sea turtles into the craft or grab at passing seaweed. A speargun or hand spear is also handy for catching fish. Be super-cautious with knives and other sharp objects in an inflatable. People have sunk their own rafts while trying to gaff fish.

Fishing line is a crucial item, not only for fishing but for tying things down so they don't float away. Carry plenty of different sized fish hooks in your kit as well as wire leaders. Pelagic fish have sharp teeth that will cut through the line. Wear heavy gloves to protect hands when handling spiny fish - the tiniest cuts can quickly fester.

One item that can save your life is a handheld desalinator. A solid unit containing a series of filters is pumped by hand, and the sea water that goes in one end comes out the other as drinkable fresh water. It is not only seafarers who can benefit from these units. An explorer on foot travelling a dry and desolate coast might also carry one, not as a substitute for normal water rations but for emergency use only. The compact *PUR Survivor 06 Watermaker* weighs around 2 kilos and is capable of producing up to a litre of water per hour. It pressurises the sea water and forces it through a semipermeable membrane, eliminating virtually all bacteria, viruses and 98.4% of the salt content. This is achieved with a simple manual pump. Tony Bullimore kept hydrated with one of these when trapped under the hull of Exide Challenger in the Southern Ocean in 1997. The entire unit is 200 mm long.

Another item of interest to the survivor is the *Hot Pak Self-Heating Meal*. These pre-cooked meals heat themselves. A measured amount of water (included in the kit) is added, activating the chemical heat pack.

The hot meal is then ready to eat in twelve minutes. The kit includes heater, water, plate and fork. No refrigeration is needed.

The HotPak Self-heating Meal has a shelf life of five years.   Photo: West Marine

The PUR Survivor 06 Watermaker   Photo: West Marine Products, U.S.A.

Emergency food rations with a five year shelf life are available. These are easily digested rations designed to minimise thirst and offer 3600 calories of balanced nutrition per packet. Sealed 125 ml foil sachets of emergency drinking water can also be obtained from marine supply stores; these are the most accurate way to measure water consumption in a survival situation. They're sold by the case, which holds eight litres total (64 packets).

Some specialized marine survival gear can be difficult to find in Australia. If you're having trouble it's worth trying the huge U.S. company West Marine (PO Box 50070, Watsonville, CA 95077-0070, U.S.A. Tel:1-800-143404, website: www.westmarine.com) from whom you can order directly. Their catalogue of equipment is over 600 pages.

A good knife is vital at sea. Floating stainless steel knives are best, preferably in a sheath which you can attach to your waist. Keep all knives sharp - you will use them constantly to cut line, fillet fish and make repairs. In the absence of a tin opener they can help you forcibly open cans of food.

Signalling potential rescuers is a major priority. Keep flares dry. Attach a V-sheet, tarp, sail, space blanket or anything large, reflective or colourful to the drifting craft. Maximise visibility.

Aside from those items listed in the Marine Survival Kit there are others that can help your cause - sail thread and stainless steel needles, rechargeable batteries, portable gas cooking stove, tool kit (hammer, nails, pliers, chisels, saw, wire, etc.), extra cord and spare clothing (wool is preferable to cotton). If capsized, most of your vessel may be underwater so hammocks or air beds can assist sleeping.

Tarps, space blankets and sails are perfect for collecting rainwater. Have a supply of sealable containers to store the water. Many self-inflating life rafts come with a plastic rain-catcher.

ABANDONING SHIP

Mishaps at sea vary in their severity. A cruising yacht with a broken mast that's still upright is in a far less perilous position than three people in an exposed dinghy carrying minimal food and water and no signalling gear. In an overturned vessel there may still be access to supplies submerged in the cabin; if so, your chances are increased. The worst survival scenarios involve persons who have gone overboard and must try to reach land before exhaustion or exposure overtakes them.

If forced to abandon ship, take as much survival gear with you as you can. Life raft and drinking water are first on your list. Don't remove clothing. Air pockets trapped in clothing help keep you afloat. A well-made survival suit is one of the best investments an offshore boatie can make. These provide protection from the effects of hypothermia and enhance flotation. A full body suit prevents the small cuts and abrasions that lead to sea sores and infections in exposed conditions. They significantly reduce the effects of wind chill in an open boat, which can be a killer in itself.

Life jacket substitute - a pair of trousers knotted at the cuffs and swung over the head (to trap air) can be used to stay afloat. Airmen forced to ditch at sea have stayed afloat for over 36 hours with this simple technique. Large inflated plastic bags are also excellent for emergency flotation. While in the water, grab anything that floats.

When relaxed the human body floats quite well in sea water, so save energy by using as little motion as possible. If rescue is not imminent and you decide to swim for land, use leisurely energy-saving strokes in a steady rhythm. Almost all swimmers underestimate distance to land. It is always farther than it looks. If the tide pushes you away from shore just float and wait for it to turn and push you back in. Fighting against current leads quickly to exhaustion and is a major cause of beach fatalities in Australia.

A common myth is that the best way to stay warm in cold water is to swim vigorously. In reality this is the quickest way to lose precious body heat and reduce survival chances. Instead, relax at the surface in your life jacket in what is called the Heat Escape Lessening Posture (H.E.L.P.). Draw your knees up to chest level and fold your arms across your chest, with elbows up against the rib cage. The idea is to protect the body's areas of highest heat loss, where large amounts of blood circulate close to the skin surface. These crucial areas are the wrists, groin and sides of the chest. The HELP position keeps the vulnerable areas covered while your life jacket protects your neck and holds your head out of the water. Having the head above water conserves body heat and makes it easier to relax while floating.

When a group is in the water, huddle together as closely as possible with sides of chests touching. Put children in the middle of the huddle and keep everyone awake.

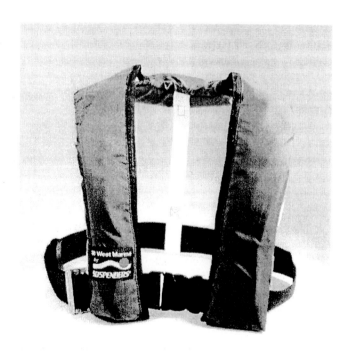

Modern life jacket design offers reliable flotation without the bulkiness found in older-style jackets.   **Photo: West Marine U.S.A.**

STAYING AFLOAT

In calm seas even nonswimmers wearing clothing can keep afloat if they can relax. The human body is naturally buoyant in salt water, and air trapped in clothes gives extra flotation. If waves prevent you floating on your back, use the following 'drown proofing' technique:

1. Take a breath, then relax face down in the water with arms extended in front of you.

2. Exhale calmly into the water, then scoop down with both hands to raise your head so your mouth *just breaks* the surface. A single relaxed leg kick will help lift you at the same time but don't kick unless you have to - your goal is sustained energy conservation. If your clothes are buoyant, pushing down with scooped hands should be enough *if you are relaxed*. Take a breath when lungs are empty, then close your mouth. A relaxed and complete exhalation is just as important as taking breaths; finish each exhalation completely before getting more air.

3. Lower your face back down and once again rest arms at the surface in front of you, exhaling normally. Don't worry about your legs; let them float out naturally behind you in the seconds before you need another breath. The key is to relax - your survival may depend on it. Breathe calmly - don't hyperventilate by gasping for air or trying to hold your breath underwater. It's all in the timing. If movements are minimalist and controlled you can achieve a fairly effortless rhythm. The trick is not to raise your head too far out of the water to inhale. Come up as high as you need to and no more.

Getting wet diminishes survival chances, so climb into a life raft if you can rather than jumping in the water and swimming for it. If there's time, put on the warmest clothes you can find before exiting the vessel. Inflatable life jackets are meant to be inflated *after* you get into the water, not on the boat. The way to enter water from a height is feet first with life jacket deflated, head up, back straight, mouth closed, nose pinched and elbows tight against your body to keep the life jacket from billowing out. While in the air, cross your ankles and keep legs straight and rigid. Once immersed pull the life jacket cord to inflate. If it malfunctions use the mouthpiece. Get clear of the vessel by swimming backwards with your legs.

If you're in the water for hours and feel yourself getting sleepy, fight it off - drowsiness is a by-product of cold exposure. If you succumb to sleep you can't maintain the HELP position, watch for swamping waves or signal rescuers. Do all you can to stay awake.

If you've just gone overboard, immediately try to attract the attention of those on board. Shout loudly and wave one arm over your head. Don't try to wave both arms as you tend to sink. If wearing a life jacket use the attached whistle. Quality life jackets also have a small attached light for use when a rescue vessel is near.

From Zero to Survival in Sixty Seconds

BE PREPARED - A leisurely boat cruise can turn into a survival situation in an instant.   In 1972 a schooner with six people on board was sunk by killer whales 500 kilometres off the coast of Costa Rica. They had only *one minute* to get organised before the yacht sank. In that time they salvaged a 3-metre fibreglass dinghy, an inflatable raft and enough food and water for three days.

They collected rain water and improvised fish hooks to catch food. Flying fish which jumped into their dinghy were eaten raw, and sea turtles floating nearby were dragged aboard. Thin strips of turtle meat were dried in the sun and the rest eaten raw. The turtle's blood was drunk immediately upon capture. They were rescued by a Japanese fishing boat after 37 days adrift. All survived.

If there has been a fire on board you may be forced to enter the water through oil flames on the surface. Go in feet first upwind of the boat and swim away underwater as far as possible. As you surface use a breast stroke to make a flame-free space for your head.

IN THE LIFE RAFT

In a dinghy, raft or boat your priorities are to prevent exposure to sun, wind and salt spray, attract rescuers and ration water supplies. Collect rainwater whenever possible and try to establish your location. Put gear in plastic bags and tie them to the craft so big waves will not send them overboard. In some cases the survivors themselves may need to be tethered to the craft. Most life rafts come with loops or other attachments for this purpose. With several persons in a raft, someone should remain on watch at all times to scan the horizon for ships or land.

Start fishing at once, but remember you should only eat when there is sufficient water. If you have no water you can still use the fish, not as food but for the drinkable fluid within their backbones. Fluids found in the stomachs of fish must be avoided as they are high in protein and will rob your body of moisture if consumed.

A raft is generally at the mercy of prevailing currents but you can use the wind to help steer it in the desired direction. Rig up a makeshift sail with a tarp or other material. The paddles that come with most rafts are valuable survival items and should be tied to the craft so they're not lost. Aside from their function as paddles they can become fishing rods, masts for sails or supports for plankton drag nets.

Check flares and keep them dry until needed. Flares are not all the same. While some types are for night use only, orange smoke flares are for signalling in daylight. Smoke is less effective in high winds. Other flares incorporate a built-in parachute that activates at a certain height to increase 'hang time' in the air. Learn what yours are meant to do and how to fire them safely. When planes or ships approach, use your flares or dye markers and flash your signal mirror toward the direction of rescuers. If you spot a ship or plane and have no flares or mirror, stand up in the raft and wave your arms to attract attention.

After sending out a distress call, try to maintain your position by using a sea anchor. A large sturdy canvas bag (such as that used to store sails) is an ideal sea anchor; a bucket also works well. Any heavy object that will slow your drift can be tried. A sea anchor has several important functions. It slows down rate of drift, which is important for trying to stay close to the spot where your original signal was activated. Sea anchors add stability and help keep the craft facing the weather so it is less likely to capsize.

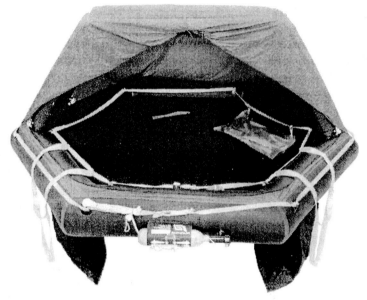

Photo: West Marine U.S.A.

Modern life rafts come with covers to keep out sun, wind and spray. In an exposed dinghy use a tarp or other material to rig up protection. Cold wind and regular spray soakings quickly lead to hypothermia. Bail out water from the bottom of the raft to avoid foot problems. Keep clothing on. It may be dampened to assist in cooling but don't leave it permanently soaked as this will lead to saltwater boils (sea sores) and leave you chilled at night. Stop dampening clothing at the first sign of skin soreness. Protect head and neck with a wide-brimmed hat, legionnaire's cap or other covering and wear sunglasses (with strap) to reduce glare.

Ration water immediately. Rations per day will depend on available supply. Military survival-at-sea manuals advocate drinking nothing the first day, about 400 millilitres for the next two or three days and 60 - 250 millilitres per day after that. Obviously a minimum of a litre a day is optimum but this may not be possible. Swish the water around in your mouth before swallowing to keep tongue and throat moist. Don't drink sea water or urine - this accelerates dehydration and can quickly lead to delirium. Don't smoke or drink alcohol.

If water supply isn't a problem you can turn your attention to whatever food you have salvaged. This too should be rationed and supplemented with fish as soon as possible. Most poisonous species inhabit inshore waters so fish caught far out to sea are generally safe to eat and nutritious. If you have no gloves, wrap your hands in cloth to pull in the line. Fish innards make good bait to catch more fish. Light from a torch can attract fish at night but conserve batteries - you may need the torch for signalling. Create lures out of coloured cloth, metal spoons, pieces of alfoil or whatever is at hand. A gaff handle with a knife *securely* tied to one end can spear fish that come alongside.

Sea turtles are often attracted to the shade beneath floating rafts. These are an excellent protein source if you can manage to pull them aboard. Fresh sea turtle blood is very nourishing but must be collected quickly. Once an incision is made in the leathery flesh you have only thirty seconds to collect the vitamin-rich flow before it coagulates.

A landing net or plankton net can be dragged through the water to catch smaller food sources. Consume these as soon as possible, especially in hot weather. Cut surplus fish or turtle meat into strips and hang it to dry in the sun.

Don't overlook sea birds as a potential food source. Birds may decide your craft is the ideal rest spot, and can be caught by hand or with a baited line. Consume the flesh, but not the blood.

Seaweed is another possible food source but it's very salty and should not be eaten unless you have plenty of fresh water. Floating seaweed is often the home of small crabs, shrimps or other creatures which can be eaten.

In a raft at sea the main problem with sharks is deciding how to handle hooked ones. Small sharks can be pulled aboard and clubbed but with large ones you should cut the line, even if it means sacrificing a precious fish hook. Shark skin is like sandpaper and doesn't do a rubber inflatable much good. Don't fish when sharks are around the raft and don't throw fish offal overboard. Keep hands and legs in the raft.

Surviving at sea is only part of the story. As you approach land you must decide the safest way to come ashore. Aim for a beach rather than rocks. If you arrive at night try to wait until daylight to beach the craft. Take note of any watercourses or habitations as you approach. You may have little choice in where you reach land, but attempt to avoid heavy waves. It's possible to ride a dinghy or raft into the beach on a breaking wave but it may be safer to turn, face the waves and paddle against them. This reduces the chance of being upended in the surf. When swimming toward shore bring your knees up in front of you so the spring in your legs absorbs any collisions with unseen rocks.

Survival Priorities
Natural Disasters

1. FLOODS -
Stay out of flood waters - they harbour hidden dangers and may be contaminated. Don't camp in dry creek beds.

2. CYCLONES -
Take shelter in a cave or ditch - a tent may not offer sufficient protection. Stay tuned to radio reports on the storm's progress. Beware of flying debris.

3. EARTHQUAKES -
In the bush the safest place is an open space. Don't run; lie down flat on the ground and wait until it passes.

4. BUSH FIRES -
Radiated heat (not flames) is the major killer. To survive you must effectively shield yourself from it.

In a bushfire you are safer in your vehicle than out of it. Roll up windows against the smoke and flames.

Keep up fluid intake. Stresses on the body are great in a fire - fight them by staying hydrated and calm.

If a fire is close and rapidly approaching it is better to prepare to shelter from it rather than try and outrun it - fires tend to win the race.

Use wet blankets, your vehicle or any nonflammable, solid barrier to shield yourself from the few minutes of intense heat as the fire's front passes. If nothing else find a ditch, lie down and cover yourself with earth or wet clothing.

Panic kills in a natural disaster - stay calm and make the most of your resources.

Natural Disasters

You don't have to go into wilderness to find yourself in a survival situation. Cyclones, floods, earthquakes and bush fires occur regularly in Australia, often in heavily populated areas. At times you may even be safer in the bush than in urban areas when such disasters occur. This is because danger is greatest where the natural environment has been disrupted - buildings, roads and other man-made structures may be destroyed, live electrical lines may be down and dams may burst.

FLOODS

There is a major flood somewhere in Australia virtually every year. They can happen anywhere in any season. Cyclones, storms and torrential rain are the normal causes of freshwater flooding, while coastal areas are subject to saltwater inundation from king tides or seismic surges. Inland floods tend to rise more slowly than those in coastal catchment areas but last longer. In flat areas the water has no easy escape route; communities can be cut off from road access for weeks.

Without a radio you might be unaware of impending flood danger. Heavy rain over a hundred kilometres away can bring flash floods surging through watercourses downstream. This is why camping in creek beds is a bad idea. A riverbed can be bone dry one minute and a muddy torrent the next, with only seconds of warning before the wall of water hits you.

Essential gear for flood emergencies includes practical clothing, candles, matches, drinking water, a supply of food and a small first aid kit which includes personal medications. A portable camping stove and basic cooking gear are useful since dry firewood for cooking may be hard to find.

Don't drink floodwater; it may be contaminated from dead animals. Catch rainwater to drink instead. Don't stay in the area if you don't need to - people have been swept away while sightseeing in flood-stricken areas. Weakened embankments can collapse at any time. Keep clear of the water's edge.

It's a good idea to boil drinking water during floods. Contaminated water causes cuts and abrasions to fester and spreads disease. Food or beverages that have been in contact with floodwater should not be consumed.

Wear sensible footwear to protect feet. When wading through flooded areas you'll encounter hidden rocks, branches and other hazards. Deep holes are especially dangerous so proceed slowly. Cold water, wind chill and strong currents weaken the body quickly. Many people perish in floods because they attempt actions beyond their physical capabilities.

If swept away in a strong current, don't try to fight it - you will be wasting valuable strength. Tuck your legs into your body so they don't snag on passing branches. Grab hold of any floating objects that might help keep your head above water. Wide, shallow stretches of river are slower moving than narrow sections and are the best places to try to exit the water.

EARTHQUAKES

Earthquakes are rare in Australia but fatalities have occurred, so the possibility must always be considered. Falling debris is the major cause of death or injury in earthquakes.

In the city the advice is to stay indoors if you're already there, taking cover under a desk, doorway or other sturdy protection. If your cooking stove is on, turn off the gas. If outdoors, move quickly away from buildings and utility wires. You are safest out in the open away from trees. In the bush an earthquake is only a real danger if you're rock climbing, standing near cliff faces or camped under trees. A steep slope with plenty of loose rock underfoot can also be trouble. If you're in the car when the shaking starts, stop as soon as you safely can and remain in the vehicle - it's the safest place.

CYCLONES

Cyclones in Australia most often occur along tropical coasts between November and April. Occasionally they spring up outside the 'regular' cyclone season or stretch further south than normal. Winds can reach 200 kilometres per hour. Cyclones start out with strengthening winds that reach gale force, often accompanied by rain squalls. As the wind increases the main danger is flying debris. Cyclonic winds can uproot trees, lift roofs off houses and send objects through the air at deadly speeds. Sudden flooding often accompanies these storms and adds to damage.

Cyclonic activity tends to weaken as it moves inland but this varies from storm to storm. Damage to inland areas can be severe as well. Cyclones might strike an area once, move away and then double back to savage the same region again.

Abnormally high sea levels are a risk during coastal cyclones. Storm tides occur when wind and low pressure force a build-up of water against the coastal shelf. Seas can rise as much as the height of a one-storey house and flood low-lying inland areas. A cyclone far out to sea generates huge waves that travel much faster than the cyclone itself. The sudden appearance of heavy swells may therefore indicate an approaching cyclone. A cyclone 1000 kilometres out to sea may take nearly three weeks to reach the coast but the waves it produces can arrive within 24 hours.

Cyclone Updates

When cyclones are detected within 800 kilometres of the coast the Bureau of Meteorology issues either a *Cyclone Watch* or a *Cyclone Warning.*

CYCLONE WATCH
This denotes that a cyclone is on the way but is not expected to reach the area within 24 hours. The purpose of this alert is to give people as much warning as possible so they can prepare. When a *Cyclone Watch* is issued, stay tuned to the radio for further announcements.

CYCLONE WARNING
When a cyclone is expected to threaten an area within 24 hours a *Cyclone Warning* is issued. Stay tuned to the radio for advice or instructions from police or local State Emergency Services.

You may be able to escape the brunt of a cyclone by travelling inland before things turn nasty, provided you have sufficient warning. If camping when the winds hit you may need to shift the tent to a safer location - severe gusts can send a tent and its occupants flying. If your sole shelter is a tent, move it to a sheltered spot out of range of falling debris. Don't forget flying hazards can move sideways as well as downwards in a fierce wind.

If caught with no tent, seek shelter wherever there is the best combination of maximum wind protection and minimum danger from falling rocks and branches. A cave is ideal. In open grassland find a ditch (or dig one if you can), lie in it and cover your head with both arms. Sunglasses will protect your eyes from flecks of debris. Cover the head with a T-shirt to fight off swirling dust.

BUSH FIRES

Bush fires pose a serious survival risk. The main cause of death in these fires is a breakdown in the body's heat regulating system. Lung damage from breathing hot gases, loss of oxygen from smoke inhalation and death from the flames themselves are also possible, but most who perish are victims of excessive radiated heat. It is important for the survivor to understand the nature of bush fires and to react in a quick but calm manner to their approach.

The key to surviving a bushfire is to find an effective way to shield yourself from heat radiation. Heat rays don't curve around corners or pass through solid objects and they are successfully reflected by barriers such as rock, metal, wood and earth. Clothing offers some protection and so does your vehicle.

Statistically the danger of exploding petrol tanks is a fallacy. If a tank has sprung a leak there is certainly a potential danger, but otherwise most petrol tanks are hard to explode. In the aftermath of some of Australia's worst bush fires petrol tank explosions have been virtually nonexistent. Far more people die because they leave the protective barrier of a vehicle and succumb to the heat outside. When sheltering in the car, keep windows closed against the heat and smoke.

As a bushfire passes, both its peak heat and its flames rarely last more than four or five minutes in one spot. Even when caught out in the open people have wrapped themselves in wet blankets, stood perfectly still and survived a passing fire. Others have come through by digging a trench, climbing in and covering themselves with earth. The natural human impulse is to flee the fire, but panicked running in intense heat offers slim survival chances.

Clothing is your first line of defence. Woollen material is a good choice, while some synthetics are highly flammable and may melt against the body. Wet your clothing down if possible and don't forget feet. Leather boots are preferable to sandshoes.

The ideal spot to wait out a coming bushfire - low elevation, plenty of bare earth and a water supply. Water is important not only for dampening clothing but because you must drink much more than usual to combat the effects of the fire's intense radiated heat. In a sparsely wooded region such as this the danger would be minimal with reasonable preparation. The most dangerous areas are those with dense eucalypt forest - the trees' natural oils provide a formidable fuel.

The burning front edge of a moving grass fire may only be a metre wide on the ground in light winds, so it may be possible to walk or run quickly through it with protective clothing. This is not the case with fires fed by stronger winds, as the width of the moving flame line can be a dozen metres. Crown fires in thick dry forest are the most dangerous because the fire feeds on both the undergrowth and the treetops. Flames from grass fires rarely reach over three metres in height, but a crown fire is a mass of solid, blazing heat from the ground all the way up to thirty metres or higher.

If trapped on foot in a bush fire look for stretches of bare earth in which to dig a depression. Then cover yourself with the spare earth or any other nonflammable material. A collection of tall boulders may become a safe refuge if you can get between them. Rivers and waterholes offer another choice; cover your exposed head with a wet shirt or other protection. Water tanks may seem a safe option, but radiated heat has been known to bring the water inside to a boil.

Remember that flame moves more quickly uphill. If trying to outrun a fire you will have a better chance on a descending slope.

A good place to park your vehicle in a bush fire is in the middle of a shallow creek, out of reach of flames.

Surviving a natural disaster is often a matter of being in the right spot at the right time. The location above would be an excellent place to shelter from a bushfire, but highly dangerous in a flood or earthquake. In a cyclone, protection from flying debris could be taken beneath the larger boulders, but rising waters would soon force a move to higher ground. Photo: Damiano Visocnik

When German aviators Bertram and Klausmann were forced to land in the harsh, isolated northern Kimberley in 1932, their ordeal was just beginning....

Two Who Survived

One of the most amazing survival stories in Australia's history is the saga of two German aviators who spent nearly two months stranded in the remote Kimberley in 1932.

On 14 May 1932, pilot Hans Bertram and his mechanic Adolf Klausmann took off in their Junkers seaplane "Atlantis" from Kupang, Timor en route to Port Darwin. They never reached their destination. Blown off course in a storm, they were forced to land the plane near the mouth of the Berkeley River, about 200 km northwest of the town of Wyndham in Western Australia. This was the beginning of a gruelling 53-day ordeal in one of the harshest, most desolate parts of the country.

Bertram wrongly believed he had landed on Melville Island in the Northern Territory and all his subsequent plans to reach civilisation were based on this error. Moments after the forced landing they encountered an Aborigine but couldn't communicate with him. Bertram's first impression of the Kimberley was shock at the sheer number of flies and mosquitoes at their landing site. Low on fuel, they took off again, flying up the coast in the hope of spotting a settlement. With the fuel gauge teetering on empty they could only fly 40 kilometres until forced to land again, this time in a sheltered bay near Rocky Island.

All survival stories are easy targets for criticism in hindsight, but second-hand evaluation is subject to a lot of misinterpretation. To truly comprehend the ordeal of Klausmann and Bertram is not possible - we were not there. However, this is a classic tale of outdoor struggle that can teach us several fundamental survival lessons. The mistakes made by these men are the same types of errors commonly made in survival situations today. It is easy to be critical of some of their decisions, but remember that these two men had no previous experience in the Australian bush. That they stayed alive for nearly two months in this harsh region is testimony to their resolve. It also shows the physical deprivations human bodies can endure when forced to do so. Put yourself in their place as you read the following account of their ordeal and consider what you might have done differently.

Bertram's first thought is to find water. They take a sip of dirty, oily water from the plane's radiator and spit it out. A decision is made to travel south on foot. They hope to come across another Aborigine who can take them to water. Two hundred metres from the plane they are stymied by a muddy inlet which threatens to suck them down like quicksand. They back-track and opt for a good night's sleep at the plane.

Next morning the men pack a pistol, water bag, matches and maps and set off again, this time walking around the swamp. Increasingly thirsty, they flavour the radiator water with mouthwash to make it more palatable. After two hours their water bag splits open on a sharp rock, spilling its contents on the ground. There are a few litres of water back at the plane but they decide to press on.

In two days they arrive at a long inlet 7 km north of Elsie Island. Walk-ing around it would take hours so they decide to swim to the other side. Halfway across, Bertram looks behind him and sees ripples - two or three crocodiles are swimming their way. The shore is still forty metres off. Bertram shouts to Klausmann, then removes his pack and swims for his life. They both make it to shore but the pack sinks out of sight. In it are their clothing, shoes and matches. They collapse on the beach, naked except for aviator hats, goggles and neckerchiefs. Their pistol somehow survives the crocodile scare. As the men rest a kangaroo hops into view. Bertram aims and misses. One of the men raises the possibility of suicide out loud, which prompts Bertram to throw the pistol into the inlet in horror.

It is the dry season and nights are cold. To protect their exposed bodies the men bury themselves in the sand at night. Faces are covered with neckerchiefs and goggles but one arm remains exposed, devoured by hordes of mosquitoes and midges during the night. In the mornings the flies take over, swarming over their scratches and minor wounds. It takes four days without water to backtrack to the moored Atlantis. They have been gone a week and now have swollen feet, sunburn and several in-fected sores.

After drinking some radiator water and resting they take stock of the situation. Without matches they make a fire lighter using the motor's starter magnet, a few litres of fuel, a bottle and some cotton. The cloth is stuffed into the bottle and a few drops of fuel are poured in. They put the magnet's wires into the bottle and turn the crank until they get a spark. This proves an economical device, needing only a few drops of fuel to get going.

"How helpless we are in this strange, wild world" writes Bertram in his journal. The men decide to make a boat using one of the plane's floats. A couple of bathrobes and a pair of trousers form the sail.

Before they go to sea, Klausmann is rummaging around the cockpit floor and finds a fish hook. He catches a single tiny fish but then loses the hook. They search everywhere but it is gone.

The next phase of their ordeal takes place in the choppy, open sea where their tiny makeshift craft drifts aimlessly for five days. Rudder and sail are too small to make any difference. They spot the Koolinda, a ship that passes within 600 metres. Their hopes of rescue are dashed when the ship steams past. No one has seen them.

They eventually reach shore to the north, five kilometres from Cape Bernier. Neither has slept during the five days at sea. At last they have some luck - near their boat's landing site they stumble upon a waterhole, the only one they have seen in twenty days. With water problems finally solved their attention is turned to food. They sample some leaves and grass but quickly become ill as a result. Climbing a hill on the 23rd day, Bertram gets a view toward the west for a distance of 25 kilometres. An endless expanse of trackless plain spreads before him. Only then does he realise they're actually in the Kimberley Plateau, not on Melville Island as originally assumed. Their only navigational aids are a compass and a large-scale map of Australia. The nearest town is Wyndham, over 200 kilometres away. For over three weeks they have been travelling directly away from it.

They walk back to their tiny 'boat' from the waterhole and encounter yet another nasty surprise. The makeshift craft has broken anchor and been destroyed, smashed to pieces by waves and rocks. Both men are extremely weak from heat, physical hardship and lack of food. They find a bush covered with small green berries, but this meal also produces violent stomach spasms. That week Bertram sees smoke and heads toward it, sure it must be an Aboriginal camp. On closer inspection it is only a bush fire. The men try to create a new boat out of what is left of the old. This fails. Bertram and Klausmann wander back toward Cape Bernier. A search plane flies directly over their heads but doesn't see them.

It is now day 36. Rain is falling for the first time and the men locate a cave above the high water mark not far from the Cape. They crawl into it with the last of their strength and mentally prepare for death. Luckily the rain continues for three more days, filling up rocky depressions near the cave. Their energy is gone but at least they needn't worry about water for a while. Klausmann's nerves are not holding up well under the strain of physical deprivation. They eat a few mangrove snails which are cracked open and gulped down raw.

Meanwhile a search plane had finally spotted the abandoned Atlantis. A sea search begins for the missing aviators. A launch containing Wyndham police and Aboriginal trackers arrives at 'Seaplane Bay'. In the plane they find a note from Bertram saying he and Klausmann had taken off on foot toward the north. In the launch they head up the coast to King George River, passing Cape Bernier where the men shelter in their cave. Unfortunately the drizzle prevents lookouts from spotting the cave. They pass it a second time on the way back to Seaplane Bay, but once again rain obscures the coast. The launch returns to Wyndham.

On the morning of their fortieth day in the bush, an Aborigine from Drysdale Mission (now Kalumburu) finds the men huddled inside their cave, awaiting death. He gives them water and a freshly caught fish, which they swallow raw. Their rescuer lights a signal fire which is answered from two kilometres away. He is joined by three companions, one of whom carries a letter from the Drysdale River Mission priests explaining that they've been searching for the men for weeks. Bertram writes a note to the mission stating their position and two of the four Aborigines set off at once to relay the message. The remaining two feed the starving aviators tinned beef and bake damper in the cave. One of their helpers goes off with his spear and returns moments later with a metre-long fish. The Aborigines collect grass to make soft beds for the weak men, while sleeping themselves on cold stones by the fire.

Later the Germans and their rescuers are joined by a dozen more Aborigines. They offer the men fish, meat and a container of bush honey. Bertram sees what he believes are flies crawling all over the honey but eats a handful anyway (they were probably native bees, which are also small and black). The next offering is a kangaroo leg but the weakened men can no longer chew properly. The Aboriginals solve the problem by pre-chewing the meat for them so they need only swallow it. Soon another kangaroo is killed nearby and cooked in a ground oven.

The residual effects of being stranded in the bush for so long take their toll on Klausmann, who suffers a mental breakdown during this period. Uncontrollable crying and ranting is interspersed with paranoia - he becomes convinced the Aborigines who rescued them are now plotting to eat them. Bertram comforts him as best he can.

While this is going on a police party has been travelling on horseback for six days from Forrest Mission near Wyndham (now known as Oombulgurri). They reach the cave on June 28th. According to leader Police Constable Marshall, the survivors' first words after a weak hello are "Do you have bread, bread, bread?" The survivors have not seen another white person for forty-five days.

Klausmann by this stage is having regular bouts of delirium and raving, and has to be subdued and put in restraints by the constables. He is shouting that the rescue party are all devils who want to kill him. It's another week before the police launch arrives to pick the party up and transport them to Wyndham. Klausmann's condition does not improve during this time but Bertram recovers well.

Constable Marshall had previously sent two Aboriginal runners back to Wyndham to deliver news that the aviators were alive and would soon be in port. One of the most impressive aspects of this entire episode is the speed with which these runners got from Cape Bernier to Wyndham. This is a distance of 200 kilometres over trackless, rugged terrain. The men ran through this rough country in under four days, an outstanding physical achievement. Anyone who has spent time in the northern Kimberley will appreciate the hardship involved.

Klausmann was still in a bad way for some time in Wyndham, but later recovered and returned home to Germany, as did Bertram. Before leaving Australia Bertram spent a couple of months in Perth doing the rounds and giving a talk called "53 Days in the Bush" to schools and organisations, raising money to get *Atlantis* back in action so he could fly it home. Klausmann returned to Europe by ship.

WHAT WENT WRONG?

The men's initial landing put their plane near the mouth of the Berkeley River. This is a fish-rich area where the men would have had good survival chances compared to more northerly parts of the coast where fresh water is scarce. A number of good-sized tributaries flow into the Berkeley near its saltwater mouth so fresh water would not have been a problem. Unfortunately the men had no idea where they were and flew away from the direction of help (at Wyndham) instead of toward it. Their inability to communicate with the Aborigine they encountered upon landing was unfortunate, as was their decision to take off again. They were hurried along by Bertram's disgust at the swarms of flies. Had they stayed put their rescue would certainly have come more quickly. The Aborigine was probably from the Forrest River Mission not far from Wyndham, and news of two stranded aviators and a seaplane would certainly have travelled fast.

At their second forced landing they only had foul tasting radiator water to drink. Later this would become a precious commodity, but initially they spurned it. Surrounded by beach sand, they could easily have created a filter by filling a tied-off trouser leg with grass and sand. By pouring the water through this they would have removed the worst of the taste. A lack of durable water containers was also a problem. Their canvas water bag was wrecked after just a few hours of travel. When they finally found a waterhole they were able to fashion a water bag from a spare rubber raincoat. Both men were in an advanced state of dehydration during much of this ordeal; the fact that they survived these stretches is astonishing. They went for several days without water during their first foray away from the plane, and endured a similar waterless period later on.

The Germans may not have known there were crocodiles in Australia. A saltwater inlet in the Kimberley is no place for a swim. Deadly jellyfish would not have been a problem at that time of year, but bronze whaler sharks are common. The horror Bertram felt at seeing the swimming crocs made him drop the bag containing their shoes and clothing, but they were both lucky to escape the water intact.

This loss of matches, clothing and shoes was a result of understandable panic. Bertram's decision to throw his pistol into the same inlet was impulsive, but may not have been a bad thing considering his companion's deteriorating state of mind as time wore on. Bertram later was furious at himself, though in retrospect he admitted that throwing the gun away may have actually ensured their survival. He believed the temptation to "end it all" would have been very strong at various stages of their predicament.

The assumption that they had landed on Melville Island wasn't helped by their inadequate maps, which were made for aviation instead of overland travel. Much of the time wasted during the first two weeks stemmed from this navigational error. They were setting course for places they could never reach.

Their ability to improvise under stress was a positive factor. Creating a fire lighter from the plane's starter magnet was an inspired achievement. The trick of burying their bodies in sand to escape insects and cold is a well known technique in desert regions. It served them well when they had to travel naked and barefoot for four days after the crocodile encounter. Lacking the convenience of a modern fly net they used goggles and neckerchiefs to keep insects out of nostrils, mouths and eyes. This may seem a trivial matter to those who have not experienced fly-plagued bush, but the energy expended in keeping insects away is energy you cannot afford to lose in such a situation.

The decision to strike out in their 'float boat' with its bathrobe sail was understandable but dangerous. The seas did not permit control of the craft's direction. Good fortune alone landed them five days later near a waterhole. Had they not found it they would have died quickly.

With the water situation in hand they began to look for food. Having no knowledge of Australian plants, their foraging efforts were more detrimental than helpful. Northern shores provide plenty of food if one knows where to look. They might have found hermit crabs amongst the coastal rock pools. These can be cracked open; the soft innards provide useful protein. Klausmann eventually sampled mangrove snails, but this was late in the ordeal when neither man had the strength to venture from the cave to hunt for bush tucker. These snails are easily plucked from mangrove roots and are a convenient food source.

The survival of Bertram and Klausmann illustrates that the human spirit can overcome huge physical and mental obstacles in the struggle for life. It shows that in the end, survival comes down to making good choices and trying to reduce the damage after you have made bad ones.

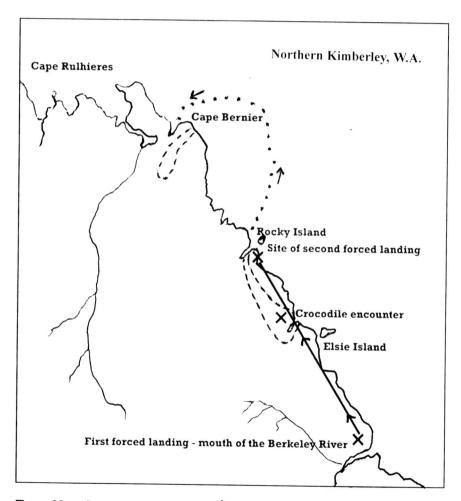

Travel by plane ———————————▶
Travel by makeshift boat • • • • • •
Travel on foot - - - - - - - - - - - - - - - -

The Germans' knowledge of the region they found themselves in was minimal, but certainly there are many Australians who would not have fared better in the same circumstances. Hopefully most of us would have avoided the swim with hungry 'salties', but otherwise would we have made similar mistakes?

The importance of survival skills and knowledge is no better demonstrated than in the food situation. The Germans had no idea how or where to look for sustenance, yet their Aboriginal saviours were able to spear fish, collect honey and kill a kangaroo at short notice once they found the men. A fish was actually speared and presented to the men within minutes of initial contact. Nutritionally, fish and bush honey were excellent choices to give the weakened men. The Aborigines nursed them back from the brink of death, their efforts playing the most significant role in their eventual recovery. Bertram commented on their culinary rituals in his journal: "We marvel at the Aborigines' careful procedures of preparation and consumption". Anyone who has seen food prepared with traditional Aboriginal methods will note a certain fastidious precision in the process. The simplicity of these methods is an illusion, quickly discovered by unskilled persons who try to emulate them.

This survival ordeal is unique not only for its length and miraculous outcome but because it combines elements of land, air and sea survival within a single experience.

In this part of the Kimberley the landscape is virtually unchanged today. It is now Aboriginal Reserve land, pristine and as harsh as when Bertram and Klausmann landed there in 1932. In 1984 the author walked through the northern Kimberley region alone from the Gibb River Road north to the Timor Sea. While trekking for one month and four hundred kilometres, not a single sign of civilisation was seen - no road, track, fence, building or evidence that human beings had ever been there. The flies, dust and heat were very much in evidence, however.

Appendix 1
Survival Training

This book provides a foundation upon which to build your outdoor survival skills. However, only practice and training can convert this knowledge into real experience. Survival training is enjoyable and builds self-confidence, creating a sense of achievement that carries over into other aspects of your life.

Survival training forces you to think, improvise and extend your personal limitations. It's no surprise that confidence-building courses for business executives often involve team challenges in a bush setting. Character, initiative and leadership quickly become evident in an environment stripped to the essentials.

Enrol in an accredited course to increase skills in a specific area. Useful survival-related courses include wilderness first aid, river rescue, outback driving, coastal navigation and a host of others. If it increases bush confidence and raises your skill level, give it a go.

STAYING ALIVE SURVIVAL SERVICES

Many courses skirt around the edges of outdoor survival but only one company in Australia provides comprehensive survival training. *STAYING ALIVE Land, Air, Sea Survival Services* is a specialist survival and self-help consultancy and training company based in Brisbane, Queensland. Courses are designed to simulate the environment in which participants are likely to travel or operate.

Director and chief instructor is Nick Vroomans, whose career as an Australian military officer included four years as Chief Instructor for the Australian Defence Force Combat Survival School. His experience includes special forces survival training with the U.S. Green Berets and S.A.S. in Cold Weather Survival (Alaska), Deep Sea Survival (Florida) and Desert, Arid and Jungle Survival (Australia).

The training courses vary in content and length depending upon the needs of participants.

Tel: (07) 3374 4554. Mobile: 0419 796 382.
Fax: (07) 3374 4664. Email: stayalivesurvival@bigpond.com.au
Address: PO Box 5116 Kenmore East QLD 4069

TRAINING YOURSELF

Whether you've completed formal survival-related training or not, the old adage 'practice makes perfect' still applies. Basic techniques can be honed during normal bush outings, but for best results some organisation is needed. The best way to practise the skills in this book is to carry it in your pack or 4WD, head bush and conduct your own survival training.

The ideal survival exercise involves spending one to four days in the bush solely for the purpose of developing skills. How much food and gear you carry is up to you. For realistic survival conditions a minimalist approach is best. For safety, these trips are best done with friends. Make sure somebody back home knows where you're going.

Solitary survival exercises can also be useful, though they are not to everyone's taste. A surprising number of people have never experienced a full 24 hours of complete solitude in their entire lives. However, many survival incidents involve enforced solitude in difficult circumstances, so those who are 'used to their own company' will find such episodes less stressful. The author regularly spends up to four weeks at a time alone in trackless bush, developing bushcraft skills and exploring pristine regions.

List the skills you want to practise and complete as many as you can during the trip. You might choose, for example, to spend a weekend on a remote coast practising distillation of salt water into fresh, hunting tidal bush foods, fishing with improvised gear or building shelter from driftwood and a tarp. Obey the rules in designated conservation areas, especially those regarding bush camping, lighting of fires and protection of vegetation and wildlife. Whether on Crown Land, Aboriginal Land, National Park or in your own backyard, leave no evidence of your practice sessions behind. Learn, improve, enjoy the experience and leave the landscape as you found it. In genuine survival situations the goal of staying alive overrides environmental concerns, but in *practising* bushcraft always be non-destructive and respectful of the land.

Keep a journal during the survival exercise to record weather conditions, terrain and other factors affecting the adventure. List the gear you've brought along - what you use and what you don't may surprise you when it's all over. Write down how long it takes to accomplish each skill and record any difficulties. This helps to gauge improvement over a succession of trips. Make entries in the log throughout the day - don't wait until nightfall.

A field guide to bush foods and a first aid booklet are useful to have along. Many bush emergencies are medical, so definitely practise skills such as bandaging, splinting and other basics. Don't just try them out on others - learn the art of 'self-aid' as well.

The ten basic commandments for every survival exercise are:
1. Don't go unless you're 100% healthy.
2. Ensure someone knows your location and return time.
3. Have a definite daily plan to try out specific skills.
4. Take an adequate first aid kit.
5. Take your pocket survival kit and a sharp knife.
6. Carry sufficient water for the duration.
7. Keep a log to record conditions and progress.
8. Carry maps, compass and suitable clothing.
9. Leave footprints behind but nothing else.
10. Enjoy yourself.

Don't rely on bush tucker. Carry enough food, even if you end up not needing it. If you sample some bush foods or catch a few fish your provisions can stay in the pack.

A survival exercise isn't meant to be an exercise in masochism. Indeed, knowing how to make yourself comfortable in adverse conditions is one of the signs of a true bush expert. The goal is not to fight the environment but to understand it. If you are prepared, confident and know where to look, even the harshest parts of Australia can yield the necessities of survival.

Avoid the temptation to cram too much practice into one weekend. Some skills take several days to fully master. Learning to build a fire in wet conditions, make a solar still or cook in a ground oven takes time; weaving a fishing net from monofilament is a true test of patience. Other skills such as building a debris hut or making fire with a bow drill are rarely successful if rushed. Be methodical in perfecting your survival skills, and speed and confidence will follow in due course.

On a local level, there are no better qualified teachers of survival skills than Aboriginal people who still use those skills today. Invaluable bush knowledge can be acquired in parts of the country where age-old methods of collecting bush tucker, making fire, hunting game and finding water are still utilised. In Arnhem Land, the Kimberley, the Red Centre and elsewhere you will find Aboriginal people more than willing to share their culture and heritage with you; this is also true with Torres Strait Islanders. This may be in the form of organised 'bush tucker tours' or similar tourist ventures. Elsewhere it's simply a matter of explaining your interest in bush survival and finding the most experienced people to take you into the bush for some hands-on experience.

Appendix 2
Suggested further reading

Albatross (*Deborah Scaling Kiley, Little, Brown and Co., 1994*). First-hand account of the sinking of the yacht Trashman off the U.S. coast, and the crew's five day fight for life in an open inflatable dinghy.

Alive (*Piers Paul Read, Pan, London 1975*). The crash of an airliner in the Andes mountains remains one of the most incredible survival stories of the 20th century. Sixteen people lived in the snow for two and a half months at an elevation of 3500 metres. Staying alive by eating the frozen bodies of their dead comrades, the survivors showed teamwork, perseverance and inventiveness in making the most of a bad situation.

Australia's Reptiles (*Steven Wilson & David Knowles, Angus & Robertson 1992*). A complete photographic reference to Australia's terrestrial reptiles. A beautiful book, ideal for reptile identification. Large format.

Bushcraft (*Richard Graves, Dymock's Book Arcade Ltd. 1975*). Written by the former leader of the Australian Jungle Rescue Detachment, this 'serious guide to survival and camping' emphasises self-reliance. Though somewhat dated, it contains a few techniques not found in other books.

Bush Food - Aboriginal food and herbal medicine (*Jennifer Isaacs, Ure Smith Press 1987*). Impressively photographed guide to natural bush foods and medicine, as utilized by indigenous Australians.

Bush Medicine (*Tim low, Angus & Robertson 1990*). Use of Australian plants and animals for medicinal purposes, both by Aboriginals and early settlers. A pharmacopoeia of natural remedies.

Bush Tucker (*Tim Low, Angus & Robertson 1992*). Large full-colour guide to edible plant and animal life in Australia.

Dangerous Australians (*Bay Books 1992*). All about the creatures that can cause us trouble, from sharks and funnel-webs to snakes and jellyfish. Good photos and accurate information on our hazardous wildlife.

Explore Wild Australia with the Bush Tucker Man (*Les Hiddins, Penguin Books 1999*). Les takes readers on a 4WD tour through some of Australia's most out of the way places. Information on bush tucker and trip planning is included. An excellent read.

Flight into Hell (*Hans Bertram, Currey O'Neil Ross 1985*). Two German aviators, attempting to fly to Port Darwin in 1932, were forced to land in the remote Kimberley where they survived for nearly two months.

Giant Book of Exploration (*The Book Company International, 1995*). A compilation of first-hand accounts of explorers, including Australian adventurers Charles Sturt, Burke and Wills, and John McDouall Stuart.

Outdoor Survival Guide (*Hugh McManners, Dorling Kindersley, 1998*). A very pictorial guide by a former British Commando.

Safe Outback Travel (*Jack Absalom, Five Mile Press 1992*). A popular no-nonsense guide to vehicle travel in the bush, written by one of the most experienced outback travellers in Australia.

SAS Survival Handbook (*John Wiseman, Harper Collins, 1996*). Comprehensive manual based on British SAS survival training. Originally published in 1986 and frequently reprinted. A reasonable reference, although much of the material is irrelevant to Australian conditions.

Saved (*Tony Bullimore, Little, Brown and Co, 1997*). The extraordinary story of Bullimore's rescue from an upturned racing yacht in the Southern Ocean, one of the most impressive peacetime air/sea rescues in Australian history.

Stay Alive (*Maurice Dunlevy, Australian Government Publishing Service, Reprinted 1993*). A compact but somewhat outdated survival guide originally produced in 1978 as a manual for government employees working in the bush.

Survive the Savage Sea (*Dougal Robertson, Elek, London 1973*). Account of a man, his wife, their three sons and a friend who survived 37 days adrift in the open sea after their yacht sank in the Pacific.

Appendix 3

PRODUCTS / SERVICES RELATING TO SURVIVAL OR OUTDOOR ADVENTURE

AUSLIG, Freecall 1 800 800 173. Australian mapping agency. Topographic maps for all of Australia.

Barrett Communications, PO Box 1214, Bibra lake WA 6965. Tel: 1 800 999 580. Suppliers of HF two-way radios and antennas.

EQUIP, PO Box 1175, Fremantle WA 6160. Tel: (08) 9319 8818. State of the art First Aid kits. Supplementary first aid packs available for wound management, survival, blisters/burns, dental etc.

Go There! Do That! Outdoor Books, PO Box 105, O'Connor ACT 2601. Tel: (02) 6230 4859. New and second-hand outdoor books; everything from polar exploration to sea kayaking.

Grant Minervani Agencies, PO Box 209, Welland SA 5007. Distributors of MSR cooking stoves (Dragonfly, Whisperlite, XGK, etc.)

High-n-Wild Mountain Adventures, 3/5 Katoomba St., Katoomba NSW 2780. Tel: (02) 4782 6224. Abseiling, canyoning, bush skills courses, rock climbing and mountaineering.

Iridium, Level 3, 616 St. Kilda Rd, Melbourne VIC 3004. Tel: 1 800 506 508. Makers of satellite telephones.

Lowrance Australia, 42/9 Powells Rd, Brookvale NSW 2100. Makers of Global Positioning Systems for boaters, walkers and outback drivers.

Mountain Designs Australia, www.mountaindesign.com.au Outdoor gear specialists, with several stores throughout Australia. Reliable, quality gear for all Australian environments.

Opal Shell Yacht Charters, 14 Graelou Rd, Lesmurdie WA 6076. Tel: (08) 9291 6923. Wilderness cruising specialists. The Opal Shell is a 60 ft. motor sailer that visits some of the most spectacular parts of the remote Kimberley coast.

Outdoor Australia, (03) 9867 6303. A magazine for outdoor enthusiasts. Often includes excellent articles on specific survival-related outdoor skills.

Outward Bound, www.outwardbound.com.au   A registered outdoor education and training program.

Rescue 3, (07) 3892 1155. rescue@powerup.com.au   International rescue courses by accredited instructors.

Staying Alive Survival Services, PO Box 5116, Kenmore East, QLD 4069. stayalivesurvival@bigpond.com.au   Australia's only complete survival training company, run by a former Chief Survival Instructor for the Australian Defence Force Combat Survival School. Offers world-class survival training that's relevant, supportive and challenging. Stockist of specially made water transpiration bags.

West Marine, PO Box 50070, Watsonville, California 95077-0070. Tel: 1-800-143404. Website: www.westmarine.com. Large U.S. company stocking marine equipment including an extensive range of safety and survival gear. Orders can be placed by phone, fax or through their website. Products include HotPak self-heating emergency meals and PUR Survivor 06 Watermaker, a hand-held filter pump desalinator.

Wilderness First Aid Consultants (The Safety Network), PO Box 320, Katoomba NSW 2780. Quality bush first aid courses and first aid kits.

Wild Magazine, PO Box 415, Prahran VIC 3181.   www.wild.com.au Tel: (03) 9826 8482.   'Australia's wilderness adventure magazine'. The comprehensive gear surveys are an extremely useful feature.

Willis's Walkabouts, 12 Carrington St., Milner NT 0810. Tel: (08) 8985 2134. Guided back-country bushwalking tours to Kakadu, the Kimberley and the Red Centre.

Photo: Gary Tischer

NOTES

NOTES

ORDER FORM

Kimberley Publications
PO Box 6095
Upper Mount Gravatt, QLD 4122

Please send me:

_____copies of AUSTRALIAN BUSH SURVIVAL SKILLS

$24.95 each (GST inclusive) plus $4.00 postage/handling

Price prior to 1 July 2000 is $22.70 plus $3.65 post - ($26.35)

NAME:

ADDRESS:

_____Post Code:_____

All orders are sent the same day received. Please make cheque or money order payable to Kimberley Publications, and post to PO Box 6095, Upper Mt. Gravatt, QLD 4122.

NOTES

ORDER FORM

Kimberley Publications
PO Box 6095
Upper Mount Gravatt, QLD 4122

Please send me:

_____ copies of AUSTRALIAN BUSH SURVIVAL SKILLS

$24.95 each (GST inclusive) plus $4.00 postage/handling

Price prior to 1 July 2000 is $22.70 plus $3.65 post - ($26.35)

NAME: _____

ADDRESS: _____

_____ Post Code: _____

All orders are sent the same day received. Please make cheque
_y order payable to Kimberley Publications and post
3ox 6095, Upper Mt. Gravatt, QLD 4122.